The Advanced Montessori Method, volume I

ISBN: 978-90-79506-27-9

Montessori-Pierson Publishing Company
Koninginneweg 161, 1075 CN Amsterdam, the Netherlands

Cover design and layout
Van de Manakker, grafische communicatie, Maastricht, the Netherlands
Printed and bound by
Wilco Printing & Binding, Amersfoort, the Netherlands

THE MONTESSORI SERIES
VOLUME 9

The Advanced Montessori Method, volume I

Scientific Pedagogy as Applied to the Education of Children

by

Maria Montessori

Maria Montessori

Formerly Entitled
Spontaneous Activity in Education

Translated from the Italian by
Florence Simmonds and
Lily Hutchinson

MONTESSORI-PIERSON PUBLISHING COMPANY
Amsterdam, The Netherlands

Available in the same series:

The Absorbent Mind
The Discovery of the Child
The Formation of Man
What You Should Know About Your Child
Education for a New World
To Educate the Human Potential
The Child, Society and the World
The Child in the Family
Education and Peace
Education for Human Development
From Childhood to Adolescence
The Advanced Montessori Method, Vol. II
Basic Ideas of Montessori's Educational Theory
The 1915 California Lectures
Psychogeometry
The 1946 London Lectures
The 1913 Rome Lectures
The Mass explained to children
Psychoarithmetic
Maria Montessori Speaks to Parents
The Secret of Childhood

Some of the titles above are also available in the Spanish language

Table of Contents

Editor's Notes

The Montessori-Pierson Publishing Company is delighted to bring out their 2016 edition of Maria Montessori's great work The Advanced Montessori Method, volume I and II – the successor to The Montessori Method written seven years earlier. It was now considered time to publish an edition that includes fresh illustrative materials whilst remaining faithful to the original translation prepared by two excellent early students of Maria Montessori's, Lily Hutchinson and Florence Simmonds.

The 1965 foreword to this title by Mario Montessori Senior is also included, as it adds insights and flavour, although it must also be read with a view to the historical context of the 1960s.

Given the approach chosen, the publisher also wanted to take advantage of the opportunity to make the edition, though historical, more accessible to the modern reader by providing explanatory footnotes. Maria Montessori was well read and hugely interested in international developments in the field of medicine, anthropology, school education, psychology, philosophy and much more; she frequently refers to names and events that probably needed no additional introduction during her time, but nearly one hundred years on today's readers will welcome some more background details in a number of instances. This exercise also gave us the opportunity to correct small errors in language and spelling.

The publisher is extremely fortunate to have benefited from the expertise and support of a small production team, and would like to thank Miep van de Manakker for her extraordinary design skills. The production of this book could not have happened without the energy, knowledge, and forty+ years of Montessori experience of Fred Kelpin, responsible for editing and coordinating all work. Fred worked as a Montessori teacher and teacher trainer in the Netherlands, and joined AMI's Executive Committee in 1980 at the invitation of Mario Montessori Senior, with his portfolio including the development of Montessori material.

2016, Alexander Henny, Publisher

Foreword

All who deal with History of Education know the impact made on orthodox educational procedures by Dr. Maria Montessori's two books, The Montessori Method and The Advanced Montessori Method.

Long out of print, the latter reappears now in a historical edition. The language reflects the literary period of the time when the first English translation was published in 1918. The terminology is necessarily that of the epoch. Positivism then gave its tinge to science.

In writing an introduction to this book I do so with a feeling of reverence and awe for its author. I wonder if anyone else could have withstood what she did throughout her life and remain what she was.

What she was can be gathered from the first part of this book. In it, vivid, fresh and vigorous the glorious figure of Maria Montessori stands forth in her vital essence.

In The Secret of Childhood, a book she wrote later, she relates how a group of children – aged three to six – changed the course of her life. Practically they were waifs, fearful of society but violent and destructive. They came from the scum of the deprived citizenry of Rome. They were dirty, greedy little vandals.

Dr. Montessori, who was a psychologist, created for them a proportioned environment in which there were varied motives of activity. She gave them exact techniques and subsequently left them free to choose their occupations and to indulge in them as long as they liked. Only that which might harm or offend others was not allowed. After a few months an incredible change took place in the behaviour of the children. Dr. Montessori could not bring herself to believe this was real.

"It took time for me to convince myself that this was not an illusion", she writes in The Secret of Childhood "after each new experience proving such a truth, I said to myself, I won't believe it yet, I'll believe it next time. Thus for a long time I remained incredulous and at the same time deeply stirred and trepidant."

But in the end she had to surrender to reality.

"One day", she relates in the same page, "in great emotion, I took my heart in my two hands as though to encourage it to raise to the heights of faith and I stood respectfully before the children, saying to myself: Who are you then? Have I perhaps met with the children who were held in Christ's arms and to whom divine words were spoken? I will follow you to enter with you into the kingdom of Heaven."

The revelations however were not over. She was due for further surprises. With the intention of eventually bringing them to reading, she had given to the children some cut-out alphabetical letters and taught them their sound (not their names).

One day, some weeks later – all of a sudden – one child with tremendous enthusiasm "burst into writing". And then another ... and another. The age of these children was four years and a half! It was incomprehensible, impossible! Is it surprising that she left her medical career, her University professorship, the direction of the feminist movement to study these children? They had given her the vision of a new world – and this was the world of the Spirit. It is to be wondered at, if she felt compelled to follow that vision and to safeguard and better the conditions which had made possible the spontaneous moral "conversion" of the children? Or to try to understand what unconscious process could have caused the joyous conquest of a cultural item, which was one of the torments in orthodox schools?

She plunged into the secret of the child. Afterwards nothing that happened to her or around her could divert her from it. And a lot happened.

The two books she wrote, The Montessori Method and this one, were hailed as a revelation. Soon however a controversy started which still continues. Religious people combated her for her positivism, positivists condemned her for using religious language, scientists ridiculed her for lack of serious objectivity and for indulging in demagogical expressions, educators accused her of megalomaniac pride for refusing to accept other educational theories ..., for introducing intellectual subjects at an age when children were immature for them ..., for restricting freedom ...

Even politics joined in. Dictatorship in several countries closed her institutions and ostracised her for her theories, so that several times she had to go into voluntary exile.

If for nothing else, Dr. Montessori should go into history for having been the most misunderstood educator of all times. Anyone else would have given up, for everything and everyone seemed to conspire to belittle and destroy her work. But she was secure in her vision and the children constant in their revelations. Nothing proved to be powerful enough to suffocate the truth inherent in her work. Banned from one country, it sprang up in another, to return enriched and full of new vigour where it had been stamped out.

This in itself shows the value of this book, which was one of the two that caused so much animosity and misunderstanding. When you read it you will hear "the apostle of the child", as she was often called inveighing against society as the prophet of old fulminated the citizens of Sodom and Gomorrah. For from the start, her activity had become essentially a social campaign in favour of childhood. She struck out at the appalling conditions in which the children lived at the epoch she wrote the book. Some of her expressions may seem exaggerated, but one must not forget that she had to rouse the social conscience and that a formidable barrier made up of millenary (even if often unconscious) prejudice, of incomprehension and of spiritual insensibility confronted her.

It is the social aim she envisaged that in itself justifies the use of these expressions which are certainly unusual in purely theoretical and scientific work. These are however but an impetuous manifestation of this aim and not the apodictical tendency they appear to be. This is illustrated and becomes very evident in her inveighing – among other things – against child fantasy and against the general attitude with regard to it of the educational and psychological trends of the time. But it cannot be denied that they exaggerated in giving the same general value to all the expressions of this fantasy, without distinguishing the normal from the abnormal; and that they confused its constructive aspects with what was purely distractive.

If she seemed to dispraise play as well as fantasy, it is not that she did not recognise the value of play. That she did so is illustrated in her later works. But at that time fantasy and play, combined with the natural child's credulity were veritable weapons in the hands of the adults who used them to make the child "behave". That is to stop him from molesting them.

"Go and play" was the most frequent expression of those who did not want to be bothered by the children. Fairy tales were used not only to enchant and amuse them, but to reduce the children to immobility, to obtain obedience with threats that otherwise the ogre might come and eat them or that the good fairy would be disgusted and would not bring them the presents they expected from her. The happiness of children when one plays an imaginative game with them covered a lot of sins at that time and not the least of them condemning the children to mental starvation. The fact that the children of that first Montessori school left the toys (The Secret of Childhood) in order to engage in what then was considered "work" is very significant in this sense.

Luckily times have changed and today there is no longer need to use fantasy to satisfy the child, but at that time it was used even in the physical field. The anecdote recounted in this book of the mother who, being too poor to give her child meat to eat with his bread, breaks the latter in two and tells him that one of them is meat, is touching. But more touching still is the fact that the child accepted the situation and was happy imagining that he now had also meat, though he realised perfectly well that what he had was only bread.

Granted that her vehemence in condemning society was not the usual scientific language; it is however not true, as some accuse, that she used it in order to impose her philosophical views and to belittle those of others. As I mentioned previously, it was a means to awaken dormant consciences, to make better understood what the children had showed to be their needs. The fact that these were a revelation for her is the clearest proof that the phenomena she witnessed were not due to any educational theory of hers.

Dr. Montessori never wished to be – and never was – a theorist of science. Her approach, if an approach there was, borders on the empirical. The intention to build a system, be it psychological, pedagogical or philosophical, never entered her mind. What she did was to elaborate an orientation. What she gave was directives which are scientifically solid, the validity of which has been proved by experiments conducted on a very vast scale, in all strata of society, the world over: directives for a practical action in educational and social fields to help the development of the human personality.

She concentrated upon the phenomena and facts as they were revealed in the various environments which she, or her assistants, or those who had been inspired by her work, worked in. She always sought to catch the essence of the phenomena which were observed and, if it were possible, to elaborate from them an essential and existentialistic "vision". To interpret and illustrate both the phenomena she was confronted with, in her practical work with the children and the conclusions she derived from them, she expressed herself in the scientific terminology of the time.

Because of this – and because the theories she refers to have been "exploded" – certain trends of Educational Psychology have proclaimed that what she says is false. This is as logical as to declare false the fact that children do come into the world because C.F. Wolff with his "Theoria Generationis" exploded the theories of the animalculists and of the ovulists. The theories prevailing at that time may have been exploded, but facts are facts and those Dr. Montessori described then continue to repeat themselves today when other theories are accepted as true. Were she endeavouring to make these facts understood in our era Dr. Montessori would naturally refer to the present theories. That is what she did at that time. She had to use what was felt in the different fields of contemporary science. But that does not mean that the theories then extant were her theories.

Has Dr. Montessori then said the "last word" in the field of education? She certainly did not think so.

If philosophers and educators accused her of being dogmatic and rigid, of having the pretension that she only was right and everyone else wrong, it was because they did not realise that, while they continued to debate from the old, she had shown the starting point of a new science of education.

Dr. Montessori realised fully well that the new science was in its infancy and that in future, as science progressed, there might be the possibility of further interpretations. Her own initial one evolved, as can be seen, in her later books.

"What I have shown in the immense potentiality of the child", she said again and again, "is the existence of an energy which previously had not been taken into consideration. But as far as its utilisation or knowledge about it is concerned, we are still at the stage of Galvani when he realised that the flexing of the legs of dead and decorticated frogs were due to some mysterious energy. He pointed this out and thus created the interest in electricity that evolved into atomic science."

The atomic era has contributed to vindicate Dr. Montessori. To cope adequately with the progress which has been created, our times require that humanity learns more and faster. Humanity itself is confronted with the constant threat of being wiped out by the immense destructive powers it has developed. And while a crying need is felt for men who are more tolerant and more equilibrated, the appalling reality is one of increasing youth criminality, of neurosis affecting almost one half of the child world-population, of college students in need of "spelling clinics".

In this dilemma, the refulgent figure of the child, Dr. Montessori pointed out, who had found his own path to mental health, who spontaneously and joyfully had taken to learning at an early age, has caught the general attention anew. All the more so because in varied scientific fields modern research has come now to the same conclusions Dr. Montessori came to fifty years ago.

Hence the publication of this historical edition. I must warn however that since 1916, when this book first appeared in Italy, immense strides have been made in the development of school subjects, so that what is dealt with in the second part of this book has become, so to say, but the corner stone of a majestic building. Unluckily, to date, little or nothing has been published to illustrate this evolution.

Amsterdam, 1965   Mario M. Montessori

To
Her Majesty
MARGHERITA OF SAVOY
First Queen of Italy

The Advanced
Montessori Method,
volume I

1
A Survey of the Child's Life

The general laws which govern the child's psychical health have their parallel in those of its physical health

Many persons who have asked me to continue my methods of education for very young children on lines that would make them suitable for those over seven years of age have expressed a doubt whether this would be possible.

The difficulties they put forward are mainly of a moral order.

Should not the child now begin to respect the will of others rather than his own? Should he not some day brace himself to a real effort, compelling him to carry out a necessary, rather than a chosen, task? Finally, should he not learn self-sacrifice, since man's life is not a life of ease and enjoyment?

Some, taking certain practical items of elementary education, which present themselves even at the age of six, and must be seriously envisaged at seven, urge their objection in this form: Now we are face to face with the ugly spectre of arithmetical tables, the arid mental gymnastics exacted by grammar. What do you propose? Would you abolish all this, or do you admit that the child must inevitably bow to these necessities?

It is obvious that the whole of the argument revolves round the interpretation of that "liberty" which is the avowed basis of the system of education advocated by me.

Perhaps in a short time all these objections will provoke a smile, and I shall be asked to suppress them, together with my commentary on them, in future editions of this work. But at the present time they have a right to exist, and to be dealt with, although indeed it is not very easy to give a direct, clear and convincing answer to them, because this entails the raising of questions on which everybody has firmly rooted convictions.

A parallel may perhaps serve to save us a good deal of the work. Indirectly, these questions have been answered already by the progress made in the treatment of infants under the guidance of hygiene. How were they treated formerly? Many, no doubt, can still remember certain practices that were regarded as indispensable by the masses. An infant had to be strapped and swaddled, or its legs would grow crooked; the ligament under its tongue had to be split to ensure its speaking eventually; it was important that it should always wear a cap to keep its ears from protruding; the position of a recumbent baby was so arranged as not to cause permanent deformity of the tender skull; and good mothers stroked and pinched the little noses of their nurslings to make them grow long and sharp instead of round and snub, and put little gold earrings through the lobes of their ears very soon after birth "to improve their eyesight". Such practices may be already forgotten in some countries; but in others they remain to this day. Who does not remember the various devices for helping a baby to walk? Even in the first months after birth, at a period of life when the nervous system is not completely developed, and it is impossible for the infant to co-ordinate its movements, mothers wasted several half-hours of the day "teaching baby to walk". Holding the little creature by the body, they watched the aimless movements of the tiny feet, and deluded themselves with the belief that the child was already making an effort to walk; and because it does actually by degrees begin to arch its feet and move its legs more boldly, the mother attributed its progress to her instruction. When finally the movement had been almost established – though not the equilibrium, and the resulting power to stand on the feet – mothers made use of certain straps with which they held up the baby's body, and thus made it walk on the ground with themselves; or, when they had no time to spare, they put the baby into a kind of bell-shaped basket, the broad base of which prevented it from turning over; they tied the infant into this, hanging its arms outside, its body being supported by the upper edge of the basket; thus the child, though it could not rise on its feet, *advanced*, moving its legs, and was said to be *walking*.

Other relics of a very recent past are a species of convex crowns which were put round the heads of babies when they were considered capable of rising to their feet, and were accordingly emancipated from the basket. The child, suddenly left to himself after being accustomed hitherto to supports comparable to the crutches of the cripple, fell perpetually, and the crown was a protection to the head, which would otherwise have been injured.

What were the revelations of Science when it entered upon the scene for the salvation of the child? It certainly offered no perfected methods for straightening the noses and the ears, nor did it enlighten mothers as to the methods of teaching babies to walk immediately after birth. No. It proclaimed first of all that Nature itself will determine the shape of heads, noses, and ears; that man will speak without having the membrane of the tongue cut and further, that legs will grow straight and that the function of walking will come naturally, and requires no intervention.

Hence it follows that we should leave as much as possible to Nature; and the more the babe is left free to develop, the more rapidly and perfectly will he achieve his proper proportions and higher functions. Thus swaddling bands are abolished, and the "utmost tranquility in a restful position" is recommended. The infant, with its legs perfectly free, will be left lying full length, and not jogged up and down to "amuse" it, as many persons imagine they are doing by this device. It will not be forced to walk before it is time. When this time comes, it will raise itself and walk spontaneously.

In these days nearly all mothers are convinced of this, and vendors of swaddling-bands, straps and baskets have practically disappeared.

As a result, babies have straighter legs and walk better and earlier than formerly.

This is an established fact, and a most comforting one; for what a constant anxiety it must have been to believe that the straightness of a child's legs, and the shape of its nose, ears, and head were the direct results of our care! What a responsibility, to which everyone must have felt unequal! And what a relief to say: "Nature will think of that. I will leave my baby free, and watch him grow in beauty; I will be a quiescent spectator of the miracle."

Something analogous has been happening with regard to the inner life of the child. We are beset by such anxieties as these: it is necessary to form character, to develop the intelligence, to aid the unfolding and ordering of the emotions. And we ask ourselves how we are to do this. Here and there we touch the soul of the child, or we constrain it by special restrictions, much as mothers used to press the noses of their babies or strap down their ears. And we conceal our anxiety beneath a certain mediocre success, for it is a fact that men do grow up possessing character, intelligence and feeling. But when all these things are lacking, we are vanquished. What are we to do then? Who will give character to a degenerate, intelligence to an idiot, human emotions to a moral maniac?

If it were really true that men acquired all such qualities by these fitful manipulations of their souls, it would suffice to apply a little more energy to the process when these souls are evidently feeble. But this is not sufficient.

Then we are no more than creators of spiritual than of physical forms.

It is Nature, "creation", which regulates all these things. If we are convinced of this, we must admit as a principle the necessity of "not introducing obstacles to natural development"; and instead of having to deal with many separate problems – such as, what are the best aids to the development of character, intelligence and feeling? – one single problem will present itself as the basis of all education: How are we to give the child freedom?

In according this freedom we must take account of principles analogous to those laid down by science for the forms and functions of the body during its period of growth: it is a freedom in which the head, the nose, and the ears will attain the highest beauty, and the gait the utmost perfection possible to the congenital powers of the individual. Thus here again liberty, the sole means, will lead to the maximum development of character, intelligence and sentiment; and will give to us, the educators, peace, and the possibility of contemplating the miracle of growth.

This liberty will further deliver us from the painful weight of a fictitious responsibility and a dangerous illusion.

Woe to us, when we believe ourselves responsible for matters that do not concern us, and delude ourselves with the idea that we are perfecting things that will perfect themselves quite independently of us! For then we are like lunatics; and the profound question arises: What, then, is our true mission, our true responsibility? If we are deceiving ourselves, what is indeed the truth? And what sins of omission and of commission must be laid to our charge? If, like Chanticleer, we believe that the sun rises in the morning because the cock has crowed, what duties shall we find when we come to our senses? Who has been left destitute, because we ourselves have forgotten "to eat our true bread"?

The history of the "physical redemption" of the infant has a sequel which is highly instructive for us.

Hygiene has not been confined to the task of anthropological demonstration, such as that which not only made generally known, but convinced everyone, that the body develops spontaneously; because, in reality, the question of infant welfare was not concerned with the more or less perfect forms of the body. The real infantile question which called for the intervention of science was the alarming mortality among infants.

It certainly seems strange in these days to consider this fact: that, at the period when infantile diseases made the greatest ravages, people were not nearly so much concerned with infantile mortality as with the shape of the nose or the straightness of the legs, while the real question – literally a question of life and death – passed unobserved. There must be many persons who, like myself, have heard such dialogues as this: "I have had great experience in the care of children; I have had nine." "And how many of them are living?" "Two." And nevertheless this mother was looked upon as an authority!

Statistics of mortality reveal figures so high that the phenomenon may justly be called the "Slaughter of the Innocents". The famous graph of Lexis, which is not confined to one country or another, but deals with the general averages of human mortality, reveals the fact that this terrible death-rate is of universal occurrence among all peoples[1].

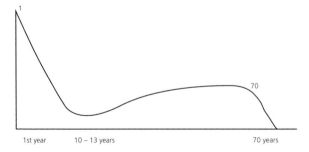

| 1st year | 10 – 13 years | | 70 years |

This must be attributed to two different factors. One is undoubtedly the characteristic feebleness of infancy; the other the absence of protection for this feebleness, an absence that had become general among all peoples. Goodwill was not lacking, nor parental affection; the fault lay hidden in an unknown cause, in a lack of protection against a dire peril of which men were quite unconscious. It is now a matter of common knowledge that infectious diseases, especially those of intestinal origin, are those most destructive to infant life. Intestinal disorders which impede nutrition, and produce toxins at an age when the delicate tissues are most sensitive to them, were responsible for nearly the entire death-toll. These were aggravated by the errors habitually committed by those in charge of infants. These errors were a lack of cleanliness which would astound us nowadays, and a complete absence of any sort of rule concerning infant diet. The soiled napkins which were wrapped round the baby under its swaddling hands would be dried in the sun again and again, and replaced on the infant without being washed. No care was taken to wash the mother's breast or the baby's mouth, in spite of fermentation so pronounced as to cause local disorder. Suckling of infants was carried out quite irregularly; the cries of the child were the sole guide whereby its feeding times, whether by night or day, were determined; and the more it suffered from indigestion and the resulting pains, the more frequently was it fed, to the constant aggravation of its sufferings. Who in those days might not have seen mothers carrying in their arms babies flushed with fever, perpetually thrusting the nipple into the little howling mouth in the hope of quieting it? And yet those mothers were full of self-sacrifice and of maternal anguish!

Science laid down simple rules; it enjoined the utmost possible cleanliness, and formulated a principle so self-evident, that it seems astounding people should not have recognised it for themselves: that the smallest infant, like ourselves, should have regular meals, and should only take fresh nourishment when it has digested what has been given before; and hence that it should be suckled only at intervals of so many hours, according to the months of its age and the modifications of physical function in its development. No infant should ever be given crusts of bread to suck, as is often done by mothers, especially among the lower orders, to still its crying, because particles of bread might be swallowed, which the child is as yet incapable of digesting.

The mothers' anxiety then was: what are we to do when the baby cries? They found to their astonishment after a time that their babies cried a great deal less, or indeed not at all; they even saw infants only a week old spending the two hours' interval between successive meals calm and rosy, with wide-open eyes, so silent that they gave no sign of life, like Nature in her moments of solemn immobility. Why indeed should they cry continually? Those cries were the sign of a state of things which must be translated by these words: suffering and death.

And for these wailing little ones the world did nothing. They were strapped up in swaddling clothes, and very often handed over to a young child incapable of responsibility; they had neither a room nor a bed of their own.

It was Science which came to the rescue and created nurseries, cradles, rooms for babies, suitable clothes for them, alimentary substances specially prepared for them by great industries devoted to the hygienic sustenance of infants after weaning, and medical specialists for their ailments; in short, an entirely new world, clean, intelligent, and full of amenity. The baby has become the *new man* who has conquered his own right to live, and thus has caused a sphere to be created for him. And in direct proportion to the diffusion of the laws of infantile hygiene, infant mortality has decreased.

When we say that in like manner the baby should be left at liberty spiritually, because creative Nature can also fashion its spirit better than we can, we do not mean that it should be neglected and abandoned.

Perhaps, looking around us, we shall perceive that though we cannot directly mould its individual forms of character, intelligence, and feeling, there is nevertheless a whole category of duties and solicitudes which we have neglected: and that on these *the life or death* of the spirit depend.

The principle of *liberty* is not therefore a principle of *abandonment*, but rather one which, by leading us from illusions to reality, will guide us to the most positive and efficacious "care of the child".

The liberty accorded to the child of today is purely physical.
Civil rights of the child in the twentieth century

Hygiene has brought liberty into the physical life of the infant. Such material facts as the abolition of swaddling bands, open-air life, the prolongation of sleep till the infant wakes of its own accord, etc. are the most evident and tangible proof of this. But these are merely means for the attainment of liberty. A far more important measure of liberation has been the removal of the perils of disease and death which beset the child at the outset of life's journey. Not only did infants survive in very much greater numbers as soon as the obstacles of certain fundamental errors were swept away, but it was also at once apparent that there was an improvement in their development. Was it really hygiene which helped them to increase in weight, stature, and beauty, and improved their material development? Hygiene did not accomplish quite all this. Who, as the Gospel says, can by taking thought add one cubit to his stature? Hygiene merely delivered the child from the obstacles that impeded its growth. External restraints checked material development and all the natural evolution of life; hygiene burst these bonds. And everyone felt that a liberation had been effected; everyone repeated in view of the accomplished fact: children should be free. The direct correspondence between "conditions of physical life fulfilled" and "liberty acquired" is now universally and intuitively recognised. Thus the infant is treated like a young plant. Children today enjoy the rights, which from time immemorial have been accorded to the vegetables of a well-kept garden. Good food, oxygen, suitable temperature, the careful elimination of parasites that produce disease; yes, henceforth we may say that the son of a prince will be tended with as much care as the finest rose-tree of a villa.

The old comparison of a child to a flower is the reality to which we now aspire; though even this is a privilege reserved for the more fortunate children. But let us beware of so grave an error. The babe is a man. That which suffices for a plant cannot be sufficient for him. Consider the depth of misery into which a paralysed man has sunk when we say of him: "he merely vegetates; as a man, he is dead", and lament that there is nothing left but his body.

The infant as a *man* – such is the figure we ought to keep in view. We must behold him amidst our tumultuous human society, and see how with heroic vigour he aspires to life.

What are the rights of children? Let us consider them for a moment as a social class, as a class of workers, for as a fact they are labouring to produce men. They are the future generation. They work, undergoing the fatigues of physical and spiritual growth. They continue the work carried on for a few months by their mothers, but their task is a more laborious, complex, and difficult one. When they are born they possess nothing but potentialities; they have to do everything in a world which, as even adults admit, is full of difficulties. What is done to help these frail pilgrims in an unknown world? They are born more fragile and helpless than an animal, and in a few years they have to become men, to be units in a highly complicated organised society, built up by the secular effort of innumerable generations. At a period in which civilisation, that is, the possibility of right living, is based upon rights energetically acquired and consecrated by laws, what rights has he who comes amongst us without strength and without thought? Like the infant Moses lying in the ark of bulrushes on the waters of the Nile he represents the future of the chosen people; but will some princess passing by perchance see him?

To chance, to luck, to affection, to all these we entrust the child; and it would seem the biblical chastisement of the Egyptian oppressor, the death of the firstborn, is to be unceasingly renewed.

Let us see how social justice receives the infant when he enters the world. We are living in the twentieth century; in many of the so-called civilised nations orphan asylums and wet nurses are still recognised institutions. What is an orphan asylum? It is a place of sequestration, a dark and terrible prison, where only too often the prisoner finds death, as in those mediaeval dungeons whence the victim disappeared, leaving no trace. He never sees any who are dear to him. His family name is eradicated, his goods are confiscated. The greatest criminal may retain memories of his mother, knows that he has had a name, and may derive some consolation from his recollections, comparable to the soothing reflections of one who having become blind recalls the beauty of colours and the splendour of the sun; but the foundling is as one born blind. Every malefactor has more rights than he; and yet who could be more innocent? Even in the days of the most odious tyranny, the spectacle of oppressed innocence kindled a flame of justice that sooner or later blazed up into revolution. The persons imprisoned by tyrants because they had happened to be witnesses of their crimes, and who were cast into dungeons where darkness and inaudible suffering were henceforth their unhappy portion, at least roused the people to proclaim the principle of equal justice for all. But who will lift up his voice for our foundlings? Society does not perceive that they too are men; they are indeed only the "flowers" of humanity. And to save honour and good name, what society would not with one accord sacrifice mere "flowers"?

The wet nurse is a social custom. A luxurious custom, on the one hand. Not very long ago, a girl of the middle, and not even the upper middle class, who was about to marry, boasted in the following terms of the domestic comfort promised her by her future husband: "I am to have a cook, a housemaid, and a wet nurse." On the other hand, the robust peasant girl who has given birth to a son, looking complacently at her heavy breasts, thinks: "I shall be able to get a good place as wet nurse." It is only quite recently that hygiene has cried shame upon those mothers whose laziness makes them refuse to suckle their own children; in our times queens and empresses who suckle their children are still cited admiringly as examples to other mothers. The *maternal duty* of suckling her own children prescribed to mothers by hygienists is based on a physiological principle: the mother's milk nourishes an infant more perfectly than any other. In spite of this clear indication, the duty is far from being universally accepted. Often in our walks we still see a robust mother accompanied by a wet nurse gorgeously attired in red or blue, with gold and silver embroideries, carrying a baby. Wealthy mothers have untidily dressed wet nurses who do not go out with them, who always follow the modern nurse, an expert in infantile hygiene, who keeps the baby "like a flower".

And what of the other child? . . . For every infant who has a double supply of human milk at his disposal, there is another child who has none. The wealth in question is not an industrial product. It is apportioned by Nature with careful precision. For each new life, the ration of milk. Milk cannot be produced by any means other than the production of life. Cow-keepers know this well; their good cows are hygienically reared, and calves are sent to the butcher. Yet what distress is felt whenever the young of some animal is parted from its mother! Is it not so in the case of puppies and kittens? When a pet dog has given birth to a litter so numerous that she cannot suckle them all, and it is necessary to destroy some of the puppies, what sincere grief is felt by the mistress of the house, whose own baby is being suckled by a magnificent wet nurse! The thing which excites her compassion above all is the eager, whimpering mother, which does not understand whether she has or has not the strength to suckle all the shapeless puppies she has borne, but which cannot lose one of them without despair. The wet nurse is quite another affair; she came of her own accord to offer her milk for sale. What the other – her own child – was to do, no one cared.

Only a clearly defined right, a law, could have protected him, for society is based on rights. These, it is true, are the rights of property, which are absolute; steal a loaf, even if you are starving, and you are a thief; you will be punished by the law and outlawed by society. The rights of property constitute one of the most formidable of the social bases. An administrator of landed estate who should sell the property belonging to his master, make money out of it for his own enjoyment, and leave the rightful owner in the direst poverty, is a criminal difficult to imagine. For who would buy a property without the signature of the owner? Society is so constituted that certain crimes would not only be punished if committed, but would also be almost impossible to commit. Yet in the case of young infants, this crime is committed every day, and is not regarded as a crime, but as a luxury. What can be a more sacred right than that of the baby to his mother's milk? He might say of this in the words of the Emperor Napoleon: "God has given it to me." There can be no doubt whatever as to the legitimacy of his claim; his sole capital, milk, came into the world with and for him. All his wealth is there: strength to live, to grow, to acquire vigour are contained in that nourishment. If the defrauded infant should become weak and rickety, what would become of him, condemned by poverty to a hard calling? What a claim for damages, what a question of accident during work with permanent injury resulting therefrom might be raised if some day the infant could present himself after the manner of a man before the tribunal of social justice!

In civilised countries rich mothers have been induced to suckle their children because hygienists have proved that this is beneficial to the baby's health, but not because it has been recognised that the "civil right" of the adult extends to the infant. These mothers consider countries where the wet nurse is still an institution as less *highly developed*, but on the same plane of civilisation as their own.

It may be asked: what if the mother is ill and *unable* to suckle her child? In such a case the child of the sick woman is the unfortunate one. Why should another have to suffer for his misfortune? However poverty stricken individuals may be, we do not allow them to take from others the wealth that is so urgently needed by them. If in these days an Emperor could be cured of terrible sufferings by immersion in a bath of human blood, he could not bleed healthy men for the purpose as a barbarian Emperor would have done. These are the things that make up our civilisation, and what differentiates us from pirates and cannibals. The rights of the adult are recognised.

But not the rights of the infant.[2] What an implication of baseness the fact carries with it: we recognise the rights of adults indeed, but not those of the child! We recognise justice, but only for those who can protest and defend themselves; and for the rest, we remain barbarians. Because today there may be peoples more or less highly developed from the hygienic point of view, but they all belong to the same civilisation – a civilisation based on the *right of the strongest*.

When we begin seriously to examine the problem of the moral education of the child, we ought to look around us a little, and survey the world we have prepared for him. Are we willing that he should become like us, unscrupulous in our dealings with the weak? That like us, his consciousness should harbour ideas of a justice which stops short at those who make no protests? Are we willing to make him like ourselves

---

2 Of course, should the child of the wet nurse have died, there can be no question of an infringement of its rights. But such cases have no relation to those in which the rich mother requires a nurse for the child she is unable to suckle herself, owing to pathological reasons.

I may draw attention to a precautionary measure which has become a law in Germany: this prohibits the acceptance of a post as wet nurse by a mother until six months after the birth of her own child. This interval is considered sufficiently long to guarantee the health of the infant. Moreover, the special care devoted to artificial feeding in Germany provides a satisfactory substitute for wet nursing, in the case of children who are deprived of maternal nourishment. Such laws and provisions are a first step towards the recognition of the 'civil rights' of poor infants.

half a civilised man in our dealings without equals, and half a wild beast when we encounter the innocent and oppressed?

If not, then before we offer moral education to the child, let us imitate the priest who is about to ascend to the altar: he bows his head in penitence and confesses his own sins before the whole congregation.

This outlawed child is like a dislocated arm. Humanity cannot work at the evolution of its morality until this arm has been put into its place; and this will also end the pains and the paralysis of the injured muscles attached to it: women. The social question of the child is obviously the more complete and profound; it is the question of our present and of our future.

If we can reconcile to our conscience deeds of such grave injustice, not to say crimes, without recognizing them as such, what minor forms of oppression shall we not readily condone in our dealings with the child?

How we receive the infants which come into the world

Let us look around. Only of late has any preparation been made to receive this sublime guest. It is not very long ago that little beds for children were first made; amongst all the innumerable tasteless, superfluous, and extravagant objects of commerce, let us see what things are intended for the child. No washstands, no sofas, no tables, no brushes. Among all the many houses, there is not one house for him and his life, and only rich and fortunate children have even a room of their own, more or less a place of exile.

Let us imagine ourselves subjected for even a single day to the miseries to which he is condemned.

Suppose that we should find ourselves among a race of giants, with legs immensely long and bodies enormously large in comparison with ours, and also with powers of rapid movement infinitely greater than ours, people extraordinarily agile and intelligent compared with ourselves. We should want to go into their houses; the steps would be each as high as our knees, and yet we should have to try to mount them with their owners; we should want to sit down, but the seats would be almost as high as our shoulders; clambering painfully upon them, we should at last succeed in perching upon them. We should want to brush our clothes, but all the clothes-brushes would be so huge that we could not lay hold of them nor sustain their weight; and a clothes-brush would be handed to us if we wanted to brush our nails. We should perhaps be glad to take a bath in one of the washstand basins; but the weight of these would make it impossible for us to lift them. If we knew that these giants had been expecting us, we should be obliged to say: they have made no preparations for receiving us, or for making our lives among them agreeable. The baby finds all that he himself needs in the form of playthings made for dolls; rich, varied and attractive surroundings have not been created for him, but dolls have houses, sitting-rooms, kitchens and wardrobes; for them all that the adult possesses is reproduced in miniature. Among all these things, however, the child cannot live; he can only amuse himself. The world has been given to him in jest, because no one has yet recognised him as a living man. He discovers that society has prepared a mockery for his reception.

That children break their toys is so well known that this act of destruction of the only things specially manufactured for them is taken to be a proof of their intelligence. We say: "He destroys it because he wishes to understand how things are made"; in reality he is looking to see if there is anything interesting inside the toys, because externally they have no interest whatever for him; sometimes he breaks them up violently, like an angry man. Then, according to us, he is destroying out of naughtiness.

It is the tendency of the child actually to live by means of the things around him; he would like to use a washstand of his own, to dress himself, really to comb the hair on a living head, to sweep the floor himself; he too would like to have seats, tables, sofas, clothes-pegs and cupboards. What he desires is to work himself, to aim at some intelligent object, to have comfort in his own life. He has not only to "behave like a man", but to "construct a man"; such is the dominant tendency of his nature, of his mission.

We have seen him in the *Case dei Bambini* happy and patient, slow and precise like the most admirable workman, and the most scrupulous *conservator* of things. The smallest trifles suffice to make him happy; it delights him to hang up his clothes on pegs fixed low down on the walls, within reach of his hands; to open a light door, the handle of which is proportioned to the size of his hand; to place a chair, the weight of which is not too great for his arms, quietly and gracefully. We offer a very simple suggestion: give the child an environment in which everything is constructed in proportion to himself, and let him live therein. Then there will develop within the child that "active life" which has caused so many to marvel, because they see in it not only a simple exercise performed with pleasure, but the revelation of a spiritual life. In such harmonious surroundings the young child is seen laying hold of the intellectual life like a seed which has thrown out a root into the soil, and then growing and developing by one sole means: long practice in each exercise.

When we see little children acting thus, intent on their work, slow in executing it, because of the immaturity of their structure, just as they walk slowly because their legs are still short, we feel intuitively that life is being elaborated with them, as a chrysalis slowly elaborates the butterfly within the cocoon. To impede their activity would be to do violence to their lives. But what is the usual method with your children? We all interrupt them without compunction or consideration, in the manner of masters to slaves who have no human rights. To show "consideration" to young children as to adults would even seem ridiculous to many persons. And yet with what severity do we enjoin children "not to interrupt" us! If the little one is doing something, eating by himself, for instance, some adult comes and feeds him; if he is trying to fasten an overall, some adult hastens to dress him; everyone substitutes an alien action to his, brutally, without the smallest consideration. And yet we ourselves are very sensitive as to our rights in our own work; it offends us if anyone attempts to supplant us; in the Bible, the sentence: "and his place shall another take" is among the threats to the lost.

What should we do if we were to become the slaves of a people incapable of understanding our feelings, a gigantic people, very much stronger than ourselves? When we were quietly eating our soup, enjoying it at our leisure (and we know that enjoyment depends upon being at liberty) suppose a giant appeared and snatching the spoon from our hand, made us swallow it in such haste, that we were almost choked. Our protest: "For mercy's sake, slowly", would be accompanied by an oppression of the heart; our digestion would suffer. If again, thinking of something pleasant, we should be slowly putting on an overcoat with all the sense of well-being and liberty we enjoy in our own houses, and some giant should suddenly throw it upon us, and having dressed us, should in the twinkling of an eye, carry us out to some distance from the door, we should feel our dignity so wounded, that all the expected pleasure of the walk would be lost. Our nutrition does not depend solely on the soup we have swallowed, nor our well-being upon the physical exercise of walking, but also upon the liberty with which we do these things. We should feel offended and rebellious, not at all out of hatred of these giants, but merely from our recognition of the innate tendency to free functions in all that pertains to life. It is something within us which man does not recognise, which God alone knows, a something which manifests itself imperceptibly to us to the end that we may complete it. It is this love of freedom which nourishes and gives well-being to our life even in its most minute acts. Of this it was said: "Man does not live by bread alone". How much greater this need must be in young children, in whom creation is still in action!

With strife and rebellion they have to defend their own little conquests of their environment. When they want to exercise their senses, such as that of touch, for instance, everyone condemns them: Do not touch! If they attempt to take something from the kitchen, some scraps to make a little dish, they are driven away, and mercilessly sent back to their toys. How often one of those marvellous moments when their attention is fixed, and that process of organisation which is to develop them begins in their souls, is roughly interrupted; moments when the spontaneous efforts of the young child are groping blindly in its surroundings after sustenance for its intelligence. Do we not all retain an impression of something having been for ever stifled in our lives?

Without being able to give any definite reason, we feel that something precious was lost on our life-journey, that we were defrauded and depreciated. Perhaps at the very moments when we were about to create ourselves, we were interrupted and persecuted, and our spiritual organism was left rickety, weak, and inadequate.

Let us imagine to ourselves certain adults, not mature and stable like the majority of grown men, but in a state of spiritual auto-creation, as are men of genius. Let us take the case of a writer under the influence of poetic inspiration, at the moment when his beneficent and inspiring work is about to take form for the help of other men. Or that of the mathematician who perceives the solution of a great problem, from which will issue new principles beneficial to all humanity. Or again, that of an artist whose mind has just conceived the ideal image which it is necessary to fix upon the canvas lest a masterpiece be lost to the world. Imagine these men at such psychological moments, broken in upon by some brutal person shouting to them to follow him at once, taking them by the hand, or pushing them out by the shoulders. And for what? The chessboard is set out for a game. Ah! such men would say, you could not have done anything more atrocious! Our inspiration is lost; humanity will be deprived of a poem, an artistic masterpiece, a useful discovery, by your folly.

But the child in like case does not lose some single production; he loses himself. For his masterpiece, which he is composing in the recesses of his creative genius, is the new man. The "caprices", the "naughtinesses", the "mysterious vapours" of little children are perhaps the occult cry of unhappiness uttered by the misunderstood soul.

But it is not only the soul that suffers; the body suffers with it. For the influence exercised by the spirit on the entire physical existence is a characteristic of man.

In an institution for deserted children, there was one extremely ugly little creature, who had nevertheless greatly endeared himself to a young woman who had the care of him. This nurse one day told one of the patronesses that the child was growing very pretty. The lady went to look at it, but found it very ugly, and thought to herself that daily habit soon accustoms us to the defects of others. Some time after this the nurse made the same remark as before, and the lady good-naturedly paid another visit; impressed by the warmth with which the young woman spoke of the child, she was touched to think that love had made the speaker blind. Several months elapsed, and finally the nurse, with a triumphant air, declared that henceforth no mistake would be possible, for the child had undoubtedly become "beautiful". The lady, astounded, had to admit that this was true; the body of the child had actually been transformed under the influence of a great affection.

When we delude ourselves with the idea that we are giving *everything* to children by giving them fresh air and food, we are not even giving them this: air and food are not sufficient for the body of man; all the physiological functions are subject to a higher welfare, wherein the sole key of all life is to be found. The child's body lives also by joyousness of soul.

Physiology itself teaches us these things. A frugal meal taken in the open air will nourish the body far better than a sumptuous repast in a closed room, where the air is impure, because all the functions of the body are more active in the open air, and assimilation is more complete. In like manner a frugal meal eaten in common with beloved and sympathetic persons is much more nutritious than the food a humble, harassed secretary would partake of at the lordly table of a capricious master. Liberty in this case is the cry that explains all. *Parva domus sed mea* (a little house, but my own), has been quoted ever since the Roman epoch to indicate which is the most healthy of houses. Where our lives are oppressed, there can be no health for us, even though we eat of princely banquets or in splendid buildings.

With man the life of the body depends on the life of the spirit

Physiology gives an exhaustive explanation of the mechanism of such phenomena. Moral activities have such an exact correspondence with the functions of the body that it is possible to appreciate by means of these the various emotional states of grief, anger, weariness, and pleasure. In *grief*, for instance, the action of the heart becomes feebler, as under a paralysing influence; all the bloodvessels contract, and the blood circulates more slowly, the glands no longer secrete their juices normally, and these disturbances manifest themselves in a pallor of the face, an appearance of weariness in the drooping body, a mouth parched from lack of saliva, indigestion caused by insufficiency of the gastric juice, and cold hands. If prolonged, grief results in malnutrition and consequent wasting, and predisposes the debilitated body to infectious diseases. *Weariness* is like a rapid paralysis of the heart; it may induce fainting, as expressed in the popular phrase "dead tired"; but a reflex action will nearly always restore the sufferer, like an automatic safety-valve; thus a yawn, that is to say, a deep spasmodic inspiration, which dilates the pulmonary alveoli, causes the blood to flow to the heart like a suction pump, and sets it in motion again. In *anger* there is a kind of tetanic contraction of all the capillaries, causing extreme pallor, and the expulsion of an extra quantity of bile from the liver. *Pleasure* causes dilatation of the bloodvessels; the circulation, and consequently all the functions of secretion and assimilation are facilitated; the face is suffused with colour, the gastric juice and the saliva are perceptible as that healthy appetite and that watering of the mouth which invite us to supply fresh nourishment to the body; all the tissues work actively to expel their toxins, and to assimilate fresh nourishment; the enlarged lungs store up large quantities of oxygen, which burn up all refuse, leaving no trace of poisonous germs. It is an injection of health.

In Italy, where after the abolition of the death penalty the punishment of solitary confinement was substituted, we have a proof even more eloquent of the influence of the spirit upon the functions of the body. With our modern measures of hygiene in prisons, the prison cell cannot be called a place of torture for the body; it is merely a place where all spiritual sustenance is withheld. It consists of a cell with perfectly bare grey walls, opening only into a narrow strip of ground enclosed by high walls, where the criminal may walk in the fresh air, because the open country is all around him, though it is hidden from his sight. What is lacking here for the body? It is provided with food, and a shelter from the weather, it has a bed and a place where it can take in fresh stores of pure oxygen; the body can rest, nay more, it can do nothing but rest. The conditions seem almost ideal for anyone who does not wish to do anything, and desires simply to vegetate. But no sound from without, no human voice ever reaches the ear of the being here incarcerated; he will never again see a colour or a form. No news from the outer world ever reaches him. Alone in dense spiritual darkness, he will spend the interminable hours, days, seasons and years. Now, experience has shown that these wretched persons cannot live. They go mad and die. Not only their minds but their bodies perish after a few years. What causes death? If such a man were a plant, he would lack nothing, but he requires other nourishment. Emptiness of the soul is mortal even to the vilest criminal, for this is a law of human nature. His flesh, his viscera, his bones perish when deprived of spiritual food, just as an oak-tree would perish without the nitrates of the earth and the oxygen of the air. This slow death substituted for violent death was, indeed, denounced as very great cruelty. To die of hunger in nine days like Count Ugolino[3] is a more cruel fate than to be burnt to death in half an hour like Giordano Bruno[4]; but to die of starvation of the spirit in a term of years is the most cruel of all the punishments hitherto devised for the castigation of man.

If a robust and brutal criminal can perish from starvation of the soul, what will be the fate of the infant if we take no account of his spiritual needs? His body is fragile, his bones are in process of growth, his muscles, overloaded with sugar, cannot yet elaborate their powers; they can only elaborate themselves; the delicate structure of his organism requires, it is true, nutriment and oxygen; but if its functions are to be satisfactorily performed, it requires joy. It is a joyous spirit which causes "the bones of man to exult."

---

3   Count Ugolino. Treacherous Italian nobleman and politician, who features in Dante's Divine Comedy. He died from hunger in a tower where he was imprisoned.

4   Giordano Bruno. He was trialled for heresy by the Roman Inquisition and burned at a stake.

2
A Survey of Modern Education

The precepts which govern moral education and instruction
Although the adult relegates the child to an existence among toys, and
inexorably denies him those exercises which would promote his internal
development, he claims that the child should imitate him in the moral
sphere. The adult says to the child: "Do as I do." The child is to become
a man, not by training and development, but by imitation. It is as if a father were to say in the morning to his little one: "Look at me, see how tall
I am; when I return this evening, I shall expect you to have grown a foot."

Education is greatly simplified by this method. If a tale of some heroic deed is read to the child, and he is told to "become a hero"; if some
moral action is narrated and is concluded with the recommendation,
"be thou virtuous"; if some instance of remarkable character is noted together with the exhortation, "you too must acquire a strong character",
the child has been put in the way of becoming a great man!

If children show themselves discontented and restless, they are told
that they want for nothing, that they are fortunate to have a father and a
mother, and to conclude, they are exhorted thus: "Children, be happy – a
child should always be joyous"; and behold! the mysterious yearnings of
the child are supposed to be satisfied!

Adults are quite content when they have acted thus. They straight-
en out the character and the morals of their children as they formerly
straightened their legs by bandaging them.

True, rebellious children occasionally demonstrate the futility of such
teachings. In these cases a good instructor chooses appropriate stories
showing the baseness of such ingratitude, the dangers of disobedience,
the ugliness of bad temper, to accentuate the defects of the pupil. It
would be just as edifying to speak to a blind man about the dangers of
blindness, and to a cripple about the difficulties of walking. The same
thing happens in material matters; a musicmaster says to a beginner:
"Hold your fingers properly; if you do not, you will never be able to
play." A mother will say to a son condemned to sit bent double all day

on school benches, and obliged by the usages of society to study continually: "Hold yourself gracefully, do not be so awkward in company, you make me feel ashamed of you."

If the child were one day to exclaim: "But it is you who prevent me from developing will and character; when I seem naughty, it is because I am trying to save myself; how can I help being awkward when I am sacrificed?" To many this would be a revelation; to many others merely a "want of respect."

There is a method by which the child may be brought to achieve the results which the adult has laid down as desirable; it is a very simple method. The child must be made to do whatever the adult wishes; the adult will then be able to lead him to the heights of goodness, self-sacrifice and strength, and the moral child will be created. To dominate the child, to bring him into subjection, to make him obedient – this is the basis of education. If this can be done by any means whatever, even by violence, all the rest will follow; and remember, it is all for the good of the child. The child could not be moulded by any other means. It is the first principal step in what is called "educating the will of the child", one which will henceforth enable the adult to speak of himself as Virgil speaks of God.

After this first step the adult will examine himself to see what are the things he finds most difficult, and these he will exact from the child in time, that the child may accustom himself to the necessary difficulties of man's life. But very often the adult also imposes conditions which he himself has not the fortitude to accept even partially . . . as, for instance, the task of listening motionless for three or four hours every day, during a course of years, to a dull, wearisome lecturer.

It is the teacher who forms the child's mind. How he teaches

The same conception governs the school: it is the teacher who must form the pupil; the development of the child's intelligence and culture are in his hands. He has a truly formidable task and a tremendous responsibility. The problems that present themselves to him are innumerable and acute; they form as it were a hedge of thorns separating him from his pupils. What must first of all be devised, to win the attention of his pupils, so that he may be able to introduce into their minds all that seems to him necessary? How is he to offer them an idea in such a manner that they will retain it in their memories? To this end, it is essential that he should have a knowledge of psychology, the precise manner in which physical phenomena are produced, the laws governing memory, the psychical mechanism by means of which ideas are formed, the laws governing the association of ideas, by means of which very gradually ideas proceed to the most sublime activities, impelling the child to reason. It is he who, knowing all these things, must build up and enrich the mind. And this is no easy matter, because, in addition to this difficult work, there is always the difficulty of difficulties, that of inducing the child to lend himself to all this endeavour, and to second the master, and not show himself recalcitrant to the efforts made on his behalf. For this reason the *moral* education is the point of departure; before all things, it is necessary to *discipline* the class. The pupils must be induced to *second* the master's efforts, if not by love, then by force. Failing this point of departure, all education and instruction would be *impossible*, and the school *useless.*

Another difficulty is that of economising the powers of the pupils, that is to say, of utilising them to the utmost without wasting them. How much rest is necessary? How long should any particular work be carried on? Perhaps ten minutes' rest may be necessary after the first three-quarters of an hour, a pause of fifteen minutes may be required, and so on throughout the day; finally, a quarter of an hour's rest may be needed after ten minutes' occupation. But what instruction is best adapted to the powers of a child during the various hours of the day? Is it best to begin with mathematics or with dictation? At what hour will the child be most inclined to exercise his powers of imagination, at 9 in the morning or at 11?

Other anxieties must assail a perfect teacher! How should he write on the blackboard so that the children seated at a distance may see? for if they do not see his work is of no avail. And how much light should fall upon the blackboard, in order that all may see clearly the white characters on the black surface? Of what size should be the script specially chosen by the master to suit distant vision? This is a serious matter, because if the child, obliged by discipline to look and learn from a distance, should put too great a strain upon his powers of visual accommodation, he may in time become short-sighted; then the teacher would have man-ufactured a blind person. A serious matter indeed!

★ ★ ★

What consideration is ever given to the state of anxiety of such a teacher? To get some idea of his anxiety we may think of a young wife about to be-come a mother, who should set herself such problems as the following: how can I create an infant, if I know nothing of anatomy; how can I form its skeleton? I must study the structure of the bones carefully. I must then learn how the muscles are attached; but how will it be possible to put the brain into a closed box? And must the little heart go on beating continu-ally until death? Is it possible that it will not weary?

In like fashion, she might ponder thus over her newborn babe: it is evident that he will not be able to walk if he does not first of all under-stand the laws of equilibrium; if he is left to himself, he will not be able to understand these till he is twenty; I must therefore prepare to teach him these laws prematurely in order that he may be able to walk as quickly as possible.

The schoolmaster is the person who builds up the intelligence of the pu-pil; the intelligence of the pupil increases in direct proportion to the efforts of the teacher; in other words, he knows just what the master has made him know and understands neither more nor less than the master has made him understand. When an inspector visits a school and questions the pu-pils he turns to the master, and if he is satisfied says: "Well done, teacher!" For the result is indubitably the work of the master; the discipline by which he has fixed the attention of his pupils, even to the psychical mechanism which has guided him in his teaching, all is due to him. God enters the school as a symbol in the crucifix, but the creator is the teacher.

A good deal of help is given to teachers in their super-human task. There is a kind of division of labour, by virtue of which more advanced experts prepare the schemata of instruction; basing them upon psy-chology, if the teaching is on a scientific plan, or on the principles laid down by one of the great pedagogues such as Herbart[5], for example;

---

5   Johann Friedrich Herbart (1776 – 1841) was a German philosopher who founded peda-gogy as an academic discipline.

moreover, the sciences, such as hygiene and experimental psychology, are further invoked to overcome many practical difficulties and to help in the arrangement of schoolrooms, the drawing up of the curriculum, timetables, etc.

Here, for instance, are notes for lessons on a psychological basis, that is to say, lessons which take account of the proper *order of succession* in which the psychical activities should develop in the mind of the child: by exercises of this kind the pupil will not only learn, but will develop his intelligence in accordance with the laws governing its formation.[6]

Object Lesson

A Candle: *Education of the sensory and perceptive faculties.*

Sight: White, solid.

Touch: Greasy, smooth.

Nomenclature: Parts of the candle: wick, surface, extremity, edges, upper part, lower part, middle part.

The candles we use are made of *wax* mixed with *stearine.* Stearine is made of the fat of oxen and sheep, and pigs. Hence they are called stearine candles. There are also *wax* candles. These are yellowish and less greasy. Wax is produced by bees. There are also tallow candles; these are very greasy and have a disagreeable smell when burning.

Memory: Have you ever seen a candlefactory? Have you ever seen a beehive? Of what are the cells of the honeycomb made? When do you light a candle? Have you ever carried a lighted candle carelessly? Did not this cause a disaster?

Imagination: Draw the outline of a candle on the blackboard.

Comparison, association, abstraction: Similarity and difference in candles of stearine, wax, and tallow.

Judgment and reasoning: Are candles useful? Were they more useful formerly, or now that we have gas and electric light?

Sentiments: Children are greatly pleased by a visit to a candlefactory. It is indeed very agreeable to see how the candles used by so many people

---

6   These two examples are taken from the wellknown review, I diritti della Scuola, Year XIV (The rights of the School).

are made. When we can satisfy our desire for instruction we feel pleasure and contentment.

Volition: What should we do with the fat of pigs if we did not know how to make it into stearine? What should we do with wax if we did not know how to utilise it? Man is able to work and to transform many products into useful substances and objects. Work is our life. Blessed be the workers! Let us also love work and devote ourselves diligently thereto.

(N.B. The children are all to listen without moving.) Any kind of lesson may be based on the same psychical plan, even a moral lesson. For instance:

Moral education derived from the observation of actions: (N.B. The actions are all invented and narrated.)

Agreeable manners. Incident: "Is it true, Miss, that the village church is more than a kilometre from here? My mother has ordered me to go there. I thought I had arrived, and I was so pleased. I have come a long way, and I am so very, very tired." "Indeed", replied the girl, who was standing at the gate of her home, "you are still a kilometre and a half from the church. But come through my gate, and take the short cut I will show you through my fields. You will get to the church in five minutes." What an amiable girl!

Successive relations of cause and effect: The village girl showed amenity to the little traveller. The latter reached the church quickly, was saved much fatigue, and felt great relief.

Memory: Have you always been pleasant to your companions? Have you always been ready to lend a comrade anything he has asked for? Have you always thanked those who have done you favours in an agreeable manner?

Comparison, association, abstraction: Comparison between an agreeable child and a boorish one.

Judgment, reasoning: Why is it necessary to be courteous to all? Is it sufficient to give help solely to show oneself to be amiable?

Sentiments: He who is amiable has a soul rich in sweetness and suavity. What sympathy he evokes in all! The disagreeable person is irritated by trifles. He excites disgust and fear in others. He who is affable shows love to his neighbour.

Volition: Children, accustom yourselves to be pleasant to everyone.

You should be pleasant when you are conferring some favour, otherwise the favour will seem irksome. When you want something, do you ask for it arrogantly? If so, it will be easier to say no than yes to you. On the other hand, if you ask politely for something, will it not be difficult to refuse you?

It will perhaps be more interesting to follow a lesson actually given, and accepted as a model for teachers in general. I therefore reproduce one of the lessons which gained a prize at a competition of teachers held in Italy.[7] In this, according to the subject or theme, only one primary psychical activity was to be dealt with, namely sensory perception. (The compositions were distinguished not by the names of the authors, but by mottoes.)

Motto: Things are the first and best teachers.

I set myself the following limits:

To give an idea of icy cold in contrast to that of heat. (This would be amply sufficient in itself, for these ideas are not grains to pick up one after the other, but sublime psychical facts of great complexity, and, consequently, very difficult to assimilate.)

Combine with the idea to be imparted, the cultivation of a sense of compassion and pity for the very poor, to whom winter brings such severe suffering; a feeling I have already tried many times to arouse.

The above is for my own guidance; what follows is for the children.

"Children, how comfortable we are here! Everything is clean; everything is in order; I am so fond of you; you are so fond of me. Isn't this true, children?

Children: I am, I am. Me too (correct).

Tell me, Gino, are you cold? You said no at once. Well, no, you are right; we are really very cosy here. There, in that corner (I point) there is a thing which gives out much . . .

Children: Heat. It is the stove.

But outside, where there is no stove, over there, towards the horizon (the children are to a certain extent familiar with this word), there is no warmth.

---

7   This was published in the review, *La Voce delle Maestre d'Asilo*, Year VIII of the Italian National Union of Kindergarten Teachers. Also published by the Montessori-Pierson Publishing Company in *The 1913 Rome Lectures* by Maria Montessori, page 153 – 155.

Children: It's cold there (an answer due to the clarity of the laws of contrast).

Last night . . . while we were asleep, while your mother perhaps was mending your clothes . . . dear mother, how kind she is! . . . well, last night, so many, many white flakes fell softly from the sky! . . . Snow, snow, exclaim the children. Children! let us say: so many snowflakes fell. How beautiful the snow is! Let us go and look at it closely.

Children: Yes, yes, yes, yes.

It is so beautiful that I see you would all like to take a little. But perhaps this is not allowed. To whom does the snow belong? (No answer). Who bought it? Who made it? You? No. I? No. Your mother? No. Then did your father buy it? (They look at me in astonishment; these are really very strange questions.) No, again. Well then the snow belongs to everyone. And if this is so, we may take a little handful of it. (Evident signs of joy.) I will hand round the boxes you made yesterday. (These children have no desks with lockers in which they may put away their little works. Using the boxes will be a good way of demonstrating the utility of their work.) They will do very well to hold the beautiful snow. (I talk to them as I distribute the boxes, that their attention may not flag.) I will take mine too, the one I made with you. It is larger than yours; so which will hold more snow, mine or yours?

Children: Yours.

Come then, children. Put a white handful into your boxes. How delightful!

(Going.) Just stop a moment; how comfortable we are here! Put one hand over your face. How warm your face is, and how warm your hand is too! We shall see whether your hands will still be so warm after you have touched the snow.

Children: They will be cold.

Yes, indeed. (Going out.) How beautiful it is! It fell down from above. The sky has given the earth a beautiful dress, all . . .

Children: White.

At this juncture my children, accustomed to that principle of healthy, ordered liberty, which is the main factor in the formation of character, touch and gather up the snow; some of them break the pure surface with little drawings. I let them. I wait a minute, then I make as it were a sudden assault upon their attention:

Children, I too will take a little snow, but together with all of you. Stop. Stand up. Look at me. Let us take away a little strip of the great cloak. Let us put it in our boxes. That's right. (Re-entering the schoolroom.) Oh! How cold it is! The children who are not wrapped up well are the coldest. Poor little things! And those who haven't that thing full of burning coal in their houses!

Children: The stove.

How cold they will be! Come now, quickly; all to your places. Put the boxes on the desk. How cold the snow is! Did you notice how cold it made your hands, which were quite warm?

Children: My hand is cold! Mine too, etc.!

In the courtyard, I saw Caroline take a little snow, and then suddenly let it fall; she was not strong enough to bear such cold. But then she tried again, and the second time she did not drop it.

Child: I didn't. I putted it (correct) quickly into my box.

Children, when the cold is as great as the cold of the snow, it is called *frost.* Say that, Guido. What is the word? Now you Giannina. And the snow which is so cold is . . . what? Who can guess?

A child: Frozen.

Say: the snow is *frozen.*

We came indoors, because it is frosty outside, and inside it is . . .

Children: Warm.

But we brought with us a frozen thing which is called . . .

Children: Snow.

★ ★ ★

What is it the stove gives us? Do you remember? [8]

Children: Heat.

I want Maria to tell me. And now, Peppino.

Do you know, our mouths also give out heat. Open yours. Not too much! Hold up one hand in front of it, the right hand. Breathe on it as I am doing. Let us breathe again; now let us send our breath outwards,

---

8   The children are expected to know that the stove gives out heat, by an effort of memory.

as I am doing. Again . . . again . . . again. That's right. Now feel. You see your mouth too gives out a little . . .

Children: Heat.

Now let us try putting a little snow into it. A little piece like this. Oh! The heat of the mouth is escaping, it has already gone at the icy touch of the snow.

Children: Our mouths are cold now.

Yes, that's right. They are very, very cold, so cold that they are what we call . . .

Children: Freezing.

Perhaps Giuseppe doesn't know. He didn't say it with the others. Say it again, that he may say it with you. Again. That will do. Bravo, Giuseppe. So our mouths were . . .

Children: Freezing.

Let us eat another little piece of snow. The snow turns to water in our mouths, because it is made of water only. Now bread is made of water too, but not only of water. What does the baker want to make the dough for bread? . . .

Children: Flour.

And what else?

Children: Salt.

And what else?

Children: Yeast.

I see Luigi is still eating snow, and Alfonso too, and Pierino. Do you like it?

Children: Yes, Signora.

Do you all like it?

Children: Yes, Signora. Me too, me too (correct).

Well, eat a little more, but not much, it might make you ill. It is so freezing (I repeat this word very often, because it expresses the idea I am trying to convey).

When it snows it is so very cold, and just think that there are many children, many people, who are not warmly dressed and have no stoves; they are very poor. They suffer very much, and some of them die; poor people! How fortunate we are, on the other hand! We have so many garments (they have learnt this word) to cover ourselves with; we have a stove at home and one at school, to warm us. How lucky we are!

A child: I have no stove at home.

I know you have not, Emilio, and I am very sorry. Children, you must be kind to Emilio and Giuseppina, because they are very . . .

Children: Poor.

Have you eaten it all?

Children: No, Signora.

Now let us go into the courtyard and throw away the rest of the snow. Then we will put the boxes on this table to dry. And tomorrow I will show you a pretty picture of country covered with snow. Come along; bring your boxes, and when you have emptied them put them back where I told you."

I intend to repeat this lesson in another form, combining others with it, and referring in it to other ideas, which bear a relation to that here set forth.

As everything in the physical and moral world is one and indivisible, bound together in closest union, human development is gravely impeded by the presenting of isolated educational facts in a desultory manner, because it is impossible to disconnect things united by a sacred and eternal law.[9]

⋆ ⋆ ⋆

In the above "model" lesson, it is claimed that only two perceptions are dealt with, those of cold and heat, and that the child has been allowed a good deal of liberty, but of a judicious kind.

Now it would be exceedingly difficult to limit the perceptions strictly to two, especially when dealing with persons placed in an environment abounding in stimuli, who have already stored up a whole chaos of images. But such being the object in view, it is necessary to eliminate as far as possible all other perceptions, to arrest those two, and so to polarise attention on them that all other images shall be obscured in the field of consciousness. This would be the scientific method tending to isolate perceptions; and it is, in fact, the practical method adopted by us in our education of the senses. In the case of cold and heat, the child is "prepared" by the isolation of the particular sense in question; he is placed

---

9 Nowadays we know that children should not under any circumstances eat snow.

blindfolded in a silent place, to the end that thermic stimuli alone may reach him. In front of the child are placed two objects perfectly identical in all characteristics perceptible to the muscular tactile sense: of the same dimensions, the same shape, the same degree of smoothness, the same resistance to pressure; for instance, two india rubber bags, filled with the same quantity of water, and perfectly dry on the outside. The sole difference is the temperature of the water in the two bags; in the hot one, the water would be at a temperature of sixty degrees centigrade; in the cold, at ten degrees centigrade. After directing the child's attention to the object, his hand is drawn over the hot bag, and then over the cold one; while his hand is on the hot bag the teacher says: it is hot! While he feels the cold one he is told: it is cold. And the lesson is finished. It has consisted merely of two words, and of a long preparation designed to ensure that as far as possible, the two sensations corresponding to these two words shall be the only ones that reach the child. The other senses, sight and hearing, were protected against stimuli; and there was no perceptible difference in the objects offered to the touch save that of temperature. Thus it becomes approximately probable that the child will achieve the perception of two sensations exclusively.

And what about the liberty of the child, we shall be asked?

Well, we admit that every lesson infringes the liberty of the child, and for this reason we allow it to last only for a few seconds: just the time to pronounce the two words: hot, cold; but this is effected under the influence of the preparation, which by first isolating the sense, makes, as it were, a darkness in the consciousness, and then projects only two images into it. As if from the screen before a magic lantern, the child receives his psychical acquisitions, or rather they are like seeds falling on a fertile soil; and it is in the subsequent free choice, and the repetition of the exercise, as in the subsequent activity, spontaneous, associative, and reproductive, that the child will be left "free". He receives, rather than a lesson, a determinate impression of contact with the external world; it is the clear, scientific, pre-determined character of this contact which distinguishes it from the mass of indeterminate contacts which the child is continually receiving from his surroundings. The multiplicity of such indeterminate contacts will create chaos within the mind of the child; pre-determined contacts will, on the other hand, initiate order therein, because with the help of the technique of isolation, they will begin to make him distinguish one thing from another.

The technique of our lessons is governed by experimental psychology. And this trend, without doubt, is in contrast to that of the past, which was governed by speculative psychology, on which the whole of the educational methods commonly in use in schools has hitherto been based.

It was Herbart who used the philosophical psychology of his day as a guiding principle to reduce pedagogic rules to a system. From his individual experience he believed he could deduce a universal method of developing the mind, and he made this the psychological basis of the methods of teaching. The German pedagogue, whose methods are now, thanks to Credaro, formerly Professor of Pedagogy at the University of Rome and afterwards Minister of Education, adopted for elementary education throughout Italy, gave a unique type of lesson on the four well known periods (the formal steps): clarity, association, system, method. These may be explained approximately as follows: presentation of an object and its analytical examination (clarity); judgment and comparison with other surrounding objects or with mnemonic images (association); definition of the object deduced from preceding judgments (system); new principles derived from the idea which is thus deepened, and which will lead to practical application of a moral order (method).

The teacher must guide the child's mind on these lines in every kind of teaching; he must, however, never substitute his own intelligence for that of the child, but rather make the child himself think, and induce him to exercise his own activity. For instance, in the association period, the master must not say: "Look at such and such an object, and at such and such another; see how much alike they are, etc. . .". He should ask the pupil: "What do you see when you look round? Is there not something which is like, etc.". Again, in the definition period, the master should not say: "A bird is a vertebrate animal covered with feathers; it has two limbs which have been transformed into wings", but by rapid questions, corrections, and analogies, he should induce the child to find the precise definition for himself. If the mental process of Herbart's four periods is to come naturally, it would be essential that great interest in the object should exist; it is interest which would keep the mind amused, or, as the famous pedagogue would say, plunged in the idea, and would maintain it in a system nevertheless embracing multilateral ideas; and hence it is necessary that "interest" should be awakened and should persist in all instruction. It is well known that a pupil of Herbart's must, to this end, supplement Herbart's four periods by a prior period, that of interest; linking all new knowledge to the old, "going from the known to the unknown", because what is absolutely new can awake no interest.

"To make oneself interesting artificially", that is, interesting to those who have no interest in us, is indeed a very difficult task; and to arrest the attention hour after hour, and year after year, not of one, but of a multitude of persons who have nothing in common with us, not even years, is indeed a superhuman undertaking, yet this is the task of the teacher, or, as he would say, his "art": to make this assembly of children whom he has reduced to immobility by discipline follow him with their minds, understand what he says, and learn; an internal action, which he cannot govern, as he governs the position of their bodies, but which he must win by making himself interesting, and by maintaining this interest. "The art of tuition", says Ardigo, "consists mainly of this: to know up to what point and in what manner one can maintain the interest of pupils. The most skilful teachers are those who never fatigue one fraction of the pupil's brain, but act in such a manner that his attention, turning now here, now there, may rest itself, and gaining strength, return to the principal argument of the discourse with renewed vigour."

A much more laborious art is that which leads the child to find by means of its own mental processes, not what it would naturally find, but what the teacher desires, although he does not say what he desires; he urges on the child to associate his ideas "spontaneously" – as the teacher associates them – and even succeeds in making the child compose definitions with the exact words he himself has fixed upon, without having revealed them. Such a thing would seem the result of some occult science, a kind of conjuring trick. Nevertheless, such methods have been and still are in use, and in some cases they form the sole art of the teacher.

When in 1862 Tolstoy was making his tours of inspection in the schools of Germany, he was struck by this method of tuition, and among the pedagogic writings describing his school, at Yasnaya Polyana, he reproduces a lesson which deserves to be recorded, although perhaps it would no longer be possible to find an example of such a lesson in any German school.

YASNAYA POLYANA, 1862.

Calm and confident, the professor is seated in the classroom; the instruments are ready; little tables with the letters, a book with the picture of fish. The master looks at his pupils; he knows beforehand all they are to understand; he knows of what their souls consist, and various other things he has learnt in the seminary.

He opens the book and shows the fish. "Dear children, what is this?" The poor children are delighted to see the fish, unless indeed they already know from other pupils with what sauce it is to be served up. In any case, they answer: "It is a fish". "No", replies the professor (all this is not an invention nor a satire, but an exact account of what I have seen without exception in all the best schools in Germany, and in those English schools which have adopted this method of teaching). "No", says the professor. "Now what is it you see?" The children are silent. It must not be forgotten that they are obliged to remain seated and quiet, each one in his place, and that they are not to move. "Well, what do you see?" "A book", says the most stupid child in the class. Meanwhile, the more intelligent children have been asking themselves over and over again what it is they do see; they feel they cannot guess what the teacher wants, and that they will have to answer that this fish is not a fish, but something the name of which is unknown to them. "Yes, yes", says the master, eagerly, "very good indeed, a book. And what else?" The intelligent ones guess, and say joyfully and proudly: "Letters". "No, no, not at all!" says the teacher, disappointed; "you must think before you speak." Again all the intelligent ones lapse into mournful silence; they do not even try to guess; they think of the teacher's spectacles, and wonder why he does not take them off instead of looking over the top of them: "Come then; what is there in the book?" All are silent. "Well, what is this thing?" "A fish", says a bold spirit. "Yes, a fish. But is it a live fish?" "No, it is not alive." "Quite right. Then is it dead?" "No." "Right. Then what is this fish?" "A picture."

"Just so. Very good!" All the children repeat: "It is a picture", and they think that is all. Not at all. They have to say that it is a picture, which represents a fish. By the same method the master induces the children to say that it is a picture, which represents a fish. He imagines that he is exercising the reasoning faculties of his pupils, and it never seems to enter his head that if it is his duty to teach children to say in these exact words, "it is a book with

*a picture of a fish", it would be much simpler to repeat this strange formula
and make his pupils learn it by heart.*

As a pendant to this old-fashioned lesson witnessed by Tolstoy in an elementary school in Germany, we may cite the following lesson recently
set forth by a distinguished French pedagogue and philosopher, whose
textbooks are classics in the schools of his own country and in those
of many foreign lands, and are also in use in the teachers' training col-
leges in Italy. As the subtitle on the title page informs us, it is one of
a series of "lessons designed to mould teachers and citizens who shall
be conscious of their duties, and useful to families, to their fatherland,
and to humanity."[10] We are therefore in the ambit of secondary schools.
The lesson we cite is a practical application of the principle of giving
lessons by means of interrogation (Socratic method), and deals with a
moral theme: rights.

*You boys have never mistaken your companion Paul for this table or this
tree? – Oh, no! – Why? – Because the table and the tree are inanimate and
insensible, whereas Paul lives and feels. – Good. If you strike the table it
will feel nothing and you will not hurt it; but have you any right to destroy
it? – No, we should be destroying something belonging to others. – Then
what is it you respect in the table? The inanimate and insensible wood, or
the property of the person to whom it belongs? – The property of the person
to whom it belongs. – Have you any right to strike Paul? – No, because we
would hurt him and he would suffer. – What is it you respect in him? The
property of another, or Paul himself? – Paul himself. – Then you cannot
strike him, nor shut him up, nor deprive him of food? –*

*No. The police would arrest us if we did. – Ah! ah! you are afraid of the
police. But is it only this which prevents you from hurting Paul? – Oh! no,
Sir. It is because we love Paul and do not want to make him suffer, and
because we have no right to do so. – You think then that you owe respect
to Paul in his life and his feelings, because life and feeling are things to
respect? – Yes, Sir.*

Are these all you have to respect in Paul? Let us enquire; think well. – His

---

10 F. Alengry, *Education based upon Psychology and Morality.*

books, his clothes, his satchel, the luncheon in it. – Well. What do you mean? – We must not tear his books, soil his clothes or his satchel, or eat his luncheon. Why? – Because these things are his and we have no right to take things belonging to others. – What is the act of taking things that belong to others called? – Theft. – Why is theft forbidden? – Because if we steal we shall go to prison. – Fear of the police again! But is this the chief reason why we must not steal? – No, Sir, but because we ought to respect the property as well as the persons of others. – Very good. Property is an extension of human personality, and must be respected as such.

And is this all? Is there nothing more to respect in Paul than his body, his books and his copybooks? Do not you see anything else? Can you not think of anything more? I will give you a hint: Paul is an industrious pupil, an honest, good-natured companion; you are all fond of him, and he deserves your affection. What do we call the esteem we all feel for him, the good opinion we have of him? – Honour . . . reputation. – Well, this honour, this reputation, Paul acquired by good conduct and good manners. These are things which belong to him. – Yes, Sir; we have no right to rob him of them. – Very good; but what do we call this kind of theft, that is, the theft of honour and reputation? And first of all, how can we steal them? Can we take them and put them in our pockets? – No, but we can speak evil of him. – How? – We could say that he had done harm to one of his companions . . . that he had stolen apples from a neighbouring orchard . . . that he had spoken ill of another. – That is so. But how could you rob him of honour and reputation by speaking thus? – Sir, people would no longer believe him if they had a bad opinion of him; he would be beaten, scolded, and left to himself. – Then if you speak evil of Paul, and what you say is false, do you give him pleasure? – No, Sir, we would cause him pain, and do him a wrong, which would be very odious and wicked of us. – Yes, boys, this lying with intent to injure would be odious and wicked, and it is called calumny. I will explain later that evil speaking differs from calumny or slander in that what is said is not untrue, and I will point out the terrible consequences of evil speaking and slander.

Now let us sum up what we have said: Paul is a living and sensitive creature. We ought not to cause him suffering, to rob him, or to slander him; we ought to respect him. The honourable things in Paul constitute rights, and make him a moral person. The obligation laid upon us to respect these rights is called duty. The obligation and the duty of respecting the rights of others is also called justice. Justice is derived from two Latin words (jure stare), meaning: to keep oneself in the right.

The duties of justice enumerated by us are to be summed up this: Not to kill . . . not to cause suffering . . . not to steal . . . not to slander. Always reflect upon the words you say in which "Not" is followed by a verb in the imperative infinitive. What does that mean?

An obligation, a command, a prohibition. – Go on, explain. The obligation of respect . . . the command to respect rights . . . the prohibition of stealing. How may all these things be summed up? In doing no evil.

Positive science makes its appearance in the schools

Positive science was invited to enter into schools as into a chaos where it was necessary to separate light from darkness, a place of disaster where prompt succour was essential.

Discoveries of medicine: distortions and diseases

The first science, indeed, to penetrate into the school was medicine, which organised a special hygiene for the occasion, a kind of Red Cross service. The most interesting part of the hygiene that penetrated into schools was that which diagnosed and described the "diseases of school children", that is to say, the maladies contracted solely as a result of study in school. The most prevalent of these maladies are spinal curvature and myopia. The first is caused by excessive sitting, and by the injurious position of the shoulders in writing. The second arises from the fact that in the spot where the child has to remain seated, there is not sufficient light for him to see clearly; or this spot is too far from the blackboard, or from the places where the child has to read, and the prolonged effort of accommodation induces myopia. Other minor generalised maladies were also described: an organic debility so widely diffused that hygiene prescribed as an ideal treatment a gratuitous distribution of cod-liver oil or of reconstituent remedies in general to all pupils. Anaemia, liver complaints, and neurasthenia were also studied as school diseases.

Thus a new field was opened to hygiene in connection with the most fertile source of professional disease, and reading and writing were carefully studied in relation to pedagogical methods, and in relation to spinal curvature and defective refraction of the eyes.

The figure of the child, that victim of unsuitable and disproportionate work, was not hereby brought into strong relief, as might have been expected, by the aid of medicine, but a new branch of "legal medicine" came into being. It was, indeed, medicine which drew attention to the diseases and deaths of the victims in orphan asylums, victims of artificial or irrational feeding, in conjunction with wet nursing; it was medicine which passed in review one by one all those individual cases which proclaim this legal fact: children have no civil rights. Medicine now entered into another sphere where the victims were not "cases", but the generality, the child-population in its entirety; and now it is the law itself which imposes duties upon them, and condemns them *en masse* to labour for many years in a manner which entails physical torture. If a branch of legal medicine has arisen in connection with criminals, how is it that none should ever have arisen in connection with the innocent?

Science has not fulfilled its mission in its dealings with children

Medicine has confined itself to the treatment of diseases artificially produced. It has diagnosed a cause of disease and left this cause undisturbed, content merely to alleviate the resultant evils befalling a multitude of victims. It has not taken up the attitude proper to its great and dignified role of "protector" of life; it has merely come forward, like the Red Cross Service during war, to heal the wounded and alleviate the condition of the suffering; it has not considered that the authority it enjoys as the guardian of health would enable it to utter the supreme cry of peace, putting an end to a war so dangerous, unjust, and inhuman.

As, in its struggle against microbes, it was the standardbearer in the most glorious of victories over death, so, fighting directly against the causes of the impoverishment of generations, it might have aspired to bear the banner of protector of posterity. Instead of this, it confined itself to the elaboration of a branch of study that mimics science: school hygiene; thus making itself the accomplice of a social wrong.

Let us glance into a recent treatise of school hygiene, which merely sums up the ideas and the work of the world at large:

"We will briefly indicate the conditions favourable to the development of spinal curvature. The age when the malady usually appears is that of second infancy, hence its name of spinal curvature of the adolescent; spinal curvature caused by rickets, which appears in early childhood, is rarer, and is of less direct interest to us here. The commonest cause, and that on which our attention should be primarily concentrated, is the vicious attitude adopted by the majority of our pupils during their school work; this cause is so universal that we may call spinal curvature the professional disease of the pupil. Doctor Legendre, in a formula which may be judged over-severe, though unhappily it is only too well founded, said of our schools that they are factories for the production of the deformed and the myopic."

"The main cause of myopia is to be found in the very conditions under which children are gathered together in schools: insufficiency of light, the over-small type common in schoolbooks, the frequent use of the blackboard on which the teacher is not always careful to make the size of the characters he traces proportionate to the distance at which they have to be read, are so many causes of ocular fatigue." "The visual keenness of a given eye," says Doctor Leprince, "decreases rapidly when the intensity of the light falls below a certain limit. The pupil, working with insufficient light, repairs the defective keenness of which this is the cause, by increasing the visual angle under which the details of the object he is looking at appear to him; in other words *he brings that object inordinately close to him.*"

"The time necessary to recognise a given letter increases greatly, when the limit of visual acuteness has been reached. Therefore, insufficient light would tend to make work slower, unless the pupil increased acuteness by approaching the object more closely. Thus myopia constitutes a positive adaptation to the defective conditions of work, enabling the pupil to work more rapidly."[11]

It would seem therefore natural to say: let the child find himself a better lighted place; if the blackboard is at some distance from him, let him come nearer to it; if the insufficient light retards his work, let him go more slowly; if the questions at issue are such harmless things as changing a place, advancing a step or two, taking a few minutes longer

---

11 Brouardel and Mosny, *Hygiene Scolaire.* Balliere, Paris, 1914, pp. 142, 143, 430, 496.

over a task – what tyrant on earth would deny such a small favour, and condemn the suppliant to blindness?

Such a tyrant is the teacher, who aspires to win the affection of his victims by means of moral exhortations.

It would be so simple to allow children, when tired of sitting, to rise, and when tired of writing, to desist, and then their bones would not be twisted. Who can look on unmoved at the spectacle of children whose spine is being deformed by using desks, just as in the Middle Ages the instep was deformed by the torture of the boot. And on what grounds is this odious torture judged to be necessary?

Because a man has substituted himself for God, desiring to form the minds of children in his own image and likeness; and this cannot be done without subjecting a free creature to torture. This is the only reason.

We will now quote the remedies by means of which a so-called science proposes to counteract spinal curvature in schoolchildren. It has determined the exact position in which a child may remain seated and at work for a long period of time without injury to the vertebrae:

"The child, seated at the table, should have his feet planted flat upon the ground, or upon a foot-rest. The legs should be at right-angles to the thighs, as should the thighs be to the trunk, save for a slight inclination of the bench itself. The trunk should be in such a position that there will be no lateral inclination of the vertebral column, the arms should be parallel with the sides of the body, the thorax should not be interfered with by the front edge of the table, the pelvic basin should be symmetrically supported, the head slightly bent forward at a distance of thirty centimetres from the level of the table; the axis of the eyes, remaining parallel with the front edge of the table, should be horizontal; the forearms, two-thirds of which should be laid on the table, should rest on it, but without leaning upon it."

To realise all these conditions, it is necessary that the desk should be *exactly fitted* to the proportions of the child; its constituent parts should agree with those of the body and limbs of the scholar.

The following are the measurements which Dufessel considered indispensable in the fashioning of a desk suitable for children:

1 Height.
2 The length of the leg, taken from below the knee, when the child is seated with the legs at right-angles to the thighs, and the feet flat on the ground. This measurement gives the required height of the seat from the foot-rest.
3 The diameter of the body from front to back, taken from the sternum; this, with five centimeters added to it, gives the proper distance from the reading-desk to the back of the seat.
4 The length of the femur, two-thirds of which represent the depth of the seat.
5 Finally, the height of the epigastric cavity above the seat, augmented by a few centimeters, indicates the height of the reading-desk.

"We may add that in view of the rapid growth of the child, these measurements should be taken twice in the course of the school year, and children should be made to change places in accordance with these measurements".

There is a little crustacean, which coming naked into the world, chooses an empty shell and adapts itself thereto; when it grows larger and the shell becomes too tight, it sallies forth and takes up its abode in a larger one. This the creature does of its own accord, without a savant to measure it or a teacher to choose a new shell for it. But to us and to scientists, a child is inferior to this lowly invertebrate!

The difficulty of keeping forty or fifty children motionless for hours in the prescribed hygienic attitude, and of finding desks exactly adapted to these growing bodies, makes this remedy impracticable, so hunchbacks continue among us. The problem remains unsolved.

Hence it has been deemed more practical to establish a kind of orthopaedic institution within the building itself in certain model schools in Rome. It consists of a costly and elaborate apparatus, to which the pupils come in turn to be suspended by the head after the method adopted in medicine to combat spinal curvature in Pott's disease (tuberculosis of the vertebral column) and rickets. Healthy children, as well as the unsound, suffer by these applications; but on the other hand, the results afford encouraging statistics. If this hanging treatment be initiated regularly at the age of six years it strikes a perfect balance with the injury caused by prolonged deterioration induced by school desks, and children are delivered from spinal disease.

Discoveries of experimental psychology: over-work; nervous exhaustion

Hygiene, making its way into the school, discovered scholar's spinal curvature and scholar's myopia; experimental psychology discovered the exhaustion due to over-work, and studied the *fatigue* of the scholar. It followed in the beaten track of medicine – that is to say, it sought to alleviate the ills it had diagnosed, and instituted a branch of science the title of which is not very clearly defined as yet, for some call it experimental psychology applied to the school, others Scientific Pedagogy.

It is necessary to remember that experimental psychology was established in 1860 by Fechner, who was a physicist accustomed to experiment on *things*, not on living creatures, and who merely adapted the methods employed in physics to psychical measurements, thus founding psycho-physics. The instruments specially invented for esthesiometric measurements were of extreme precision; but the results obtained showed such anomalies that by mathematical law they could not be attributed to "errors of measurement", but were obviously due to "errors of method". Indeed, for the measurement of liquids it is necessary to have an instrument different from that which we use in measuring solids, although we are still in the domain of physics; we cannot measure a stuff by the quart, nor wine by the yard; how much more then must the methods of measuring physical substances and spiritual energy differ?

After psycho-physics, psycho-physiology was introduced by Wundt. Wundt, a physiologist, applied the methods of study proper to physiological functions to psychical study. He did not make the exact metrical instrument his aim; but he measured nervous reactions exactly in *time*. Fechner's primitive researches made it possible to produce instruments so exact that they can measure the sound made by a drop of water falling from the height of a metre, while Wundt's researches have resulted in chronometers which can measure the thousandth part of a second. But the spirit did not correspond to the exactness of research – the results showed by their oscillations that nothing was being measured – that the object to be measured escaped. It will suffice to mention that in measuring the nervous currents in rate of transmission of impulse along the nerves and also in the ganglion cells of the final marrow, Exner arrived at a rapidity of eight metres, and Bloch at a rapidity of 194 metres, in the same unit of time.

In spite of this startling contrast between the precision of the means of research and the huge variations in the results, which were shown by mathematical law to be absurd, experimental psychology carried on extensive studies, under the illusion that it rested upon a mathematical basis.

It is from this science that a branch has been detached with which to penetrate into the school, for the purpose of giving spiritual help to the scholar, and fresh vigour to pedagogy.

Methods of research are no longer merely those antiquated psycho-physical and psycho-physiological methods formerly in favour; experimental psychology, henceforth emancipated from its origins, has developed independently. It now relies on purely psychological tests for its researches, and although it does not exclude the methods adopted in the laboratory, and the use of such accurate and trustworthy instruments as the esthesiometer and the ergograph, the school itself has become the chief field of experiment.

For example: one of the most familiar tests of attention is to give a printed page to be read over, with directions to strike out every a on the page; the time taken to complete this task is measured by the chronometer.

Counting aloud from one to a hundred, and at the same time carrying on arithmetical operations in writing, is a measure of the distribution of the attention, provided the time taken be calculated by the chronometer, and all errors be noted. To make several persons perform similar exercises at the same time enables us to study comparative individual activities. In schools, exercises in dictation which have been previously determined, may be given to a group of scholars, care being taken to note the time occupied in performing the exercise and to compare the errors. This is also an easy and practical means of obtaining collective results.

These experiments all psychologists agree should be carried out without interrupting the usual routine of the school. They are to be regarded as an addition, an *extra*, and may be summed up as a means of scientific research, throwing light upon the regular psychical conditions of school studies.

The principal results of such experiments have been: the multiplicity of mistakes made, and the difficulty of fixing attention; that is to say, they reveal the weariness, the degree of fatigue in children.

This gave the alarm! Old-fashioned pedagogy was concerned solely with what children ought to do. The idea that their nervous energies might be impaired was first called into being by the warning note of science.

Researches into the causes of fatigue became more and more frequent, and coupled with such researches was the less immediate enquiry as to how fatigue could be "combatted" or "alleviated". All the factors relating to the question were studied: age, sex, the degree of intelligence, the type of individual, the influence of the seasons, the influence of the various times of the day, of the various days of the week, of habit, intervals of relaxation, interest, variety of work, the position of the body, and, finally, position in reference to the cardinal points.

Science is confronted by a mass of unsolved problems

The outcome of all these researches is a growing mass of unsolved problems. It has not been established whether males are more easily fatigued than females; whether the intelligent are more subject to fatigue than the unintelligent. With regard to the individual type, Tissié's[12] conclusion seems to be the most noteworthy: "Each individual becomes fatigued or not according to his degree of will." In connection with the seasons it appears that fatigue increases from the first to the last day of school, but it is uncertain whether this is due to the influence of the seasons, or whether, as Schuyten[13] affirms, the scholar's gradual exhaustion is due to the scholastic system. With regard to the time of day, "it is still a question whether the fatigue produced is less when the pupil works spontaneously, but this problem is a difficult one to solve". The days of the week when fatigue is least evident are Monday and Friday [14],

---

12 Philippe Tissié (1852 – 1935) was a French physician and hygienist. Among others he wrote *La fatigue et l'entraînement physique.* (Paris 1897).

13 Medard Carolus Schuyten (1866 – 1948) was a Belgian pedologist.

14 Thursday is a day of rest for school children in Italy.

but researches made in this connection are not definitive; as to habit, intervals of rest, interest: "in connection with these factors which are antagonistic to fatigue, it has been questioned whether they actually diminish fatigue, or merely cloak it, but no decision has been reached". A great variety of interesting researches have been made into the question of change of work with identical results – namely, that frequent change of work causes greater fatigue than continuous work of one kind, and that a sudden interruption is more fatiguing than persistence. The following experiment (quoted by Claparède) was made by Schultze: One day the girls were required to add up figures for twenty-five minutes, and then to copy out passages for another twenty-five minutes. Another day they performed the same work, but it was differently divided; they had to add for fifty minutes and to copy for another fifty minutes. Now these last tests gave results infinitely superior to the first. And yet it is well known that, in spite of such results, constant interruption and change of work are commonly practised in schools, as part of a scientific plan for combatting fatigue.

One of the researches directly relating to schools is that of the ponogenic coefficient [15] of the various subjects of instruction, that is to say, of the degrees of fatigue induced by these. Wagner is of opinion *a priori* that one hundred, the maximum coefficient, must be assigned to mathematics; in this case, we should get the following ponogenic coefficients in schools, for each subject:

Mathematics	100
Latin	91
Greek	90
Gymnastics	90
History and Geography	85
French and German	82
Natural History	80
Drawing, Religion	77

We may note the arbitrary and surprising manner in which such results are established; nevertheless, in the name of "experimental science" it is possible to make such deductions as the following:

---

15 Ponogenic is 'making tired', causing intellectual fatigue.

"It would be interesting to enquire if the order of the ponogenic co-efficients varies with the age of the children, which would enable us to know on the one hand when the brain is best fitted for the study of any particular subject and when therefore it would be most judicious to make it predominate in the programme; on the other hand, it would help us in the arrangement of the daily timetable; we should take, if possible, the most fatiguing subjects at the beginning of the day." (Claparède, *op. cit.*)[16]

Another recent research is that made into the toxins produced by fatigue; Weichardt succeeded in isolating these toxins, and in fabricating anti-toxins with which he experimented successfully on rats. The experiments were also repeated in a clinic. With regard to the appearance of the toxins, it was found that they were abundantly produced during the performance of "wearisome" work, whereas there were only traces of them to be found when the work was "interesting".

Throughout this science so packed with researches which give as their result unsolved problems, we perceive that not one of the factors taken into consideration can alleviate fatigue; interruption and change of work merely aggravate it. The one means by which *surmenage* (exhaustion due to overwork) can be eliminated is to make work pleasant and interesting, to give joy in work rather than pain.

"The necessity of making education and instruction attractive has been propounded by all pedagogues worthy of the name, such as Fenelon, Rousseau, Pestalozzi, Herbart, and Spencer", says Claparède, "but it is still unrecognised in the everyday practice of the schools." *(op. cit.)*

"By common consent, the first duty of the educator is that of doing no harm: first do no harm, a precept also accepted in the practice of medicine. To obey it to the letter is, indeed, *impossible, because every method of scholastic education is in some way prejudicial to the normal development of the child. But the educator will seek to alleviate the injury which instruction necessarily entails." (op. cit.)*

This is indeed cold comfort, after all these studies and researches! A confession that problems have arisen at every step, and that not a single one has been solved! Indeed, underlying all this is the *problem of problems:*

---

16 Edouard Claparède (1873 – 1940) was a Swiss child psychologist.

how to make that place attractive and joyous where hitherto the body has been tortured and contorted, and the blood poisoned by weariness! It is impossible to educate without doing harm; but we must do harm that will give pleasure! This is truly an embarrassing position! And this is why an interminable string of notes of interrogation serves as the decorative motive of this new science, which might be more appropriately styled: *ignorabimus*.

And it is for this reason that the considerations indicated by hygiene and psychology now tend to do away altogether with the sum total of irreparable evils, "commuting the sentence", that is to say, abbreviating hours of study, cutting down the curriculum, avoiding written exercises. Thus a new spectre, that of ignorance, and henceforth the abandonment of the child for the greater part of the day, present themselves as a substitute for the spectre of destruction. Meanwhile our epoch demands an intensive care of the new generation, and the preparation of a culture ever vaster and more complex.

True, it would appear that today a way of escape may be offered by the discovery of the anti-toxin for fatigue. "Just think!" exclaims Claparède, "a serum against fatigue. How valuable this would be!" From this point of view, I should say that the ponogenic coefficients might find a more practical and rational application than that of the revelation of "programmes"; indeed these coefficients indicating the production of toxins would appear destined to determine the dose of anti-toxin necessary to nullify the evil effects resulting from each different subject of instruction. In the not far distant future, when these auxiliary sciences of the school and pedagogy shall have made due progress, we shall perhaps see, side by side with the orthopaedic ward, a physio-chemical clinic, where every evening the pupils, as they leave the beneficent suspensory apparatus which counteracts injury to their skeletons, may enter with a kind of ponogenic prescription regulated by the teaching they have undergone, and receive an injection which will deliver them from the poisonous effects of fatigue!

This reads like an irony of the worst kind, perhaps; but this is not the case. Where the orthopaedic institution is already an accomplished fact, we may very soon see the chemical clinic established. If a problem of liberty is to be solved with machines, and if a problem of justice is to be regarded from the chemical point of view, similar consequences will be the logical end of sciences developed upon such errors.

It is obvious that a real experimental science, which shall guide education and deliver the child from slavery, is not yet born; when it appears, it will be to the so-called "sciences" that have sprung up in connection with the diseases of martyred childhood as chemistry to alchemy, and as positive medicine to the empirical medicine of bygone centuries.

I think it will be of interest here to record the impressions of a person who, leaving the field of mathematics, entered upon the study of biology and experimental psychology.

It is an account of a young English engineer, who had evidently mistaken his vocation, and who, after studying my method for two years, returned to the universities of his own great country as a student of biology.

This is his opinion of experimental psychology:

"In psychology we are studying the most modern experimental researches. At present we are engaged upon Thought and Imagination. I must confess that I do not find this course very illuminating, though I agree that it is necessary to know something of these researches. In modern psychology there is nothing at all adequate to the subject of our method. These investigators seem to me like persons looking at a tree, and noting the most obvious of its external forms: the shape of a leaf, a stem, etc. doing all this with great gravity and using very precise language (perhaps believing that this constitutes science), but often confusing the function of *definition* with that of *description*.

In this manner descriptions of wonderful fascinating things are reduced to arid definitions, in order to be clothed in their science, and thus are rendered powerless to inspire thought. They never meditate; they read a great deal; they think in mental images which no more represent facts than a diagram on the blackboard represents a living organ; and these images differ among different psychologists, but their language is always the same. They do all this believing they are making progress, and instead of training their pupils to observe for themselves without prejudice, they instil their own prejudices into the minds of the students, cramming them with definitions and descriptions of the strangest and most amorphous kind, which effectually prevent them from thinking for themselves.

But within the tree there is the fundamental structure which they have not begun to examine, though the revelation of this would explain all the external data. The details would diminish in importance; all these details issuing from a single root might be classified in the simplest manner. This "science" reminds me of that antiquated lore which dealt with the constellations, when the laws of planetary motion were not yet known, and the so-called science confined itself to descriptions of the "Great Bear", the "Crab", the "Goat", etc.

I detest those dryasdusts who, unaware of their own ignorance, write enormous arid tomes with an air of great majesty, as if they were revealing absolute knowledge, books that lie heavy on the minds of the students, making them dry as their teachers. But the students, seem to me to care only about passing their examinations and to have no thought of discovering new knowledge; and the professors "serve" them to this end. Thus we are all in a state of servitude due to a mistaken system of education, which calls loudly for reform.

3

My Contribution to Experimental Science

The organisation of psychical life begins with the characteristic phenomenon of attention

My experimental work with little children from three to six years old has been, in fact, a practical contribution to research which has for its aim the discovery of the treatment required by the soul of the child, a treatment analogous to that which hygiene prescribes for its body.

I think, therefore, that it is essential to record the fundamental fact which led me to define my method.

I was making my first essays in applying the principles and part of the material I had used for many years previously in the education of deficient children, to the normal children of the San Lorenzo quarter in Rome, when I happened to notice a little girl of about three years old deeply absorbed in a set of solid insets, removing the wooden cylinders from their respective holes and replacing them. The expression on the child's face was one of such concentrated attention that it seemed to me an extraordinary manifestation; up to this time none of the children had ever shown such fixity of interest in an object; and my belief in the characteristic instability of attention in young children, who flit incessantly from one thing to another, made me peculiarly alive to the phenomenon.

I watched the child intently without disturbing her at first, and began to count how many times she repeated the exercise; then, seeing that she was continuing for a long time, I picked up the little arm-chair in which she was seated, and placed chair and child upon the table; the little creature hastily caught up her case of insets, laid it across the arms of her chair, and gathering the cylinders into her lap, set to work again. Then I called upon all the children to sing; they sang, but the little girl continued undisturbed, repeating her exercise even after the short song had come to an end. I counted forty-four repetitions; when at last she ceased, it was quite independently of any surrounding stimuli which might have distracted her, and she looked round with a satisfied air, almost as if awaking from a refreshing nap.

I think my never-to-be-forgotten impression was that experienced by one who has made a discovery.

This phenomenon gradually became common among the children: it may therefore be recorded as a constant reaction occurring in connection with certain external conditions, which may be determined. And each time that such a polarisation of attention took place, the child began to be completely transformed, to become calmer, more intelligent, and more expansive; it showed extraordinary spiritual qualities, recalling the phenomena of a higher consciousness, such as those of conversion.

It was as if in a saturated solution, a point of crystallisation had formed, round which the whole chaotic and fluctuating mass united, producing a crystal of wonderful forms. Thus, when the phenomenon of the polarisation of attention had taken place, all that was disorderly and fluctuating in the consciousness of the child seemed to be organizing itself into a spiritual creation, the surprising characteristics of which are reproduced in every individual.

It made one think of the *life of man* which may remain diffused among a multiplicity of things, in an inferior state of chaos, until some special thing attracts it intensely and fixes it; and then man is revealed unto himself, he feels that he has begun to live.

This spiritual phenomenon which may co-involve the entire consciousness of the adult, is therefore only one of the constant elements of the phenomena of "internal formation". It occurs as the normal beginning of the inner life of children, and accompanies its development in such a manner as to become accessible to research, as an experimental fact.

It was thus that the soul of the child gave its revelations, and under their guidance a method exemplifying spiritual liberty was evolved.

The story of this initiatory episode soon spread throughout the world, and at first it seemed like the story of a miracle. Then by degrees, as experiments were made among the most diverse races, the simple and evident principles of this spiritual "treatment" were manifested.

Psychical development is organised by the aid of external stimuli, which may be determined experimentally

The contribution I have made to the education of young children tends, in fact, to *specify* by means of the revelations due to experiment, the form of liberty in internal development.

It would not be possible to conceive liberty of development, if by its very nature the child were not capable of a spontaneous organic development, if the tendency to develop his energies (expansion of latent powers), the conquest of the means necessary to a harmonious innate development, did not already exist. In order to expand, the child, left at liberty to exercise his activities, ought to find in his surroundings something *organised* in direct relation to his internal organisation which is developing itself by natural laws – just as the free insect finds in the form and qualities of flowers a direct correspondence between form and sustenance. The insect is undoubtedly free when, seeking the nectar which nourishes it, it is in reality helping the reproduction of the plant. There is nothing more marvellous in Nature than the correspondence between the organs of these two orders of beings destined to such a providential co-operation.

The secret of the free development of the child consists, therefore, in organizing for him the means necessary for his internal nourishment, means corresponding to a primitive impulse of the child, comparable to that which makes the newborn infant capable of sucking milk from the breast, which by its external form and elaborated sustenance, corresponds perfectly to the requirements of the infant.

It is in the satisfaction of this primitive impulse, this internal hunger, that the child's personality begins to organise itself and reveal its characteristics; just as the newborn infant, in nourishing itself, organises its body and its natural movements.

We must not therefore set ourselves the educational problem of seeking means whereby to organise the internal personality of the child and develop his characteristics; the sole problem is that of offering the child the necessary nourishment.

It is by this means that the child develops an organised and complex activity which, while it responds to a primitive impulse, exercises the intelligence and develops qualities we consider lofty, and which we supposed were foreign to the nature of the young child, such as patience and perseverance in work, and in the moral order, obedience, gentleness, affection, politeness, serenity; qualities we are accustomed to divide into different categories, and as to which, hitherto, we have cherished the illusion that it was our task to develop them gradually by our direct interposition, although in practice we have never known by what means to do so successfully.

In order that the phenomenon should come to pass it is *necessary* that the spontaneous development of the child should be accorded *perfect liberty*; that is to say, that its calm and peaceful expansion should not be disturbed by the intervention of an untimely and disturbing influence; just as the body of the newborn infant should be left in peace to assimilate its nourishment and grow properly.

In such an attitude ought we to await the *miracles* of the inner life, its expansions and also its unforeseen and surprising explosions; just as the intelligent mother, only giving her baby nourishment and rest, contemplates it seeing it *grow*, and awaits the manifestations of nature: the first tooth, the first word, and finally the action by which the baby will one day rise to his feet and walk.

But to ensure the psychical phenomena of growth, we must prepare the "environment" in a definite manner, and from this environment offer the child the external means directly necessary for him.

This is the *positive* fact which my experiment has rendered concrete. Hitherto the liberty of the child has been vaguely discussed; no clearly defined limit has been established between liberty and abandonment. We were told: "Liberty has its limits", "Liberty must be properly understood". But a special method indicating "how liberty should be interpreted, and what is the intuitive *quid* which ought to co-exist with it", had not been determined.

The establishment of such a method should open up a new path to all education.

$$\star \; \star \; \star$$

It is therefore necessary that the environment should contain the means of auto-education. These means cannot be "taken at random"; they represent the result of an experimental study which cannot be undertaken by all, because a scientific preparation is necessary for such delicate work; besides, like all experimental study, it is laborious, prolonged, and exact. Many years of research are required before the means really *necessary* for *psychical development* can be set forth. Those educationalists who leave the great question of the liberty of the pupil to the good sense or to the preparation of the master are very far from solving the problem of liberty. The greatest scientist or the person most fitted by nature to teach, could never of himself discover such, because, to preparation and natural gifts, the further factor of *time* must be added – the long period of preparatory experiment. Therefore a *science* which has already *provided the means* for self-education must exist beforehand. Today, he who speaks of liberty in the schools ought at the same time to exhibit objects – approximating to a scientific apparatus – which will make such liberty possible.

The scientific instrument must be constructed upon a basis of *exactitude*. Just as the lenses of the physicist are constructed in accordance with the laws of the refraction of light, so the pedagogic instrument should be based on the *psychical manifestations* of the child.

Such an instrument may be compared to a systematised "mental test". It is not, however, established upon a basis of external measurement, for the purpose of estimating the amount of instantaneous psychical reaction which it produces; it is, on the contrary, a stimulus which is itself determined by the psychical reactions it is capable of producing and maintaining permanently. It is the psychical reaction, therefore, that in this case determines and establishes the systematic "mental test". The psychical reaction which constitutes the sole basis of comparison in the determination of the tests, is a *polarisation of the attention*, and *the repetition of the actions* related to it. When a stimulus corresponds in this manner to the "reflex personality", it serves, not to *measure* but to *maintain* a lively reaction; it is therefore a stimulus to the "internal formation". Indeed, upon such activity, awakened and maintained, the accompanying organism initiates its internal elaborations in relation to the stimuli.

This does not penetrate into the ancient ambit of pedagogy as a science that *measures* the personality, as the experimental psychology introduced in schools has hitherto done, but as a science that *transforms* the personality, and is therefore capable of taking its stand as a true and real pedagogy. Whereas the ancient pedagogy in all its various interpretations started from the conception of a "receptive personality" – one, that is to say, which was to receive instruction and to be passively formed, this scientific departure starts from the conception of an *active* personality – reflex and associative – developing itself by a series of reactions induced by systematic stimuli which have been determined by experiment. This new pedagogy accordingly belongs to the series of modern sciences, and not to antique speculations, although it is not directly based on the purely metric studies of "positive psychology". But the "method", which informs it – namely, experiment, observation, evidence or proof, the recognition of new phenomena, their reproduction and utilisation – undoubtedly places it among the experimental sciences.

External stimuli may be determined in quality and quantity

Nothing can be more interesting than such experiments. By their means external stimuli may be determined with the greatest precision, both as regards quality and quantity. For instance, very small objects of various geometric forms will only attract the fugitive attention of a child of three years old; but by increasing the dimensions gradually, we arrive at the limit of size when these objects will fix the attention; then such objects excite an activity which becomes permanent, and the resulting exercise becomes a factor of development. The experiment is repeated with a number of children, and thus the dimensions of a series of objects are established.

It is the same with colours and with every kind of *quality*. In order that a quality should be felt to such a degree as to fix the attention, a certain extension and a certain intensity of the stimulus are necessary, which may be *determined* by the degree of psychical reaction shown by the child; as, for instance, the minimum chromatic extension sufficient to attract the attention to the coloured tablets, etc. Quality, therefore, is determined by a psychical experiment demonstrating the activity it produces in a child, who will continue the exercise with the same object for a long time, thus elaborating a phenomenon of internal development, of self-formation.

Among the characteristics of the objects, one must be pointed out, which demands the highest degree of activity in the intelligence: they contain in themselves *control of error.*

To make the process one of self-education, it is not enough that the stimulus should call forth activity, it must also direct it. The child should not only persist for a long time in an exercise; he must persist without making mistakes. All the physical or intrinsic qualities of the objects should be determined, not only by the immediate reaction of attention they provoke in the child, but also by their possession of this fundamental characteristic, the control of error, that is to say the power of evoking the effective collaboration of the highest activities (comparison, judgment). For instance, one of the first objects which attract the attention of the child of three years old, the solid insets (a series of cylinders of various dimensions to be placed in or taken out of a block with corresponding holes) contains the most mechanical control, because if a single mistake be made in placing the cylinders, one of these must be left out at the end of the exercise. Hence a mistake is an obstacle only to be overcome by correction, for without it the exercise cannot be completed. On the other hand, the correction is so easy that the child makes it himself. The little problem suddenly presenting itself to the child, almost like the unexpected object of a jack-in-the-box, has "interested" him.

It is, however, noteworthy that the "problem" thus presented is not in itself the stimulus to interest; it is not that which incites to the repetition of the act – to the progress of the child. What interests the child is the sensation, not only of placing the objects, but of acquiring a new power of perception, enabling him to recognise the difference of dimension in the cylinders, a difference which he did not at first notice. The problem presents itself solely in connection with the error, it does not accompany the normal process of development. An interest stimulated merely by curiosity, by a "problem", would not be that formative interest which wells up from the needs of life itself, and therefore directs the building up of the spiritual personality. If it were only the problem which should lead the soul to find itself, order might be dissipated by it, as by any other external cause which tends to seduce life into false paths. I lay, perhaps, excessive stress upon this point, in answer to very important objections and observations that have been made to me.

Indeed, in the second series of objects designed to educate the eye to appreciate dimensions, the control of error is not mechanical, but psychological; the child himself, whose eye has been educated to recognise differences of dimension, will see the error, provided the objects be of a certain size and attractively coloured. It is for this reason that the next objects contain, so to say, the control of error in their own size and in their bright colours. A control of error of a totally different kind, and of a much higher order, is that offered by the material of the arithmetical frame, in which the control will consist in the comparison of the child's own work with that of a model, a comparison which denotes a remarkably intelligent effort of will on the part of the child, and places him thenceforth in the true conditions of conscious auto-education. But, however slight the control of error may be, and in spite of the fact that this diverges more and more from an external mechanism, to rely upon the internal activities which are gradually developing, it always depends, like all the qualities of the objects, upon the fundamental reaction of the child, who accords it prolonged attention, and repeats the exercises.

On the other hand, the experimental criterion is different, in determining the *quantity of the objects*. When the instruments have been constructed with great precision, they provoke a spontaneous exercise so co-ordinated and so harmonious with the facts of internal development, that at a certain point a new psychical picture, a species of higher plane in the complex development is revealed.

The child turns away spontaneously from the material, not with any signs of fatigue, but rather as if impelled by fresh energies, and his mind is capable of abstractions. At this stage of development, the child turns his attention to the external world, and observes it with an order which is the order formed in his mind during the period of the preceding development; he begins spontaneously to make a series of careful and logical comparisons which represents a veritable spontaneous acquisition of "knowledge". This is the period henceforth to be known as the period of "discoveries", discoveries which evoke enthusiasm and joy in the child.

This more elevated level of development is extremely fruitful in its last ascent. It is essential that the child's attention should not be directed to the objects when the delicate phenomenon of abstraction begins. For instance, the teacher who invites the child to continue his operations with the material at such a moment, will retard his spontaneous development and place an obstacle in his way. If the enthusiasm which leads the child to rise to greater heights and experience so many intellectual emotions be extinguished, a path of progress has been closed. Now the same error may be committed by an *excessive quantity* of the educative material; this may dissipate the attention, render the exercises with the objects mechanical, and cause the child to pass by his psychological moment of ascent without perceiving it and seizing it. Moreover, such objects are then futile, and, by their futility, "the child may lose his soul".

The thing to be exactly determined is: what is *necessary* and *sufficient* as a response to the internal needs of a life in process of development, that is, of upward progression, of *ascent?* Now in determining the "quantity" we must be guided by the expression and at the same time by the active manifestations of the child. Those children who have long been occupied with these determined objects, showing every sign of absorbed attention, will, all of a sudden, begin to rise gradually and insensibly, like an aeroplane when it completes its short journey upon the ground. Their apparent indifference to the objects is revealed in its true essence by the intense and radiant expression of the face, which is animated by the liveliest joy. The child may seem to be doing nothing, but this will only be for a moment; very soon he will speak, and so will reveal what is happening within him, and then his ebullient activity will carry him along in a series of explorations and discoveries. He is saved.

Now take the case of other children in whom the same primitive phenomenon is taking place, but who are surrounded by too great a profusion of objects. At the moment of maturity they are seen to be caught, obstructed, almost palpably entangled in the toils that bind them to earth. A diminution of the absorbed attention bestowed upon the new objects, instability, and consequently fatigue, manifest themselves in an obvious extinction of internal activity. The child's bearing deteriorates, he indulges in loud, empty laughter, rude actions, and indolence. He demands "other objects", and then again other objects, because he has remained imprisoned "in the vicious circle of vanities", and is no longer sensible to anything but the desire to alleviate his weariness. Like the adult who during a chaotic life commits kindred errors, he becomes undisciplined, feeble, and "in peril of perdition". If someone does not help him by wresting from him the futile objects, and pointing out his heaven to him, he will hardly have the energy to save himself.

These two extreme types will give an idea of the criteria by which we experimentally determine the quantity of the material necessary for development.

Over-abundance debilitates and retards progress; this has been proved again and again by my collaborators.

If, on the other hand, the material be insufficient, and the primary auto-exercise incapable of leading the child on to that maturity which causes him to ascend, there will be no explosion of that spontaneous phenomenon of abstraction which is the second stage of an auto-education advancing in infinite progression. The same fundamental phenomenon of absorbed and prolonged attention which leads to repetition of the acts, guides us in determining the stimuli suitable to the age of the child. A stimulus which will cause a child of three years old to repeat an act forty times in succession, may only be repeated ten times by a child of six; the object which arouses the interest of a child of three, no longer interests a child of six. Nevertheless, the child of six is capable of fixing his attention for a much longer period than a child of three, when the stimulus is suited to his activities; if, indeed, a little child of three may achieve as his maximum the repetition of an act forty times in succession, the child of six is capable of repeating two hundred times an act which interests him. If the maximum period of continuous work on the same object may be half an hour for the child of three, it may be over two hours for the child of six.

Hence, to establish systematic tests for a certain purpose, such as that of preparing children to write, without taking their ages into account, is valueless. For example, my system of writing is based upon the direct preparation of the movements which physiologically concur to produce writing: i.e. manipulation of the instrument of writing and the tracing of the letters of the alphabet. The children, filling in the contours of the insets with innumerable parallel strokes in the one case, and touching the sand-paper letters in the other, fix the two muscular mechanisms so perfectly, that the final result is an "explosion" of "spontaneous writing" extraordinarily uniform in all the children because, as if all moulded to a common form, they have fixed the necessary movements by touching the same alphabet, and therefore reproduce its forms faithfully. To bring this about, to establish a real motor-mechanism, it is essential that the exercise should be repeated over and over again. Now the children who take most interest in filling in the figures with parallel strokes, and, above all, in touching the letters, are, at most, between four and five years old. If we offer the same material to a child of six he will not touch the letters often enough, and he will always write imperfectly, in comparison with the child who has begun the exercise at a suitable age. This applies also to all the other details of the system. It is therefore possible to determine experimentally with, I believe, a precision not hitherto attained what is the mental attitude of the child at various ages, and hence, if the fitting material for development be offered, what will be the average level of intellectual development according to age.

Here we have an indication of the possibility of *determining* the means of development so exactly as to establish a true correspondence between internal needs and external stimuli, just as actual as the correspondence which exists between the insect and the flower.

He who has all this material ready to his hand has an easy task in bringing about the natural development of the psychic life of the child. With such objects at his disposal, every teacher may realise the ideal of *liberty in the school.*

This long, occult experiment – suggested to me, as I have already said, by Itard and Seguin – is, in fact, my initial contribution to education. All this preparatory work has served for the determination of the method now well known, but it is also the key to its continuation.

The material of development is necessary only as a startingpoint

In the organisation of the external means of development, there remains a material impress of the internal development, and of that which the soul needs in its progress, during its course, and in its flights. The material part does not contain the impress of the whole soul, any more than the impress of the foot is the impress of the whole body; the aviation-ground is not the sphere of action proper to the aeroplane, but it is the part of *terra-firma* necessary for flight, and it is also the resting place, the refuge, the *hangar* to which the aeroplane must always return. Thus in psychical formation there is a necessary material part from which the spirit rises, and where it should find repose, refuge and a point of support. Without this it could not grow and rise "freely".

In order that it may be a true support it ought "to reproduce its forms" and contain them in the part corresponding to the peculiar functions of the material aid. Thus, for instance, in the first period of the psychical life, the material corresponds to the primitive exercises of the senses – it is in quality and quantity determined by the sensory needs given by nature – and permits an exercise of the activities sufficient to *mature* a superior psychical state of observation and abstraction. Vice versa, nothing corresponds in the material to the subsequent career which the childish spirit accomplishes with such delight and with so much acquisition of knowledge. But we then see the spirit eager for higher kinds of exercise – and now we witness the same primitive phenomenon of attention, which will exercise itself henceforth upon the alphabet and arithmetical material, repeating in a more complex form methodical exercises of the intelligence by linking auditory images with the visible and motor images of the spoken and written word; and in the positive study of quantities, proportions, and number. The same concomitant phenomena of "patience" and "perseverance" then manifest themselves, together with those of vivacity, activity and joy, characteristic of the spirit when the internal energies have found their *keyboard*, the gymnasium in which they exercise themselves freely and tranquilly.

And the spirit, organised in this manner under the guidance of an order which corresponds to its natural order, becomes *fortified*, grows *vigorously*, and manifests itself in the *equilibrium*, the *serenity*, the self-control which produce the wonderful *discipline* characteristic of the behaviour of our children.

The external material, then, should present itself to the psychical requirements of the child as a staircase which helps him to ascend, step by step, and on the steps of this staircase there will of necessity be disposed the means of *culture*, and of the higher *formation*. Therefore, the psychical exercises require new material, and this, if it is to fulfil its purpose, must contain new and more complex forms of objects capable of fixing the attention, of making the intelligence ripen in the continual exercise of its own energies, and of producing those phenomena of persistence in application and of patience to which will be added elasticity, psychical equilibrium, and the capacity for abstraction and spontaneous creation. Thus, in the subsequent development of the children, we see them applying themselves to those exercises of the memory which seem to us most arid, because a desire has been born in them, not only to retain the images they encounter in the world, but also to "acquire knowledge rapidly" by a determined effort. An example of this is seen in the surprising yet common phenomenon of committing the multiplication table to memory, whereas the memorizing of poems and prose extracts, although this is sometimes a passion, causes us no surprise.

Very interesting again is the *detachment* the child shows at a certain point from the aids of arithmetical calculation; at a certain stage of maturity he desires to "reason in the abstract" and make "abstract calculations with numbers", as if obeying an internal impulse which seeks to liberate the soul from every material bond and at the same time to effect an economy of time. Hereupon we see children of eight years old become eager and precocious calculators.

Children thus launched upon the enterprises of self-education acquire a remarkable "sensibility" as to their own internal needs. Just as the newborn infant whose food is rationally regulated, is silent and tranquil during the two hours of digestion and assimilation, and cries out the moment the hour for a fresh meal has struck, so do these children "ask for help", ask for "new materials", new "forms of work", as soon as they have accomplished their mysterious phenomena of internal maturation, and ask for them *determinately, indicating their most immediate need*, just as one in physical want would be able to state distinctly whether he were hungry, thirsty, or sleepy. A child, in like manner, asks for reading, or grammatical exercises, or means for observing Nature. His sensibility manifests itself in a lucid and intense desire, to which the teacher has only to respond.

It is evident that some *external* basis is necessary in the progressive development of such phenomena, and that the teacher who is to respond to the requests of the child in conscious evolution, cannot do so adequately by haphazard means; he must be guided by conditions previously determined by experience. In other words, those external means already alluded to several times, that *staircase*, the steps of which lead the soul upwards, must have been already *established by experience*, just as all the preceding means of the first development of the infant were established.

The construction of the ascending stairway, of the external means of support for the soul in process of evolution, is gradually amplified, like an inverted cone, the apex of which touches the very beginnings of psychical life, resting upon that primitive impulse which attracts the child of two and a half to the sensory stimuli, just as hunger leads the newborn infant to perform the wonderful complex action of sucking. And as these external means multiply, they are complicated more and more by the growing psychical needs of the child, and comprise within themselves the principles of culture.

The highest external organisation is not based solely upon psychological necessities, but also upon those factors which take into account the cultural aspect itself. Each subject of study, as, for instance, arithmetic, grammar, geometry, natural science, music, literature, should be presented by means of external objects upon a well-defined systematic plan. The essentially psychological character of the preliminary work must now be supplemented by the collaboration of specialists in each subject, in order to ensure the establishment of that aggregate of means necessary and sufficient to incite to auto-education.

This is the experimental preparatory work, which establishes those means of development, those external *impressions*, necessary to unfold the inner life, and an *exact* correspondence to the psychical needs of *formation* is essential in their construction.

Up to a certain point, they might correspond with the so-called didactic or objective material of the old methods. Their significance, however, is profoundly different. The objective material of the old schools was an aid to the teacher in making his explanations comprehensible to a collective class listening passively to him. The objects were related solely to *the things to be explained*, and these were chosen at random, that is to say, without any scientific criterion of their relation to the psychical needs of the child.

Here, on the other hand, *the means of development* are experimentally determined with reference to the psychical evolution of the child; and their aim is not to give mere instruction; they represent the means which induce a spontaneous interpretation of the internal energies.

The external material is then offered, and *left freely* to the natural individual energies of the children. They choose the objects they prefer; and such preference is dictated by the internal needs of "psychical growth". Each child occupies himself with each object chosen for as long as he wishes; and this desire corresponds to the needs of the intimate maturation of the spirit, a process which demands persevering and prolonged exercise. No guide, no teacher can divine the intimate need of each pupil and the time of maturation necessary to each; but only leave the child *free*, and all this will be revealed to us under the guidance of nature.

Psychical truths

It is necessary to adopt a scientific point of view in order to interpret the facts that reveal themselves in children when they are developed upon this system, and to divest oneself completely of the old scholastic conception according to which the progress of the child is assessed according to his proficiency in the various subjects of study. Here, almost like the naturalist, it is essential to observe the development of certain phenomena of life. It is true that we prepare special "external conditions"; but the psychical effects are directly bound up with the spontaneous development of the internal activity of the child.

Hence there is no direct correspondence between teacher and child; instruction is certainly not a cause of the effects observed. It is the objects of the method which, as "re-agents", provoke special psychical reactions; these may be summed up as an awakening, as an organisation of the personality. Discipline, as the first result of an order establishing itself within, is the principal phenomenon to be looked for as the "external sign" of an internal process that has been initiated.

During the first days when a new school is opened, we may consider a certain initial disorder as characteristic, especially if the teacher is making her first experiment, and consequently is handicapped by her own over-sanguine expectations. The immediate response of the child to the material does not take place; the teacher is perhaps discomfited by the fact that the children do not throw themselves, as she had hoped, upon the objects, choosing them according to their individual taste. If, indeed, the pupils are very poor children, this phenomenon does nearly always happen at once; but if they are well-to-do children, already sated by the variety of their possessions and by the most costly toys, they are very rarely attracted at first by the stimuli presented to them. This naturally leads to disorder when the mistress makes a kind of chain of that "liberty" she is to respect, and a dogma of the correlation existing between the stimulus and the childish soul. Experienced teachers, on the other hand, understand better that liberty begins when the life that must be developed in the child is initiated, and they possess a tact which greatly facilitates orientation in the initial period.

However, an experience under the most difficult conditions, as between a teacher making her first experiment and a class of wealthy children, is more instructive and gives us a clearer picture of the fundamental psychical phenomenon, which may be compared to the order which springs up out of chaos.

I quote, in this connection, various descriptions, some of which have been already published, among them those given by Miss George of her first school in the United States, and that of Mlle. Dufresne in England.

The initial disorder is eloquently set forth by Miss George: "They (the children) at first snatched the objects out of each other's hands; if I tried to show an object to any particular pupil, the others dropped what they themselves were holding and gathered aimlessly and noisily round us. When I had finished explaining the nature of an object, all the children snatched at it and quarrelled for its possession. The children showed no interest in the material: they passed from one object to another without persevering in the use of any .... One of the children was so incapable of keeping still that he could not remain seated long enough to run his fingers round one of the little circular objects we give the children. In many cases the movements of the children were quite aimless; they ran round the room without any apparent object. During these movements they made no attempt to respect the objects about them; indeed, they stumbled against the table, upset the chairs and stepped upon the material; sometimes they began an occupation at one spot and then ran off in another direction; they took up the objects and cast them aside capriciously."

Miss Dufresne describes the initial disorder of her first attempt as follows: "I must confess that the first four weeks were disheartening, the children could not settle to a task for more than a few moments; they showed no perseverance, no initiative; at times they followed one another like a flock of lambs when one child took up an object, all the others wanted to imitate him; sometimes they rolled on the floor and overturned the chairs."

From an experiment with rich children here in Rome, we get the following laconic description: "The greatest difficulty was the question of discipline. The children showed a complete lack of attraction to their work and seemed disinclined to begin upon it."

These persons, who were all working independently, are all agreed later in their accounts of the initiation of order: the phenomenon is identical; at a given moment, a child begins to show an intense interest in one of the exercises. It is by no means necessary that it should be that exercise pertaining to the object determined as the first of the series; it may be any other object that fixes the attention of the child so deeply; the important factor is not the external object, but the internal action of the soul, responding to a stimulus, and arrested by it.

Now when a child once shows this deep interest in anyone of the objects we present to him as something answering to his psychical needs, he goes on to show a like interest in all the objects, and begins to develop activities as by a natural phenomenon. When once the initiation has taken place, it leads to a progression which goes on steadily and develops of its own accord. Moreover, the phenomenon is not that of the slow and gradual progression that might be produced by a measured and systematic external action; rather it has the "explosive" character of unsuspected facts that establish themselves suddenly, and make us think of the crises of physiological life, so characteristic in the period of growth. Thus it is from one day to another that the baby cuts a tooth, from one day to another that he utters his first word, from one day to another that he takes his first step; and when the first tooth has been cut, the whole set of teeth will come; when the first word has been uttered, language will be developed; when the first step has been taken, the power of walking has been established once and for all.

Similar crises occur in the first achievement of psychic order, which is the beginning of progressive evolution in the inner life.

I quote the following sentences from Miss George's description of the advent of discipline:

"In a few days that nebulous mass of whirling particles – the disorderly children – began to take definite form. The children seemed to begin to find their own way; in many of the objects they had at first despised as silly playthings, they began to discover a novel interest, and, as a result of this new interest, they began to act as independent individuals." Miss

George's subsequent expression is: "They became extremely individual." "Thus it came to pass that an object of absorbing interest to one child had not the slightest attraction for another; the children were strongly differentiated in their manifestations of attention . . ." "The battle is only definitively won, when the child discovers some particular object which spontaneously excites great interest in him. Sometimes this enthusiasm awakens unexpectedly, or with curious rapidity."

"On one occasion I had tried a child with nearly all the objects of the series without exciting the smallest spark of interest; then I casually showed him the two tablets of red and blue colours, and called his attention to the difference of tint. He seized them at once with a kind of thirstiness, and learnt five different colours in a single lesson; during the following days he took nearly all the objects of the series which he had at first despised, and little by little mastered them all."

"A child who at first had very little power of concentrating his attention, found an outlet from this state of chaos by means of one of the most complex objects of the material, the so-called length-rods; he played with these continually for a whole week and learned to count and make simple additions. He then began to turn to the cylinders and the insets, the simpler objects, and showed interest in every part of the system."

"Directly the children find their objects interesting, their disorderliness disappears at once; their mental restlessness is at an end and they amuse themselves with the blocks, the colours, etc."

It is very interesting to follow Miss George again in her description of the special qualities that develop after such a phenomenon. She illustrates the birth of individuality by a pretty anecdote:

"There were two sisters, one of three years old, the other of five. The child of three could hardly be said to exist as an individual, so minutely did she imitate her elder sister; for example, the elder child had a blue pencil and the little one was not happy till she too had a blue pencil; when the elder sister ate bread and butter, whatever the little one had of a different kind, she would touch nothing but bread and butter, and so on. This child took no interest in anything in the school, but merely followed her sister, imitating everything she did. One day the little one became interested in the pink cubes, built up the tower with the liveliest interest, repeated the exercise several times, and completely forgot her sister. The older girl was so astonished at this, that she called her little sister and said to her: How is it that while I am filling in a circle you are building the tower? From that day the younger child became a personality; she began to develop independently, and was no longer merely the shadow or reflection of her sister."

These interesting facts concerning the spontaneous development of qualities which hitherto were non-existent in the individual, and which exploded *after* the fundamental phenomenon – of intense and prolonged interest in a task – had manifested itself, have been confirmed by repeated experiments in a great variety of places made by persons who had had no sort of communication one with another.

Thus, for instance, Miss Dufresne speaks of a little girl of four years old, who seemed quite incapable of carrying a glass of water even only half full, without spilling it; so much so, that she turned away from such a task, knowing she could not accomplish it. One day she became absorbed in work with one or other of the objects, and after this, she began to carry glasses of water with the greatest ease; and as some of her companions were now painting with water-colours, it became her great delight to carry water to them all without spilling a single drop.

Another most significant fact is related by Miss Barton, an Australian teacher. Among her pupils was a little girl who had not yet developed articulate speech, and only gave utterance to inarticulate sounds; her parents had had her examined by a doctor to find out if she were normal; the doctor declared the child to be perfectly normal, and considered that though she had not as yet developed speech, she would do so in time. This child became interested in the solid insets, and amused herself for a long time taking the cylinders out of the cavities and putting them back in their places; and after repeating the work with intense interest, she ran to the teacher, saying: "Come and see!"

A phenomenon of constant occurrence when the children begin to be interested in the work and to develop themselves is the lively joy which seems to possess them. Certain psychologists would say, it is the "sentimental note" corresponding to the intellectual acquisition; a physiologist, making an exact comparison, might affirm that joy is the indication of internal growth, just as an increase in weight is the indication of bodily growth.

The children themselves seem to have the "sensation" of their spiritual growth, a consciousness of the acquisitions they are making by thus amplifying their own personalities; they demonstrate with joyous effusion the higher process which is beginning within them. "All the children", says Miss George, "show that pride we ourselves experience when we have really produced something novel. They skip round me and throw their arms about my neck, when they have learnt to do some simple thing, saying: "I did it all alone, you did not think I could have done that; I did it better today than yesterday."

It is after these manifestations that a true discipline is established, the most obvious results of which are closely related to what we will call "respect for the work of others and consideration for the rights of others". Henceforward a child no longer attempts to take away another's work; even if he covets it, he waits patiently until the object is free; and very often a child becomes interested in watching a companion at work on some object he would like to use himself. Afterwards, when discipline has been established by these internal processes, it will happen all at once that a child will work quite independently of the others, almost as if to develop his own personality; but no "moral isolation" results from such work; on the contrary, there is a mutual respect and affection between the children, a sentiment which unites instead of separating; and hence is born that complex discipline which, moreover, contains within itself the sentiment that must accompany the order of a community.

Miss Dufresne says: "After the Christmas holidays, when school began again, there was a great change in the class. It seemed that discipline was establishing itself, without any effort on my part. The children appeared to be too much absorbed in their work to indulge in any of the disorderly actions which had marked their conduct in the beginning. They went spontaneously to the cupboards to choose the objects which had bored them formerly. They took the geometrical insets, the graduated cylinders, and began to touch the outlines of the wooden forms with their fingers; the younger children showed a preference for the buttoning and lacing frames; they took one after the other without any signs of fatigue, and seemed delighted with the new objects. An atmosphere of industry pervaded the schoolroom. The children who had hitherto chosen objects on the impulse of the moment, henceforth manifested a desire for some sort of rule, a personal and internal rule; they concentrated their efforts on their task, working accurately and methodically, and showing real satisfaction in surmounting difficulties. This precision in work produced an immediate effect on their characters. They became capable of controlling their nerves."

The instance which struck Miss Dufresne most was that of a little boy of four and a half, who at first had seemed very nervous and excitable and had disturbed the whole class: "The imagination of this child had been developed in an extraordinary manner, so that when an object was given to him, he took no notice of the actual form of the object, but personified it, and further personified himself, talking perpetually, pretending to be someone else and seeming incapable of fixing his attention upon the objects. While his mind was in this chaotic state he was unable to perform any precise action; he could not, for instance, button a single button . . . All at once a miracle seemed to take place within him. I noted the great change in him with astonishment. He took one of the exercises as his favourite task, then went on to choose all the others in succession, and thus calmed his nerves."

I will choose from various individual studies made by two mistresses of a Children's House at Rome for well-to-do children, those of two children of very different characters. One of these children came to the school too late, when he was too old, and had already developed in another environment. The other was a little creature of the normal age for entrance to the Children's Houses. The older child (a boy of five) had already been to a Froebelian Kindergarten, where he was considered very troublesome because of his restlessness. "For the first few days he was a torment to us, because he wanted to work, but could not settle to any occupation. He said of everything: 'This is a game,' and ran about the classroom, or annoyed his companions. At last he began to take an interest in drawing." Although normally drawing comes *after* the sensory exercises, he was left at liberty to do what he wished; the teachers rightly thought that it would be useless to insist that the child should apply himself to a different task. Indeed, this child, having passed the age when the primary materials answer to the physical needs of childhood, was for the first time attracted by an exercise of a higher order, that of drawing. "Whereas at first the child had passed from one occupation to another, and had even take up the letters of the alphabet, but had never settled to work with anyone of the objects, now suddenly discipline was established. We do not know exactly at what moment the change took place, but discipline was maintained and perfected, and reached a higher level in proportion to the growing interest of the child in every kind of occupation. Interest having been primarily aroused by drawing, the child spontaneously went on to the rods used in the teaching of length, then to placing the plane geometric insets, and so gradually worked through all the earlier sensory stimuli which the teacher had passed over." Thus we see that the older child chooses the objects in inverse order, proceeding almost methodically from the most difficult to the elementary.

The other child of three was also quite undisciplined. The teachers were beginning to despair of producing order in this case, when the child began to take an interest in the solid insets and in one of the frames. Thereupon he worked steadily and ceased to disturb his companions.

★ ★ ★

In our Houses of Childhood for poor children in Rome, directed by Signora Maccheroni, it was possible to make more methodical observations, and these were represented by diagrams, in order to demonstrate the course of the phenomena more clearly.

The transverse line AB represents the quiescent state; the phenomena of order (work) are represented above; those of disorder below. When a child has become calm after the first strong attraction to a task, a permanent state of order may be established in him. At this stage the conditions most favourable to work may be studied.

Primitive curve of ordered work

This is the manner in which it develops; individual type of a morning of disciplined work:

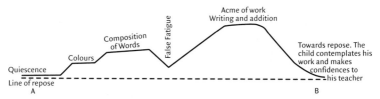

The child keeps still for a while, and then chooses some task he finds easy, such as arranging the colours in gradation; he continues working at this for a time, but not for very long; he passes on to some more complicated task, such as that of composing words with the movable letters, and perseveres with this for a long time (about half an hour). At this stage he ceases working, walks about the room, and appears less calm; to a superficial observer he would seem to show signs of fatigue. But after a few minutes he undertakes some much more difficult work, and becomes so deeply absorbed in this, that he shows us he has reached the acme of his activity (additions and writing down the results). When he contemplates his handiwork for a long time, then approaches the teacher, and begins to confide in her.

The appearance of the child is that of a person who is rested, satisfied, and uplifted.

The apparent fatigue of the child between the first and second period of work is interesting; at that moment the aspect of the child is not calm and happy as at the end of the curve; indeed, he shows signs of agitation, moves about, and walks, but does not disturb the others. It may be said that he is in search of the maximum satisfaction for his interest, and is preparing for his "great work".

But, on the other hand, when the cycle is completed, the child detaches himself from his internal concentration; refreshed and satisfied, he experiences the higher social impulses, such as desiring to make confidences and to hold intimate communion with other souls.

A similar process became in time the general process in a class of disciplined children. Signorina Maccheroni sums up this complex phenomenon as follows:

Whole class at work

In the first period of the morning, up to about 10 a.m., the occupation chosen is generally an easy and familiar task.

At 10 o'clock there is a great commotion; the children are restless, they neither work nor go in quest of materials. The onlooker gets an impression of a tired class, about to become disorderly. After a few minutes the most perfect order reigns once more; the children are promptly absorbed in work again; they have chosen new and more difficult occupations.

When this work ceases, the children are gentle, calm and happy.

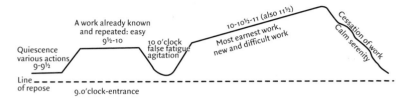

If in the period of "false fatigue" at 10 a.m. an inexperienced teacher, interpreting the phenomenon of suspension or preparation for the culminating work as disorder, intervenes, calling the children to her, and making them rest, etc. their restlessness persists, and the subsequent work is not undertaken. The children do not become calm; they remain in an abnormal state. In other words if they are interrupted in their cycle, they lose all the characteristics connected with an *internal process regularly and completely carried out.*

* * *

The single curve of individual orderly work is not general, nor strictly constant in the type described. But it may be considered as the average type of work in the level of order achieved. It will be interesting, first of all, to consider the curve of children in whom *order has not yet been established.* Poor children hardly ever show themselves to be in such a state of utter confusion as rich ones; they are *always* more or less attracted by the objects, and respond to them with a certain interest from the very first moment. Such interest, however, is at first superficial. They are attracted mainly by curiosity, by a desire to handle "pretty things". They amuse themselves for some time, it is true, with single objects, changing and selecting them, but without developing any deep interest. The characteristic of this period, which may be altogether lacking in a class of well-to-do children, is that of *alternations of disorder.* The following diagram represents this period.

Individual Differences

Stage preceding the evolution of order

Individual curve of a poor child

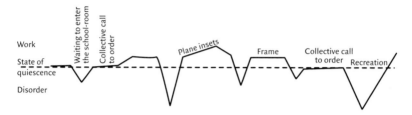

The various curves of work are to be found below the line of quiescence, in the state of disorder. It was only when the children were called to order collectively that this child was still, unless it was rising towards work; in this case, however, it did not persevere, and the curve drops suddenly below. It should be noted that in the irregular course of this diagram we may trace a period of easy work preceding a period of difficult work (frame, plane insets) and between these two the maximum decline into disorder.

Curve of Work

Of a very poor child, almost entirely neglected by its parents, and very turbulent

Period of disorder

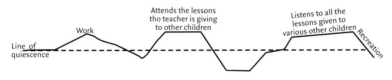

The child in question (O) seemed to have a tendency to learn from others; he ran away from work or was attracted by it only for a brief moment; and seemed incapable of receiving direct teaching. If any attempt was made to teach him something, he grimaced and ran away. He wandered about, disturbing his companions, and seemed quite intractable; but he listened attentively to the lessons the teacher gave to the other children.

Advance towards order

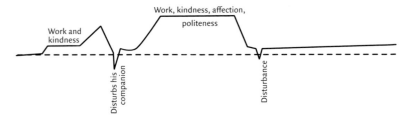

When he began to work, after having learned how to do so, he perse-
vered, and the normal process is apparent in the diagram; that is to say,
preliminary work, a pause (during which the child relapsed slightly and
momentarily into his habit of disturbing his companions), then the
curve of great application, and of final repose (during which, however,
he again relapsed into his characteristic defect). The summits of the diagram show not only interest in the work, but a marked kindliness; the
child was not only calm, but seemed full of beatitude and gentleness;
when at the height of his labours he frequently looked round at his companions, and blew little kisses to them on his fingers, but without relaxing his attention. It seemed as if a fount of love were gushing up from
the fullness of his internal satisfaction, from the depths of a soul that
had appeared at first so rough and uncouth.

Curve of work of a weak child

The diagram is made up of curves that fall upon the line of quiescence;
unity of curve is lacking, hence unity of effort. The culminating point
of work is reached after a preliminary task of an easier kind; and the supreme task (colour) is briefly resumed, after the great impetus has been
exhausted. The phase of rest is not clearly defined; the child turns to a very
easy task (solid insets). A certain feebleness of character seems to manifest itself in the half-hearted mental processes. The child makes many
successive efforts to rise; but he can neither make the decisive vigorous

effort, nor come to a definite decision to cease working. The child is calm, but his state of calm has no variations; he is neither lively nor serene, nor does he show strong affectionate impulses.

Course of progress

When the whole class is disciplined, the course of development of the internal activities may be observed.

It must be remembered that the material of development affords graduated exercises passing from the most rudimentary sensory exercises to exercises in writing, calculating and reading. The children are free to choose the exercises they prefer; but of course, as the teacher initiates them in each exercise, they only choose the objects they know how to use. The teacher, observing them, sees when the child is sufficiently matured for more advanced exercises, and introduces them to him, or perhaps the child begins them for himself after watching other children more advanced.

We must bear such conditions in mind in order to follow "progress" in work.

The two curves represent stages of greatest development as compared with the primary curve of orderly work. The stage of unrest between the easy and the more difficult work tends to disappear; the child seems more *sure of himself;* he goes more directly and readily to the choice of his culminating exercise.

Consequently, two successive phases of uninterrupted work are left; one may be called the *phase of preparation,* the other the *phase of serious work.* The phase of preparation lasts a very short time, the *serious work* is of much longer duration; it is noteworthy that the period of *rest,* with its characteristic air of *comfort* and *serenity,* sets in after the *maximum effort has spontaneously spent itself.* On the other hand, it happens invariably that any external interruption of the effort causes the child to show signs of fatigue (restlessness), or to become inattentive.

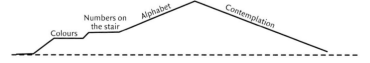

In the first curve, the initial work consists of two easy tasks, carried on for a short time, and from these the child passes directly to the serious work.

The finale is a spell of rest full of thought, the child ceases to work, but contemplates his finished task for a long time in silence; before preparing to put it away, or, after having contemplated his own work, he goes quietly to watch that of the others.

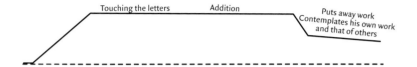

In the second curve there is a very noticeable parallelism with the line of repose; the child pursues his labours almost uniformly, and the sole difference between the initial work and the serious work is in their different duration. The contemplative period becomes henceforth an obvious "period of internal work", almost a period of "assimilation" or "internal maturation". Observation of the work of others becomes increasingly frequent, as if it were a spontaneous "comparative" study between the child himself and his companions; or as if an active interest in the contemplation of the external surroundings were developing: the period of discovery. We may say that *the child studies himself in his own productions and puts himself into communion with his companions and his environment.*

At this stage the completion of an entire cycle will exercise an influence more and more far-reaching on the personality of the child. Not only is he spurred on to a work of intimate concentration immediately after his culminating effort, he preserves a permanent attitude of thought, of internal equilibrium of sustained interest in his environment. He becomes a personality who has reached a higher degree of evolution. This is the period when the child begins to be "master of himself" and enters upon that characteristic phenomenon I have called the "phenomenon of obedience". He *can obey*, that is, he can control his actions, and therefore can direct them in accordance with the desires of another person. He can break off a piece of work when interrupted, without becoming disorderly or showing symptoms of fatigue. Moreover, work has become his habitual attitude, and the child can no longer bear to be idle. When, for instance, we call some of the children who are in this stage to the lessons for teachers, in which they are to serve as the "subjects of study", they lend themselves with ready docility to that which we ask of them, they submit to the measurements of height, heads, etc. and they perform the exercises we suggest, responding always with *interest*, and not merely with resignation, as if they were conscious of collaborating with us. But when they have to *wait*, seated on one side till they are called forward, they cannot sit idle; they work at something. Inactivity has become intolerable to them. Very often, while I am giving the lesson, the children take the lacing or tying frames, or cover the floor with words made with the movable letters; and where this is feasible, some of the children will draw or paint in these moments of waiting.

All these things have now become expressions of intelligent activity, which form part of their psychical organism.

But to ensure the continuance of this attitude and of the development of personality, it is essential that *some real task* should be performed each day; for it is from the completed cycle of an activity, from methodical concentration, that the child develops equilibrium, elasticity, adaptability, and the resulting power to perform the higher actions, such as those which are termed acts of obedience. This makes one think of the method prescribed by the Catholic religion for the preservation of the forces of spiritual life: that is, a period of "spiritual concentration", which opens up the possibility of acquiring "moral powers". It is from methodical "meditation" that the moral personality must draw its powers of solidification, without which the "inner man", incoherent and unbalanced, fails to possess itself and dispose of itself for noble ends.

Children have always need of the period of concentration, and serious work from which they derive the capacity for final development.

The following diagram represents a very lofty stage of childish development:

Superior stage

Average type

Touches the letters — Writes — Reads the slips — Recreation: looks at picture-books

Line of quiescence

Even the preparatory work is now of a higher kind: as soon as the child comes into school, he will choose, for instance, the letters of the alphabet, or will write, then (his strenuous work) he will read. For recreation he will choose an intelligent pastime, such as looking at illustrated books.

All his intellectual occupations are of a higher order, as are also his moral attributes (obedience, serenity, perseverance).

Taking the line of quiescence as a level of development, it follows that the level has become higher.

In a superior stage, the line of work tends to become straight, parallel to the line of quiescence.

Meanwhile it has been established that it is possible to determine *degrees of development*, or *averages* of internal development, by means of which individual variations may be studied. In the primordial type the characteristics are *disorderly conduct*, and *incapacity to concentrate attention*; in such a case there is no real line of work, and the main part of the diagram remains below the line of quiescence. For the type in which the phenomenon of permanent concentration of attention on a task has manifested itself, the average characteristic diagram of normal orderly work of the first degree is now established: i.e. *preliminary* work followed by a period of restlessness, and then *strenuous work* followed by a state of repose.

Afterwards we distinguish a second degree, where the average is characterised by the disappearance of the period of unrest, and the strenuous work is brought to a close in contemplation; this is the stage of discoveries, of generalised observation, of obedience; work has become a habit.

This is followed by a general elevation, to be recognised by the choice of higher preliminary work; disciplined behaviour has become a habit.

During this progression the diagram of work tends to become straight, and parallel to the line of quiescence.

A recapitulatory table of development

Diagrams of average developments

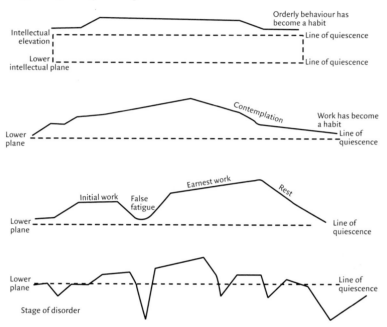

The rise in the level of the plane is related to the qualities of more advanced intellectual work; and the straightening of the line is related to qualities of internal construction and of the *organisation of the personality*; qualities which would be considered of a *moral order*, such as serenity, discipline, self-mastery as manifested in obedience and in the various activities of the child.

When work has become a habit, the intellectual level rises rapidly, and organised order causes good conduct to become a *habit*. Children then work with order, perseverance, and discipline, persistently and naturally; the permanent, calm and vivifying work of the physical organism resembles the respiratory rhythm.

The pivot, the medium of this construction of the personality, is working in freedom, in accordance with the natural wants of the inner life; thus *freedom in intellectual work* is found to be the *basis of internal discipline*.

The great achievement of the "Children's Houses" (*Case dei Bambini*) is to produce *disciplined children*.

It is this internal organisation which gives them a special "type", or character, the type or character *required* to continue the free exercise of activities for the *conquests of culture* in successive stages.

The elementary school period presents itself insensibly as a continuation of the "Children's Houses". In these, *behaviour is a habit* superposed on and fused with the earlier *habit of work*. Henceforth it will be sufficient to present the material of further culture, and the child, gradually exercising himself upon it, will pass from one intellectual stage of culture to another.

The difference shown in the successive ages arises from an intellectual interest which is no longer merely the impulse to exercise oneself by repetition of the exercises, but is a higher interest directed to the work itself, and tending to complete an external work, or to complete a branch of knowledge as a whole. Thus the child creates and seeks for things organised in themselves; for instance, he desires to compose a design by means of combinations of geometrical figures with the metal insets, and devotes himself to this work with the greatest intensity until he has completed it. Again, we see a child occupied for seven or eight consecutive days with the same work. Another child becomes interested in the potentialities of numbers or in the arithmetical frame, and perseveres with the same work for days, until his knowledge of it has matured.

Upon a basis of interior order produced by internal organisation, the mind them builds up its castle with the same leisurely calm with which a living organism grows spontaneously after birth.

We can give but a primary idea at present of the *practical possibility* of determining *average levels* of interior development according to age. We shall further require many perfect experiments, in which homogeneous children, completely suitable environment, and trained teachers will afford adequate material or observation. Then students will be able to undertake a scientific work, which will perhaps be characterised by a precision superior even to that with which it is at present possible to measure the body, and give the mathematical averages of growth.

We must consider, however, that the indications available today represent a long, systematic toil, and that they rest upon the still greater labour of finding external material means for natural development.

This will give some idea of the difficulty of scientific researches, which many still believe it possible to make by means of arbitrary and superficial tests such as those of Binet and Simon!

★ ★ ★

The study of the child cannot be accomplished by an "instantaneous" process; his characteristics can only be illustrated cinematographically.

"External means", organised in accordance with the needs of psychical life, are of fundamental importance; for how is it possible to judge of individual differences in the acquisition of internal order, in the ascent to abstraction, in the progressive stages of intellectual development, in the achievement of discipline, without the existence of pre-determined and unvarying external means which, like so many points of support, lead the child in process of formation towards his goal?

In order to determine *individual differences* logically, there must be a *constant work* or *aim*; and this is the external means on which each personality builds itself up. When the external support is the same, and corresponds in general to the psychical needs of a given age, a difference of internal construction is *due to the individual himself*. On the other hand, if the means were different, the variations in reaction might be attributed to differences in the means.

Finally, it is obvious that in all scientific research, the *instrument of measurement* must be fixed. But each *thing to be measured* requires a special instrument, and the constant instrument in psychical measurement should be "the method of education".

A series of formulae, such as the Binet-Simon tests, can neither measure anything, nor give even an approximate idea of intellectual levels of intelligence according to age; as to the children who respond, whence is their response derived? How far is this due to the intrinsic activity of the individual, and how far to the action of environment? And if the portion due to environment be ignored, who can determine what intrinsic psychical value should be given to the response?

In each personality we must recognise two parts: one is the individual, natural, spontaneous activity by means of which elements may be taken from the environment wherewith the personality may be elaborated internally, constructed and augmented, and hence *characterised*; another part is the external instrument with which all this may be done. For instance, a child who at the age of four can recognise sixty-four colours shows that he possesses remarkable activity in the perception of colours, and in the arrangement of them in gradation in his mind, etc.; but he also shows that he has had the means to accomplish this achievement; he has had, for instance, sixty-four colour-tablets, with which he has been able to practise at his leisure and undisturbed, as long as was necessary for such assimilation. The psychical factor P is the sum of two factors, one internal, the other external:

$$P=I+E$$

of these the unknown, non-directly measurable factor I may be indicated by X:

$$P=X+E$$

If we were to compare two children, one of whom has had at his disposal the sixty-four colours in the conditions described above, and another who has been left to himself in poor surroundings, where grey and brown tints prevail, and who seems dull and unobservant, etc. we should find a very remarkable psychical difference. Such a difference is not, however, intrinsic; it might well be that, subjected to the same conditions as the first child, the second would recognise the sixty-four colours. The judgment we should give in such a case would be based upon an external factor, not upon internal potentialities. We should really be appraising two different environments, not two different individuals.

To enable us to judge of individual differences, it would be necessary for the two children to have had *the same means of development*. In this case, if at the same age they were not equally capable of distinguishing the sixty-four colours, but if, for instance, one of the two could recognise only thirty of these, a true individual psychical difference would be apparent. One of the tests proposed by one of the greatest authorities on experimental psychology in Italy to determine the intellectual level of sub-normal (backward or deficient) children, was to make a child pick out the largest and the smallest cube in a series. This choice, in common with nearly all the tests proposed for the same purpose, was considered quite independently of the influence of *culture* and *education*; and it was appreciated as the expression of an intimate, personal activity of the intelligence itself. But if one of the deficient children I had educated on my method had been subjected to the tests, he would, in virtue of a long sensory training, have chosen the largest and the smallest cube very much more easily than the children selected by the psychologist from his special schools; and my deficient child might even have been not only younger, but even more backward intellectually than the other. The test would therefore have measured the different methods of education, whereas the psychical differences between the two children, really existent by reason of age or of intellectual attainment, would have remained absolutely obscure.

Man is a fusion of personality and education, and education includes the series of experiences he undergoes during his life. The two things cannot be separated in the individual: intelligence without acquirement is an abstraction. That which holds good for all living beings: that the individual cannot be divorced from his environment is more profoundly true in its application to psychical life, because the content of environment, constituting the means of auto-experience which evolves man, is an essential part of him, and, indeed, is the individual himself. Nevertheless, we all know that the psychical individual is not his environment, but a life in himself.

Given the formula

$$P=X+E$$

in which X is the internal and intrinsic part peculiar to the individual life, it may be said that every individual has his X. But in order to *approach* to direct knowledge of X, it is essential to know P and E.

He who carries out an examination, or supposes himself to be performing a "psychical measurement" by dwelling on psychical results, is in reality measuring a mixture of two unknown quantities, one of which, being external to the individual, nullifies the results of research.

Hence, to study individual differences in isolated activities, such as the perception of colours, musical sounds, the letters of the alphabet; or the capacity for observation of surroundings and the detection of errors; or co-ordination of movements, language, etc. it is essential to have first determined a *constant* element: the means of development offered by environment.

Here a simple and clearly defined difference between pedagogy and psychology manifests itself: pedagogy determines experimentally the means of development and the method of applying them while respecting the internal or personal liberty of the individual; psychology studies average reactions or individual reactions in the species or the individual. But the two things are two aspects of a single fact, which is the development of man; the individual and the environment are the two factors X and E of the same product: the psychical entity.

Isolated psychical researches of a moral order must also, if they are to be of any real value, be based upon prolonged observation *after the internal activities have become orderly*; because it is easy to make errors of judgment in a chaos. In clinical psychiatry or in criminal pathology, when we speak of "keeping a subject under observation" for purposes of diagnosis, we mean placing him in special surroundings, under hygienic and disciplinary conditions, etc. and observing him for some time in such an environment. Such a process has a value still more extensive and profound in the case of normal individuals in process of evolution. In such a case it is necessary not only to offer orderly external surroundings, but to reduce the chaotic internal world of the child to order, and, after this, to observe him for a considerable time.

We may offer as an illustration the following observations made upon two of the most interesting children who attended our schools. They were admitted into the training school for teachers during my last International Course in Rome.

Aspects of the two children
During the period they were retained as subjects for anthropological observation in the class-room for teachers

There was a considerable clamour among the students; some were talking, some laughing. In the centre of the room stood the pedometer [17]. The behaviour of the two children was almost identical. They were sitting apart quietly, working at the lacing frames which they had gone spontaneously to fetch from a neighbouring room; they did not look up

---

17 An instrument on a rectangular board on which on one side the height of a child can be measured while sitting on a wooden seat. On the other side the height can be measured while standing upright.

Measuring sitting and standing height.

at the noise, nor join in the laughter. Their attitude was that of persons at work and anxious not to lose any time. When invited by a single gesture to come and be measured, they obeyed in a wonderful manner, leaving off work at once, and moving with smiles, as if fascinated; they evidently felt pleasure in obeying, and an internal delight which came from the consciousness of being able to work, and of being ready to leave something that they liked doing, at a summons to something of a higher order. They arranged themselves very carefully on the pedometer to be measured; when any modification was necessary in the position of the body, it sufficed to murmur a word in their ears and the almost imperceptible movement required was made with the utmost exactitude; they could control their voluntary movements and direct them; they were able to translate the words they heard into actions: *this enabled them* to obey, and this constituted for them a fascinating internal conquest. When the measuring was over, nothing was said; they waited expectantly for a moment, then gave an intelligent glance and a smile, which was, as it were, their greeting; they had understood, and they returned voluntarily to their corner to take up their frames and resume their work. Presently they were wanted again, and the same actions were repeated.

When we think that children of their age (about four and a half), when left to themselves, will roam about, upsetting objects almost unconsciously, and requiring either someone to submit to their caprices, or to call them roughly to order, we shall recognise the internal perfection achieved in these two little ones, who have arrived at that stage of development in which work has become a *habit*, and obedience a fascinating acquisition.

The anthropometric measurements had shown that one of the children, O, was normal in measurement (weight, stature, length of torso) and the other, A, below the normal measurements.

Here are some notes made by the teacher on the conduct of these two children when they were in the state of disorder, or undisciplined:

O: violent, turbulent, spiteful to his companions, never applies himself to anything, but looks on at what the others are doing and then interrupts them; or listens to the individual lessons given by the teacher with a scornful and cynical expression. The father of the child says that at home he is violent, overbearing and intractable.

A: is quiet. But he has almost a mania for spying on his companions, and pointing out to the teacher every little action that might be considered wrong or incorrect. Both the children are very poor. O is almost entirely neglected by his family.

Later judgment the teacher was enabled to form of these two children after they had reduced themselves to order by means of work:

O: All the turbulence shown by O in his home resolved itself into a struggle for bread; the father, who was very poor but also neglectful, denied the child bread; the child did not resign himself, did not cry, but struggled constantly, with all the means at his disposal, in order to obtain his portion of bread. When the teacher asked the father why he denied the child bread, he replied: "Because, when he has eaten it, he asks for more".

In school, this child ran from group to group, from lesson to lesson, disturbing the others and passing over everything, because he was struggling to win his spiritual food after the same fashion.

He is a child who has an overpowering will to live: self-preservation seems to be his most strongly developed tendency.

When his life was assured, the child became not only gentle, but remarkable for his sweetness and delicacy of feeling. He was the child who, in his joy when he had learnt or completed some task, looked round lovingly at his companions, and blew little kisses to them from his fingers. Whereas for the other children who had entered into the phase of order or discipline, the teacher's note is: "work", for O the note is: "work and kindness".

Before the daily hot meal was instituted, the children used to bring their own luncheons, which varied very much; two or three of the children were very generously provided and had meat, fruit, etc. O was seated next to one of these. The table was set, and O had nothing to put upon his plate but the piece of bread he had so strenuously acquired; he glanced at his neighbour as if to regulate himself by the time the latter would take over his meal, but with no trace of envy; on the contrary, with great dignity he tried to eat his piece of bread very slowly, in order that he might not finish before the other, and thus make it evident that he had nothing more to eat while the other was still busy. He nibbled his bread slowly and seriously.

What a sense of his own dignity – subduing the desires of an appetite exposed to temptation – existed in this child, together with his sense of the fundamental needs of his own life, by which he was impelled to struggle and to conquer what was "necessary". And there was further that exquisite sensibility, which manifested itself in the affectionate expression of his mobile face, and in the effusion of a general tenderness which looked for no return.

A very remarkable thing was that this child, whom we might have expected to find ill-nourished, gave normal anthropological measurements and weight for his age. Born in poverty and neglect, he had defended himself; the normality of his body was due to an heroic effort.

A: This child was always calm and quiet; he very soon entered upon the phase of active, ordered, willing and thorough work. He applied himself with intense earnestness and perseverance. He would be the type of the clever, well-behaved child of the ordinary school. Very often he came to school without any food. His *goodness* had a *passive* character which became a mortal danger to himself; he accepted malnutrition without revolt; he profited greatly by the means of psychical life that were offered him, but he would never had been able to conquer them for himself. His goodness continued to be of the same type after as before the period of order; he showed neither agitation nor expansion. His anthropological measurements, which were below the normal, already indicated that he had started on life's pilgrimage with the gait of the victim; he belonged to the company of those "who must be saved by others".

The characteristic moral trait was "espionage". The teacher, when observing him, noticed that the child did not work simply like the others, but came to her very frequently to know if what he was doing was well or ill done. And this not only during his work with the materials, but also in reference to every act of a moral nature he accomplished; his great preoccupation seemed to be, to know whether he was doing right or wrong. Then he endeavoured to do right with the most scrupulous exactitude. With regard to his spying tendencies, the teacher noted that the child never showed any animosity towards his companions; he watched them attentively, and then proceeded to say of them as he would say of himself: So and so did this; was it right or wrong? The child was then careful to avoid what had been pronounced "wrong" in others.

What appeared to be his spying proclivities were, in fact, a manifestation of the problem that dominated his childish conscience: the problem of right and wrong. The limited experience of his own life did not suffice him; he wanted to benefit by the experience of all the others in order to learn what things were right and what were wrong; almost as if the one feeling that absorbed him was the desire to do right and avoid wrong, and as if this were his sole aspiration. The case of this child recalls a popular superstition expressed in such terms as "too good to live". The child A seemed destined for the fate thus suggested. The needs of the body did not greatly concern him, and he seemed equally indifferent to those of the mind; goodness was the mainspring of his being. If society does not note such dispositions and assume the special protection of such frail lives, children of this type go forward to premature death like angels gazing heavenwards.

These two accounts, due to Signorina Maccheroni's observation, correct a superficial judgment which, in an ordinary school, would have become a permanent record of character: one child would have been branded as *violent*, the other as a *spy*.

If we call that science which led to the translation of these words into *hero* and *angel*, and touched so many hearts in the vicinity of these two children, when they had been interpreted by their wonderful instructress, we shall be able to assert that "the judgment of love is the judgment of knowledge". The mercy of Christ in judging is here illustrated.

★ ★ ★

"Psychical action", then, starts from a principle which may be translated thus: "that the child lives". All the rest comes as a consequence.

This action of fundamental life manifests itself as a *polarisation* of the internal personality: almost as a point of crystallisation, around which, provided there be homogeneous material and an undisturbed environment, *the definitive form composes itself*.

This initial action is a task *repeated* with a special intensity of attention.

In my "biographical chart",[18] therefore, I do not give a long formula of analytical studies, but I give a "guide to psychological observations", founded upon the synthetical conception which I have sought to illustrate. Those who have not been *initiated* into this method of observation will gain no light from such a guide, which lies entirely outside the conceptions of psychological study now obtaining in connection with the observation of pupils. But those who have been initiated will understand it without the aid of illustration.

Our teachers have also a terminology by means of which they understand each other, without having recourse to the ordinary expressions, which do not convey an exact idea of the action they see in process of development. Thus they never say: The child is developing, or progressing,

---

18 The main part of the biographical charts consists of questions to be asked about the pupil's history, questions referring to the conditions of the family and to the physical development of the child specifically with regard to diseases, etc. This chart also includes an anthropological part, which guides the measurements we take to study the pupil from a morphological point of view.

the child is good or naughty, etc. The only phraseology they use is: The child is *becoming disciplined* or *is not becoming disciplined.* It is internal order that they await; and on this principle of being or not being, all or nothing depends.

This evokes a much deeper conception than that of "growth". To say that a living creature *grows is* to make a very superficial statement, seeing that he grows indeed, *but in virtue of the fact* that, within, an orderly and regular disposition of substances is in progress.

When, for instance, the embryo of an animal is formed, it grows; but anyone who has observed it internally must have been struck by a fact much more marvellous than that of the visible external "growth". A wonderful internal grouping of the cells takes place; some form, as it were, a leaf which folds over and makes the intestines, others separate to form the nervous system, one group isolates and specialises itself to make the liver, and thus an organisation of parts, more and more pronounced, together with a minute differentiation of each individual arrangement of the cells, is carried on. The future functions of the body all depend upon the possibility of the cells so establishing themselves.

The important point is not that the embryo *grows,* but that it *co-ordinates.* "Growth" comes through and by order, which also makes life possible. An embryo which grows without coordinating its internal organs is not vital. Here we have not only the impulse, but the mystery of life. The evolution of internal order is the essential condition for the realisation of vital existence in a life which possesses the impulse to exist.

Now the sum of the phenomena indicated in the "guide to psychological observation" actually represents the evolution of spiritual *order* in the child.

Guide to psychical observation

WORK

Note when a child begins to occupy himself for any length of time upon a task.

- What the task is and how long he continues working at it (slowness in completing it and repetition of the same exercise).
- His individual peculiarities in applying himself to particular tasks.

- To what tasks he applies himself during the same day, and with how much perseverance.
- If he has periods of spontaneous industry, and for how many days these periods continue.
- How he manifests a desire to progress.
- What tasks he chooses in their sequence, working at them steadily.
- Persistence in a task in spite of stimuli in his environment which would tend to distract his attention.
- If after deliberate interruption he resumes the task from which his attention was distracted.

CONDUCT

Note the state of order or disorder in the acts of the child.

- His disorderly actions.

Note if changes of behaviour take place during the development of the phenomena of work.

Note whether during the establishment of ordered actions there are:

- cries of joy;
- intervals of serenity;
- manifestations of affection.
- The part the child takes in the development of his companions.

OBEDIENCE

Note if the child responds to the summons when he is called.

Note if and when the child begins to take part in the work of others with an intelligent effort.

Note when obedience to a summons becomes regular.

Note when obedience to orders becomes established.

Note when the child obeys eagerly and joyously.

Note the relation of the various phenomena of obedience in their degrees

- to the development of work;
- to changes of conduct.

4
The Preparation of the Teacher

The possibility of observing the developments of the psychical life of the child as natural phenomena and experimental reactions transforms the *school itself in action* into a kind of scientific laboratory for the psychogenetic study of man. It will become – perhaps in the near future – the experimental field *par excellence* of the psychologist. To prepare such a school as perfectly as possible is therefore not only to prepare "a better method for the education of children", but also to prepare the materials for a renovated science. Everyone now knows that students of natural science require in their laboratories an organisation directed to the *preparation* of the material to be observed. To observe a simple cell in movement, it is necessary to have a hollow glass slide with cavity for the hanging drop; to have ready "fresh solutions" in which the living cells may be immersed to ensure their continued vitality; to have ready soils for cultures, etc. For all these ends there are special avocations, those of the so-called "preparers", who are not the assistants or helpers of the professor, but *employees* who were at one time upper servants, and then become superior workmen. At the present day they are, however, nearly always themselves scientific graduates. For, indeed, their task is a most delicate one; they must possess biological, physical and chemical knowledge, and the more thoroughly they are "prepared" by a culture analogous to that of the masters of research themselves, the more rapid and secure is the march of science.

It is strange to think that among all these laboratories of natural science, only that of "experimental psychology" has judged it possible to dispense with an organisation for the preparation of the subjects to be observed. If today a psychologist were told to arrange the work of his preparer, he would take this to mean the preparation of his "instruments", thus adopting more or less the standard of laboratories of *physics*.

But the idea of preparing the living being which produces the phenomenon would not enter his mind; and yet, if merely to observe a cell, a living microbe, the scientist needs a "preparer", how much greater must be the necessity for such an assistant when the subject to be observed is man!

Psychologists consider that they can prepare their "subjects" by arresting their attention with a word, and explaining to them how they are to proceed in order to respond to the experiment; any unknown person met by chance in the laboratory will serve their purpose. In short, the psychologist of today behaves somewhat like the child who catches a butterfly in flight, observes it for a second and then lets it fly away again; not like the biologist who takes care that his preparations are properly carried out in a scientific laboratory.

On the other hand, the picture of psychological development, which is shown to us in our experiments, even though it be incomplete, demonstrates the subtlety with which it is necessary to present to the child the means of his development and, above all, to respect his liberty; conditions which are essential to ensure that psychical phenomena be revealed and may constitute a true "material for observation"; all this demands a special environment and the preparation of a practical staff, forming a whole infinitely superior in complexity and in organisation to the ordinary natural science laboratories. Such a laboratory can only be the most perfect school, organised according to scientific methods, where the teacher is a person answering to the "preparer"-graduate.

True, not all schools would achieve this lofty scientific ideal. But it is indisputable that schools and teachers should all be directing their efforts towards the domain of the experimental sciences. The psychical salvation of children is based upon the means and the liberty to live, and these should become another of the "natural rights" accorded to the new generations; established as a social and philosophic conception, it should supersede the present "obligation to provide instruction", which is a burden not only on State economy but also on the vigour of posterity. If the psychical phenomena of the children in the national schools do not tend to enrich psychology, they become ends in themselves, just as the beauty of Nature is an end in itself.

The new school, indeed, must not be created for the service of a science, but for the service of living humanity; and teachers will be able to rejoice in the contemplation of lives unfolding under their eyes, without sharing the spectacle with science, wrapped in a holy egoism which will exalt their spirits as does every intimate contact with living souls.

It is unquestionable that with this method of education the preparation of the teacher must be made *ex novo*, and that the personality and social importance of the instructress will be transformed thereby.

Even after the first desultory experiments hitherto made, a new type of mistress has been evolved; instead of facility in speech, she has to acquire the power of silence; instead of teaching, she has to observe; instead of the proud dignity of one who claims to be infallible, she assumes the vesture of humility.

★ ★ ★

This transformation has a parallel in that undergone by the university professor, when the positive sciences began to play their part in the world. What a difference between the dignified old-world professor, draped in a robe often ermine-trimmed, seated on his high chair as on a throne, and speaking so authoritatively that students were not only bound to believe all he said, but to swear *in verba magistri*, and the professor of today, who leaves the high places to the students that they may be able to see, reserving for himself the lowest station on the bare floor; while the students are all seated, he alone stands, often clad in a grey linen shirt like a workman.

The students know that they will be on the way to the highest degree of progress when they are capable of "verifying" the theses of the professor – nay, more, of giving a further impetus to science, and inscribing their own names among those quoted as having contributed to its wealth or having discovered new truths.

Dignity and hierarchy in these schools have been superseded by interest in the chemical or physical or natural phenomena to be produced; and in presence of this all the rest disappears. The whole arrangement of the laboratory is subject to the same purpose; if the phenomenon requires light, all the walls are of glass; if darkness be necessary, the laboratory is so constructed that it may be transformed into a *camera obscura*. The one thing of importance is the production of the phenomenon, be this a bad smell or a perfume, an electric spark or the colours of Geissler's tubes, a resonance with Helmholtz's resonators, or the geometrical arrangement of a fine dust on a metallic plate in vibration; the shape of a leaf or the contraction of a frog's muscle, the study of the blind spot in the eye or the rhythm of cardiac pulsation, all is equal and all is included; the eager and absorbing quest is the quest of truth. It is this which the new generation demands from science, not the oratorical art of the professor, the noble gesture, the quip that lightens the weight of the discourse, the lively peroration of the carefully elaborated harangue, and all those expedients which were once developed by a special art for the express purpose of capturing the attention. It is passion for knowledge rather than attention which now animates our young people, who often come out of university halls remembering neither the voice nor the appearance of their professor.

But this does not connote the absence of love and respect for the master. Only the veneration a modern student feels in the depths of his heart for the great scientist and benefactor of humanity, who stands before him unassumingly dressed in a linen shirt, differs essentially from the fear tempered by ridicule which the gown and wig once inspired.

The transformation of schools and teachers must now proceed on the same lines.

When in a school everything revolves around a fundamental fact, and this fact is a natural phenomenon, the school will have entered the orbit of science. Then the teacher must assume those "characteristics" which are necessary in the presence of science.

Among its devotees we find "characteristics" independent of the content of thought; in short, physicists, chemists, astronomers, botanists and zoologists, though their content of knowledge is entirely different, are nevertheless all students of the positive sciences, and have characteristics which differentiate them from the metaphysicians of the past. These characteristics are related, not to the content, but to the method of the sciences. If, therefore, pedagogy is to take its place among the sciences, it must be characterised by its method; and the teacher must prepare herself, not by means of the content, but by means of the method.

In short, she should be distinguished by *quality* even more than by *culture*.

The fundamental quality is the capacity for "observation"; a quality so important that the positive sciences were also called "sciences of observation", a term which was changed into "experimental sciences" for those in which observation is combined with experiment. Now it is obvious that the possession of senses and of knowledge is not sufficient to enable a person to observe; it is a habit which must be developed by *practice*. When an attempt is made to show untrained persons stellar phenomena by means of the telescope, or the details of a cell under the microscope, however much the demonstrator may try to explain by word of mouth what ought to be seen, the layman cannot see it. When persons who are convinced of the great discovery made by De Vries go to his laboratory to observe the mutations in the varied minute plants of the Aenothera, he often explains in vain the infinitesimal yet essential differences, denoting, indeed, a new species among seedlings which have hardly germinated. It is well known that when a new discovery is to be explained to the public, it is necessary to set forth the coarser details; the uninitiated cannot take in those minute details which constituted the real essence of the discovery. And this because they are unable to observe.

To observe it is necessary to be "trained" and this is the true way of approach to science. For if phenomena cannot be *seen* it is as if they did not exist, while, on the other hand, the *soul of the scientist* is entirely possessed by a passionate interest in what he sees. He who has been "trained" to see, begins to feel interest, and such interest is the motive-power which creates the spirit of the scientist. As in the little child internal *co-ordination* is the point of crystallisation round which the entire psychical form will coalesce, so in the teacher interest in the phenomenon observed will be the centre round which her complete new personality will form spontaneously.

The quality of observation comprises various minor qualities, such as *patience*. In comparison with the scientist, the untrained person not only appears to be a blind man who can see neither with the naked eye nor with the help of lenses; he appears as an "impatient" person.

If the astronomer has not already got his telescope in focus, the layman cannot wait until he has done so; while the scientist would be performing this task without even perceiving that he was carrying out a long and patient process, the layman would be fuming and thinking in great perturbation: "What am I doing here? I cannot waste time like this". When microscopists expect visits from a lay public, they prepare a long row of microscopes already in focus, because they know that their visitors will wish to see "at once" and "quickly" and that they will wish to see "a great deal".

We can easily imagine a scientist whose contributions to the work of the laboratory are of the highest order, who holds chairs and possesses civil dignities and honours of every sort, amiably consenting to show a lady a cellular tissue under the microscope. As if it were the most natural thing in the world, he would proceed as follows, with solemn and serene gravity. He would cut off a minute portion of a piece of tissue preserved in a spirit, and would carefully clean the slide on which the subject was to be placed and the slide that was to cover it; he would clean again the lenses of the microscope, focus the preparation and make ready to explain. But undoubtedly the lady all this time will have been on the point of saying a hundred times: "Excuse me, Professor, but really . . . I have an engagement . . . I have a great deal to do . . ." When she has looked without seeing anything, her lamentations are bitter: "What a lot of time I have wasted!" And yet she has nothing to do, and fritters away all her time! What she lacks is not time but patience. He who is impatient cannot appraise things properly; he can only appreciate his own impulses and his own satisfactions. He reckons time solely by his own activity. That which satisfies him may be absolutely empty, valueless, nugatory; no matter, its value lies in the satisfaction it gives him; and if it gives him satisfaction, it cannot be said to be a waste of time. But what he cannot endure and what impresses him as a loss of time is a tension of the nerves, a moment of self-control, an interval of waiting without an immediate result. There is, indeed, a popular Italian proverb: *aspettare e non venire e una cosa da morire* (to wait for what does not come is a killing business). These impatient persons are like those busy-bodies who always make off when there is really work to be done.

A thorough *education* is indeed necessary to overcome this attitude; we must master and control our own wills, if we would bring ourselves into relation with the external world and appreciate its values. Without this preparation we cannot give due weight to the minute things from which science draws its conclusions.

The capacity for sustained and accurate application to a task the object of which is apparently of very small importance, is indeed a most valuable asset to him who hopes to advance in science. Let us call to mind what a physicist does to place an instrument absolutely level; how patiently he turns first one screw and then another, tries again and again, slowly and carefully: and to what end? to procure an absolutely horizontal direction for a surface. When this measure of comparison is established in hard metal, how carefully it must be preserved to ensure that the oscillations of temperature shall not modify the length even in the most infinitesimal degree; for this would be fatal to the scientific use of the instrument in measuring horizontals. And yet how slight a thing in itself is involved! the preservation of a measure . . . When the great chemist wishes to find out whether *traces* of a substance can give a reaction he seems to be playing with his phials like a little boy; he takes a retort and fills it with the substance he wishes to study, and then empties it; afterwards he fills it with water, and watches for the reaction; the reaction takes place; then again he empties the retort, fills it anew with water, and sees whether there is a further reaction. Thus he establishes the degree of dilution in which the substance will leave traces. In this case the minimum is the important thing; it was to find this imperceptible, negligible minimum that the great man acted like a child.

This attitude of humility is an element of patience. In all things the scientist is humble; from the external action of descending from his professorial throne to work standing at a little table, from the taking off of his robes to don the workman's shirt, from having laid aside the dignity of one who states an authoritative and indisputable truth to assume the position of one who is seeking the truth together with his pupils, and inviting them to verify it, to the end not that they should learn a doctrine, but that they should be spurred to activity by the truth – from all this, down to the tasks he carries out in his laboratory. He considers nothing too small to absorb all his powers, to claim his entire attention, to occupy all his time. Even when social honours are heaped upon him, he maintains the same attitude, which is to him the only true honour, the real source of his greatness. A microbe, an excretion, anything, may interest the man of science, even though he be a senator or a Minister of

State. The example of Cincinnatus[19] is not to be compared with that of the modern scientist, for these workers surpass Cincinnatus immeasurably in their power of bringing glory and salvation to humanity.

But the highest form of humility in men of science is their ready self-abnegation, not only in externals, but even in spiritual things, such as a cherished ideal, convictions that have germinated in their minds. Confronted with truth, the man of science has no pre-conceptions; he is ready to renounce all those cherished ideas of his own that may diverge therefrom. Thus, gradually, he purifies himself from error, and keeps his mind always fresh, always clear, naked as the Truth with which he desires to blend in a sublime union.

Is not this, perhaps, the reason why the specialist in infantile diseases has at present a social dignity and authority far superior to those of a schoolmaster? Yet the specialist merely seeks for truth among the excretions of the child's diseased body; but the master veils its soul with errors.

But how would it be if the master should seek the truth in the soul of the child? What an incomparable dignity would be his! To raise himself to this height, however, he would have to be initiated into the ways of humility, of self-abnegation, of patience; and to destroy the pride which is built on the void of vanity. After this he, too, might put on the spiritual vesture of the scientist, saying to the people: What did you see in the other true sciences? Reeds shaken by the wind? Men clothed in soft raiment? No, you saw prophets; but I am more than a prophet; I am he who crieth in the wilderness: prepare ye the way of the Lord, make His paths straight.

★ ★ ★

More, indeed, than the other men of science; for they must always remain extraneous to the object of their study: electric energy, chemical energy, the life of microbes, the stars, are all things diverse and remote from the scientist. But the object of the schoolmaster is man himself; the

---

19 Lucius Quinctius Cincinnatus (519 BC – 430 BC) served Rome as a dictator when enemies attacked the town. Cincinnatus defeated the enemies and then resigned in order to return to his humble farm.

psychical manifestations of children evoke something more in him than *interest in the phenomenon*; he obtains from them the revelation of himself, and his emotions vibrate at the contact of other souls like his own. All life may be his portion, not merely a part of life. Then those *virtues*, such as *humility* and *patience*, which spring up in the man of science within the limitations of the external aims he has fixed for himself, may here enfold the entire soul. Then it will no longer be a question of the "patience of the man of science", or the "humility of the man of science", but of the virtues of man in all their plenitude.

That spiritual expansion of the man of science which is, as it were, compressed into a tube, like rays of light passing through the cylinders of the telescope, may here be diffused on the horizon like the dazzling splendour of the sun. The so-called virtues are the *necessary means*, the *methods of existence* by which we attain to truth; but the delight of the scientist in his work must vary in proportion as this truth is manifested in a physical force, a protozoan, or the soul of man. The one name seems scarcely suitable for the two forms. We understand at once that, in comparison with the *schoolmaster*, the scientist must be to some extent a limited and arid being. The nobility of his spirit is lofty as man, but its dimensions are those of a brute force or an inferior life.

The spiritual life of man may blend with the virtues of the man of science only when the student and the subject of study can be fused together. Then science may become a well-spring of wisdom, and true positive science may become one with the true knowledge of the saints. There is a real mechanism of correspondence between the virtues of the man of science and the virtues of the saints; it is by means of humility and patience that the scientist puts himself in contact with material nature; and it is by means of humility and patience that the saint puts himself in contact with the spiritual nature of things, and as a consequence, mainly with man. The scientist is virtuous only within the limits of his material contacts; the saint is "all compact" of such virtue; his sacrifices and his enjoyments are alike illimitable. The scientist is a seer within the limits of his field of observation; the saint is a spiritual seer, but he also *sees* material things and their laws more clearly than other men, and invests them with spirit.

The modern scientist knows that every living thing is marvellous, and that the simplest and most primitive most readily reveal natural laws which help us to interpret the most complicated beings. St. Francis indeed knew this: "Come closer, o my sister", he said to the grasshopper chirping beneath the fig-tree near the window of his cell; "the smaller the creature, the more perfectly does it reveal the power and goodness of the Creator."

Each tiny thing is worthy of the scientist's minute attention; he counts the articulations which make up the claws of an insect, and knows the veinings of its most delicate wings; he finds interesting details where the ordinary eye would not linger for a moment. St. Francis also observed these things, but they awoke in him a feeling of spiritual joy and called forth a hymn of praise: "Who, who gave me these little fairy feet, furnished with healthy and flexible little bones, to enable me to spring swiftly from branch to branch, from twig to twig? Who further gave me eyes, *crystal globes that revolve* and see before and behind, to spy out all my enemies, the predatory kite, the black crow, the greedy goose? And he gave me wings, *delicate tissues of gold and green and blue*, which reflect the colour of the skies and of my trees."

The vision of the teacher should be at once precise like that of the scientist, and spiritual like that of the saint. The preparation for science and the preparation for sanctity should form a new soul, for the attitude of the teacher should be at once positive, scientific and spiritual.

Positive and scientific, because she has an *exact* task to perform, and it is necessary that she should put herself into immediate relation with the truth by means of rigorous observation, that she should strip off all illusions, all the idle creations of the fancy, that she should distinguish truth from falsehood unerringly, that, in fact, she should follow the example of the scientist, who takes account of every minute particle of matter, every elementary and embryonic form of life, but eliminates all optical delusions, all the confusion which impurities and foreign substances might introduce into the search for truth. To achieve such an attitude *long practice is necessary, and a wide observation of life* under the guidance of the biological sciences.

Spiritual, because it is to man that his powers of observation are to be applied, and because the characteristics of the creature who is to be his particular subject of observation are spiritual.

I would therefore initiate teachers into the observation of the most simple forms of living things, with all those aids which science gives; I would make them microscopists; I would give them a knowledge of the cultivation of plants and train them to observe their physiology; I would direct their observation to insects, and would make them study the general laws of biology. And I would not have them concerned with theory alone, but would encourage them to work independently in laboratories and in the bosom of free Nature.

This complex programme of observation must not exclude the physical aspects of the child. Thus the direct and immediate preparation for a higher task should be the knowledge of the physical needs of the child, from birth to the age when psychical life is beginning to develop in his organisation and becomes susceptible to treatment. By this I do not mean merely a theoretical course of anatomy, physiology and hygiene; but a "practice" among little children, which aims at following their development closely, and foresees all their physical needs. The teacher, in other words, should prepare herself according to the methods of the biological sciences, entering with simplicity and objectivity into the very domain in which students of the natural sciences and of medicine are initiated, when they make their first experiments in the laboratory, before penetrating into the more profound problems of life related to their special study. In like manner those young men who in our universities are destined to study vast and complex sciences, must in the beginning undertake the quiet and restful work of preparing an infusion, or the section of a rose-stalk, and thus experience, as they observe through the microscope, that emotion born of wonder, which awakens the consciousness and attracts it to the mysteries of life with a passionate enthusiasm. It was thus that we, accustomed hitherto to read in school only ponderous and arid printed books, felt that the book of Nature was opening before our spirit, infinite in its possibilities of creation and of miracle, and responding to all our latent and uncomprehended aspirations.

This should also be the book of the new teacher, the primer that should mould her for her mission of directing infant life. Such a preparation should generate in her consciousness a conception of life capable of transforming her, of calling forth in her a special "activity", and "aptitude" which shall make her efficient for her task. She should become a providential "force", a maternal "force".

But all this is but a part of the "preparation". The teacher must not remain thus on the threshold of life, like those scientists who are destined to observe plants and animals, and who are accordingly satisfied with what morphology and physiology can offer. Nor is it her mission to remain intent upon "derangements in the functions of the body", like the medical specialist in infantile disease, who is content with pathology. She must recognise that the methods of those sciences are limited. When she chants her introit and sets foot upon those steps which in the temple of life ascend to the spiritual tabernacle, she should look upwards, and feel that among the adoring host in the vast temple of science, she is a priestess.

Her sphere is to be vaster and more splendid; she is about to observe "the inner life of man". The arid field which is limited to the marvels of organic matter will not suffice for her; all the spiritual fruits of the history of humanity and of religion will be necessary for her nourishment. The lofty manifestations of art, of love, of holiness, are the characteristic manifestations of that life which she is not only about to observe but to serve, and which is her "own life"; not a thing strange to her, and therefore cold and arid; but the intimate life she has in common with all men, the true and only real life of Man.

The scientific laboratory, the field of Nature where the teacher will be initiated into "the observation of the phenomena of the inner life", should be the school in which free children develop with the help of material designed to bring about development. When she feels herself aflame with interest, "seeing" the spiritual phenomena of the child, and experiences a serene joy and an insatiable eagerness in observing them, then she will know that she is "initiated".

Then she will begin to become a "teacher".

5
Environment

Not only must the teacher be transformed, but the school environment must be changed. The introduction of the "material of development" into an ordinary school cannot constitute the entire external renovation. The school should become the place where the child may live in freedom, and this freedom must not be solely the intimate, spiritual liberty of internal growth. The entire organism of the child, from his physiological, vegetative part to his motor activity, ought to find in school "the best conditions for development". This includes all that physical hygiene has already put forward as aids to the life of the child. No place would be better adapted than these schools to establish and popularise reform in the clothing of children, which should meet the requirements of cleanliness and of a simplicity facilitating freedom of movement, while it should be so made as to enable children to dress themselves. No better place could be found to carry out and popularise infant hygiene in its relation to nutrition. It would be a work of social regeneration to convince the public of the economy they might effect by such practices, to show them that elegance and propriety in themselves cost nothing – nay, more, that they demand simplicity and moderation, and therefore exclude all that superfluity which is so expensive.

The above applies more especially to schools which, like the original Children's Houses, might be instituted in the very buildings inhabited by the parents of the pupils.

Certain special requirements must be recognised in the rooms of a free school: psychical hygiene must play its part here as physical hygiene has already done. The great increase in the dimensions of modern classrooms was dictated by physical hygiene; the ambient air space is measured by "cubature" in relation to the physical needs of respiration; and for the same reason, lavatories were multiplied, and bathrooms were installed; physical hygiene further decreed the introduction of concrete floors and washable dadoes, of central heating, and in many cases of meals, while gardens or broad terraces are already looked upon as essentials for the physical well-being of the child. Wide windows already admit the light freely, and gymnasia with spacious halls and a variety of complex and costly apparatus were established. Finally, the most complicated desks, sometimes veritable machines of wood and iron, with foot-rests, seats and desks revolving automatically, in order to preclude alike the movements of the child and the distortions arising from immobility, are the economically disastrous contribution of a false principle of "school-hygiene". In the modern school, the uniform whiteness and the washable quality of every object denote the triumph of an epoch in which the campaign against microbes would seem to be the sole key to human life.

Psychical hygiene now presents itself on the threshold of the school with its new precepts, precepts which economically are certainly no more onerous than those entailed by the first triumphant entry of physical hygiene.

They require, however, that schoolrooms be enlarged, not in deference to the laws of respiration, for central heating, which makes it possible to keep windows open, renders calculations based on cubic measure negligible; but because space is necessary for the liberty of movement which should be allowed to the child. However, as the child's walking exercise will not be taken indoors, this increase of space will be sufficient if it permits free movement among the furniture. Still, if an ideal perfection is to be achieved, we may say that the "psychical" class-room should be twice as large as the "physical" classroom. We all know the sense of comfort of which we are conscious when a good half of the floor space in a room is unencumbered; this seems to offer us the agreeable possibility of moving about freely. This sensation of well-being is more intimate than the possibility of breathing offered to us in a room of medium size crowded with furniture.

Scantiness of furniture is certainly a powerful factor in hygiene; here physical and psychical hygiene are at one. In our schools we recommend the use of "light" furniture, which is correspondingly simple and economical in the extreme. If it be washable, so much the better, especially as the children will then "learn to wash it", thus performing a pleasing and very instructive exercise. But what is above all essential is, that it should be "artistically beautiful". In this case beauty is not produced by superfluity or luxury, but by grace and harmony of the line and colour, combined with that absolute simplicity necessitated by the lightness of the furniture. Just as the modern dress of children is more elegant than that of the past, and at the same time infinitely simpler and more economical, so is this furniture.

In a "Children's House" in the country, at Palidano, built to commemorate the Marchese Carlo Guerrieri Gonzaga,[20] we initiated the study of "artistic" furnishing. It is well known that every little corner of Italy is a storehouse of local art, and there is no province which in bygone times did not contain graceful and convenient objects, due to a combination of practical sense and artistic instinct. Nearly all these treasures are now being dispersed, and the very memory of them is dying out, under the tyranny of the stupid and uniform "hygienic" fashions of our day. It was therefore a delightful undertaking on the part of Maria Maraini to make careful inquiries into the rustic local art of the past, and to give it new life by reproducing, in the furniture of the "Children's Houses", the forms and colours of tables, chairs, sideboards and pottery, the designs of textiles and the characteristic decorative motives to be met with in old country-houses. This revival of rustic art will bring back into use objects used by the poor in ages less wealthy than ours, and meanwhile may be a revelation in "economy". If, instead of school benches, such simple and graceful objects were manufactured, even this school furniture would show how beauty may be evolved from ugliness by eliminating superfluous material; for beauty is a question, not of material, but of inspiration. Hence we must not look to richness of material, but to refinement of spirit for these practical reforms.

If similar studies should be made some day upon the rustic art of all the Italian provinces, each of which has its special artistic traditions, "types of furniture" might arise which would in themselves do much to elevate the taste and refine the habits. They would bring to the enlightenment of the world an "educational mode", because the time-honoured artistic

---

20 The Marquis Carlo Guerrieri Gonzaga was the father of Maria Guerrieri Gonzaga Maraini. She founded the Children's House Palidano and, together with Dr. Montessori, initiated the manufacture of Montessori materials in Gonzaga.

feeling of a people with a very ancient civilisation would breathe new life into those moderns who seem to be suffocating under the obsession of physical hygiene, and to be actuated solely by a despairing effort to combat disease.

We should witness the humanisation of art, rising amidst the ugliness and darkness of those who have accustomed themselves to think only of death. Indeed, the "hygienic houses" of today with their bare walls and white washable furniture, look like hospitals; while the schools seem veritable tombs, with their desks ranged in rows like black catafalques – black, merely because they have to be of the same colour as ink to hide the stains which are looked upon as a necessity, just as certain sins and certain crimes are still considered to be inevitable in the world; the alternative of avoiding them has never occurred to anyone. Class-rooms have black desks, and bare, grey walls, more devoid of ornament than those of a mortuary chamber; this is to the end that the starved and famishing spirit of the child may "accept" the indigestible intellectual food which the teacher bestows upon it. In other words, every distracting element has to be removed from the environment, so that the teacher, by his oratorical art, and with the help of his laborious expedients, may succeed in fixing the rebellious attention of his pupils on himself. On the other hand, the spiritual school puts no limits to the beauty of its environment, save economical limits. No ornament can distract a child really absorbed in his task; on the contrary, beauty both promotes concentration of thought and offers refreshment to the tired spirit. Indeed, the churches, which are *par excellence* places of meditation and of repose for the life of the soul, have called upon the highest inspirations of genius to gather every beauty within their precincts.

Such words may seem strange; but if we wish to keep in touch with the principles of science, we may say that the place best adapted to the life of man is an artistic environment; and that, therefore, if we want the school to become "a laboratory for the observation of human life", we must gather within it things of *beauty*, just as the laboratory of the bacteriologist must be furnished with stoves and soils for the culture of bacilli.

Furniture for children, their tables and chairs, should be light, not

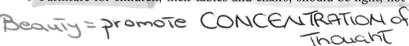

only that they may be easily carried about by childish arms, but because their very fragility is of educational value. The same consideration, leads us to give children china plates and glass drinking-vessels, for these objects become the denouncers of rough, disorderly, and undisciplined movements. Thus the child is led to correct himself, and he accordingly trains himself not to knock against, overturn, and break things; softening his movements more and more, he gradually becomes their perfectly free and self-possessed director. In the same way the child will accustom himself to do his utmost not to soil the gay and pretty things which enliven his surroundings. Thus he makes progress in his own perfection, or in other words, it is thus he achieves the perfect co-ordination of his voluntary movements. It is the same process by which, having enjoyed silence and music, he will do all in his power to avoid discordant noises, which have become unpleasant to his educated ear.

On the other hand, when a child comes into collision a hundred times with an enormously heavy iron-bound desk, which a porter would have difficulty in moving; when he makes thousands of invisible ink-stains on a black bench; when he lets a metal plate fall to the ground a hundred times without breaking it, he remains immersed in his sea of defects without perceiving them; his environment meanwhile is so constructed as to hide and therefore to encourage his errors, with Mephistophelian hypocrisy.

Free movement. – It is now a hygienic principle universally accepted that children require movement. Thus, when we speak of "free children", we generally imply that they are free to move, that is, to run and jump. No mother nowadays fails to agree with the children's doctor that her child should go into parks and meadows and move about freely in the open air.

When we talk of liberty for children in school, some such conception of physical liberty as this rises at once in the mind. We imagine the free child making perilous leaps over the desks, or dashing madly against the walls; his "liberty of movement" seems necessarily to imply the idea of "a wide space", and accordingly we suppose that, if confined to the narrow limits of a room, it would inevitably become a conflict between violence and obstacles, a disorder incompatible with discipline and work.

But in the laws of "psychical hygiene", "liberty of movement" is not limited to a conception so primitive as that of merely "animated bodily liberty". We might, indeed, say of a puppy or a kitten what we say of children: that they should be free to run and jump, and that they should be able to do so, as in fact they often do, in a park or a field, with and like the children. If, however, we wish to apply the same conception of motor liberty to our treatment of a bird, we should make certain arrangements for it; we should place within its reach the branch of a tree, or crossed sticks which would afford foothold for its claws, since these are not designed to be spread out on the ground like the feet of creeping things, but are adapted to gripping a stick. We know that a bird "left free to move" over a vast, illimitable plain would be miserable.

How, then, is it that we never think thus: if it be necessary to prepare different environments for a bird and a reptile in order to ensure their liberty of movement, must it not be a mistake to provide the same form of liberty for our children as that proper to cats and dogs? Children, indeed, when left to themselves to take exercise, show impatience, and are prone to quarrel and cry; older children feel it necessary to invent something whereby they may conceal from themselves the intolerable boredom and humiliation of walking for walking's sake, and running for running's sake. They try to find some object for their exertions; the younger children play pranks. The activity of children thus left to themselves has rarely a good result; it does not aid development, save as regards the physical advantage of general nutrition, that is, of the vegetative life. Their movements become ungraceful; they invent unseemly capers, walk with a staggering gait, fall easily and break things. They are evidently quite unlike the free kitten, so full of grace, so fascinating in its movements, tending to perfect its action by the light jumping and running which are natural to it. In the motor instinct of the child there appears to be no grace, no natural impulse towards perfection. Hence we must conclude that the movement which suffices for the cat does not suffice for the child, and that if the nature of the child is different, his path of liberty must also be different.

If the child has no "intelligent aim" in his movements, he is without internal guidance, thus movement tires him. Many men feel the dreadful emptiness of being compelled to "move without an object". One of the cruel punishments invented for the chastisement of slaves was to make them dig deep holes in the earth and fill them up again repeatedly, in other words, to make them work without an object.

Experiments on fatigue have shown that work with an intelligent object is far less fatiguing than an equal quantity of aimless work. So much so, that the psychiatrists of today recommend, not "exercise in the open air" but "work in the open air", to restore the individuality of the neurasthenic.

"Reconstructive" work – work, that is to say, which is not the product of a "mental effort", but tends to the co-ordination of the psycho-muscular organism. Such are the activities which are not directed to the production of objects, but to their preservation, as, for instance, dusting or washing a little table, sweeping the floor, laying or clearing the table, cleaning shoes, spreading out a carpet. These are the tasks performed by a servant to preserve the objects belonging to his master, work of a very different order to that of the artificer, who, on the other hand, produced those objects by an intelligent effort. The two classes of work are profoundly different. The one is simple; it is a co-ordinated activity scarcely higher in degree than the activity required for walking or jumping; for it merely gives purpose to those simple movements, whereas productive work entails a preliminary intellectual work of preparation, and comprises a series of very complicated motor movements, together with an application of sensory exercises.

The first is the work suitable for little children, who must "exercise themselves in order to learn to co-ordinate their movements".

It consists of the so-called exercises of practical life, which correspond to the psychical principle of "liberty of movement". For this it will be sufficient to prepare "a suitable environment", just as we should place the branch of a tree in an aviary, and then to leave the children free to follow their instincts of activity and imitation. The surrounding objects should be proportioned to the size and strength of the child: light furniture that he can carry about; low dressers within reach of his arms; locks that he can easily manipulate; chests that run on castors; light doors that he can open and shut readily; clothes-pegs fixed on the walls at a height convenient for him; brushes his little hand can grasp; pieces of soap that can lie in the hollow of such a hand; basins so small that the child is strong enough to empty them; brooms with short, smooth, light handles; clothes he can easily put on and take off himself; these are sur-roundings which invite activity, and among which the child will gradu-ally perfect his movements without fatigue, acquiring human grace and dexterity, just as the little kitten acquires its graceful movement and fe-line dexterity solely under the guidance of instinct.

The field thus opened to the free activity of the child will enable him to exercise himself and to form himself as a man. It is not movement for its own sake that he will derive from these exercises, but a powerful coefficient in the complex formation of his personality. His social senti-ments in the relations he forms with other free and active children, his collaborators in a kind of household designed to protect and aid their development; the sense of dignity acquired by the child who learns to satisfy himself in surroundings he himself preserves and dominates – these are the coefficients of humanity which accompany "liberty of movement". From his consciousness of this development of his person-ality the child derives the impulse to persist in these tasks, the industry to perform them, the intelligent joy he shows in their completion. In such an environment he undoubtedly *works himself*, and fortifies his spir-itual being, just as when his body is bathed in fresh air and his limbs move freely in the meadow, he works at the growth of his physical or-ganism and strengthens it.

Children's house

6
Attention

The phenomenon to be expected from the little child, when he is placed in an environment favourable to his spiritual growth, is this: that suddenly the child will fix his attention upon an object, will use it for the purpose for which it was constructed, and will *continue* to repeat the same exercise indefinitely. One will repeat an exercise twenty times, another forty times, and yet another two hundred times; but this is the first phenomenon to be expected, as initiatory to those acts with which spiritual growth is bound up.

That which moves the child to this manifestation of activity is evidently a primitive internal impulse, almost a vague sense of spiritual hunger; and it is the impulse to satisfy this hunger which then actually directs the consciousness of the child to the determined object and leads it gradually to a primordial, but complex and repeated exercise of the intelligence in comparing, judging, deciding upon an act, and correcting an error. When the child, occupied with the solid insets, places and displaces the ten little cylinders in their respective places thirty or forty times consecutively; and, having made a mistake, sets himself a problem and solves it, if he becomes more and more interested, and tries the experiment again and again; he prolongs a complex exercise of his psychical activities which makes way for an internal development.

It is probably the internal perception of this development, which makes the exercise pleasing, and induces prolonged application to the same task. To quench thirst, it is not sufficient to see or to sip water; the thirsty man must drink his fill; that is to say, must take in the quantity his organism requires; so, to satisfy this kind of psychical hunger and thirst, it is not sufficient to see things cursorily, much less "to hear them described"; it is necessary to possess them and to use them to the full for the satisfaction of the needs of the inner life.

This fact stands revealed as the basis of all psychical construction, and the sole secret of education. The external object is the gymnasium on which the spirit exercises itself, and such "internal" exercises are primarily "in themselves" the end and aim of action. Hence the solid insets are not intended to give the child a knowledge of dimensions, nor are the plane insets designed to give him a conception of forms; the purpose of these, as of all the other objects, is to make the child exercise his activities. The fact that the child really acquires by these means definite knowledge, the recollection of which is vivid in proportion to the fixity and intensity of his attention, is a necessary result; and, indeed, it is precisely the sensory knowledge of dimensions, forms and colours, etc. thus acquired, which makes the continuation of such internal exercises in fields progressively vaster and higher, a possible achievement.

Hitherto, all psychologists have agreed that instability of attention is the characteristic of little children of three or four years old; attracted by everything they see, they pass from object to object, unable to concentrate on any; and generally the difficulty of fixing the attention of children is the stumbling-block of their education. William James speaks of "that extreme mobility of the attention with which we are all familiar in children, and which makes their first lessons such rough affairs . . . The reflex and passive character of the attention . . . which makes the child seem to belong less to himself than to every object which happens to catch his notice, is the first thing which the teacher must overcome . . . The faculty of voluntarily bringing back a wandering attention, over and over again, is the very root of judgment, character and will . . . An education which should improve this faculty would be *the education par excellence*".[21]

Thus man, acting by himself alone, never successfully arrests and fixes that *inquiring* attention which wanders from object to object.

In fact, in our experiment the attention of the little child was not artificially maintained by a teacher; it was an object which fixed that attention, as if it corresponded to some internal impulse; an impulse which evidently was directed solely to the things "necessary" for its development. In the same manner, those complex co-ordinated movements achieved by a newborn infant in the act of sucking are limited to the first

---

21   William James (1842 – 1910) American philosopher, psychologist and physician in *The Principles of Psychology* (1890) *Volume I*.

and unconscious need of nutrition; they are not a conscious acquisition directed to a purpose.

Indeed, the conscious acquisition directed to a definite purpose would be impossible in the movements of a newborn infant's mouth, as also in the first movements of the child's spirit.

Therefore it is essential that the external stimulus which first presents itself should be verily the breast and the milk of the spirit, and then only shall we behold that surprising phenomenon of a little face concentrated in an intensity of attention.

Behold a child of three years old capable of repeating the same exercise fifty times in succession; many persons are moving about beside him; someone is playing the piano; children are singing in chorus; but nothing distracts the little child from his profound concentration. Just so does the suckling keep hold of the mother's breast, uninterrupted by external incidents, and desists only when he is satisfied.

Only Nature accomplishes such miracles.

If, then, psychical manifestations have their root in Nature, it was necessary, in order to understand and help Nature, to study it in its initial periods, those which are the simplest, and the only ones capable of revealing truths which would serve as guides for the interpretation of later and more complex manifestations. This, indeed, many psychologists have done; but, applying the analytical methods of experimental psychology, they did not start from that point whence the biological sciences derive their knowledge of life: that is the liberty of the living creatures they desire to observe. If Fabre had not made use of insects, while leaving them free to carry out their natural manifestations, and observing them without allowing his presence to interfere in any way with their functions; if he had caught insects, had taken them into his study, and subjected them to experiment, he would not have been able to reveal the marvels of insect life.

If bacteriologists had not instituted, as a method of research, an environment similar to that which is natural to microbes, both as regards nutritive substances and conditions of temperature, etc. to the end that they "might live freely" and thus manifest their characteristics; if they had confined themselves to fixing the germs of a disease under the microscope, the science which today saves the lives of innumerable men and protects whole nations from epidemics would not exist.

Freedom to live is the true basis for every method of observation applied to living creatures.

Liberty is the experimental condition for studying the phenomena of the child's attention. It will be enough to remember that the stimuli of infant attention, being mainly sensory, have a powerful physiological concomitant of "accommodation" in the organs of sense; an accommodation, physiologically incomplete in the young child, which requires to develop itself according to Nature. An object not adapted to become a useful stimulus to the powers of accommodation in process of development would not only be incapable of sustaining attention as a psychical fact, but would also, as a physiological fact, weary or actually injure the organs of accommodation such as the eye and ear. But the child who *chooses* the objects and perseveres in their use with the utmost intensity of attention, as shown in the muscular contractions which give mimetic expression to his face, evidently experiences *pleasure*, and pleasure is an indication of healthy functional activity; it always accompanies exercises which are useful to the organs of the body.

Attention also requires a *preparation* of the ideative centres in relation to the external object for which it is to be demanded: in other words, an internal, psychical "adaptation". The cerebral centres should be excited in their turn by an internal process, when an external stimulus acts. Thus, for instance, anyone who is expecting a person, sees him arriving from a considerable distance; not only because the person presents himself to the senses, but because he was "expected". The distant figure claimed attention because the cerebral centres were already excited to that end. By means of similar activities a hunter is conscious of the slightest sound made by game in woods. In short, two forces act upon the cerebral cell, as upon a closed door: the external sensory force which knocks, and the internal force which says: Open. If the internal force does not open, it is in vain that the external stimulus knocks at the door. And then the strongest stimuli may pass unheeded. The absentminded man may step into a chasm. The man who is absorbed in a task may be deaf to a band playing in the street.

The central action that constitutes attention is the factor of the greatest psychological and philosophic value, and the one which has always represented the maximum among the practical values in pedagogy. The whole art of teachers has consisted, in substance, in preparing the attention of the child to make it *expectant* of their instruction, and in securing the cooperation of those internal forces which should "open the door" when they "knock". And as the thing which is quite unknown, or that which is inaccessible to the understanding, can awaken no interest, the fundamentals of the art of teaching were to go gradually from the known to the unknown, from the easy to the difficult. It is the pre-existent "known" which excites expectation and *opens the door* to the novel "unknown"; and it is the already present "easy work" which opens new ways for penetration, and puts the attention into a state of expectation.

Thus, according to the conceptions of pedagogy, it should be possible to "prepare good offices for oneself", the co-operation of the psychical concomitants of the attention. Everything would depend on skilful manipulation between the known and the unknown and similar things: the clever teacher would be like the great military strategist, who prepares the plan of a battle upon a table; and man would be able to *direct* man, leading him wheresoever he pleases.

This, moreover, has long been the materialistic principle which governs psychology. According to Herbert Spencer, the mind is at first, as it were, an indifferent clay on which external impressions "rain", leaving traces more or less profound. "Experiences" are, according to him and the English empiricists, the constructive factors of the mind even in its highest activities. Man is what experience has made him; hence, in education, by preparing a suitable structure of experiences, it is possible to *build up the man*. A conception not less materialistic than that which presented itself for a moment before the marvellous progress of organic chemistry, when the series of syntheses succeeded that of analyses. It was then believed that as a species of albumen might be manufactured synthetically, and as albumen is the organic basis of the cells, and as the human ovum is nothing but a cell, man himself might one day be manufactured on the chemist's table. The conception of man as the creator of man was quickly discredited in the material domain; but the psychical *homunculus* still persists among the practical conceptions of pedagogy.

No chemical synthesis could put into the cell, apparently nothing more than a simple clot of nucleated protoplasm, that *activity sine matter*, that potential vital force, that mysterious factor which causes a cell to develop into man.

And the elusive attention of children would seem to tell us that the psychical man is subject to analogous laws of auto-creation.

The most modern school of spiritualistic psychologists, to which William James belonged, recognised in the concomitant of attention a fact bound up with the nature of the subject, a "spiritual force", one of the "mysterious factors of life".

.. From whence his intellect
Deduced its primal notices of thought,
Man therefore knows not; or his appetites
Their first affection; such in you as zeal
In bees to gather honey.
(Dante's, Purgatorio, Canto XVIII in the translation of Francis Cary.)

There is in man a special attitude to external things, which forms part of his nature and determines its character. The internal activities act as cause; they do not react and exist as the *effect* of external factors. Our attention is not arrested by all things indifferently, but by those which are congenial to our tastes. The things which are useful to our inner life are those which arouse our interest. Our internal world is created upon a selection from the external world, acquired for and in harmony with our internal activities. The painter will see a preponderance of colours in the world, the musician will be attracted by sounds. It is the quality of our attention which reveals ourselves, and we manifest ourselves externally by our aptitudes; it is not our attention which creates us. The individual character, the internal form, the difference between one man and another, are also obvious among men who have lived in the same environment, but who from that environment have taken only what was necessary for each. The "experiences" with which each constructs his *ego* in relation to the external world do not form a *chaos*, but are *directed* by his intimate individual aptitudes.

If there were any doubt as to the natural force which directs psychical formation, our experiences with little children would furnish a decisive proof. No teacher could procure such phenomena of attention by any artifices; they have evidently an internal origin. The power of concentration shown by little children from three to four years old has no counterpart save in the annals of genius. These little ones seem to reproduce the infancy of men possessing an extraordinary power of attention, such as Archimedes, who was slain while bending over his circles, from which rumours of the taking of Syracuse had failed to distract him; or Newton, who, absorbed in his studies, forgot to eat; or Vittorio Alfieri, who, when writing a poem, heard nothing of the noisy wedding procession which was passing with shouts and clamour before his windows.

Now, these characteristics of the attention of genius could not be evoked by an "interesting" teacher, however subtle his art; nor could any accumulation of passive experiences become such an accumulator of psychical energies.

If there be a spiritual force working within the child by which he may open the door of his attention, the problem which necessarily presents itself is a problem of liberty, rather than a problem of pedagogic art affecting the construction of his mind. The bestowal of the nourishment suitable to psychical needs by means of the external objects, and readiness to respect liberty of development in the most perfect manner possible, are the foundations which, from a logical point of view, should be laid down for the construction of a new pedagogy.

It is no longer a question of attempting to create the homunculus, like the chemists of the nineteenth century; but rather of taking the lantern of Diogenes and going in search of the man. A science should establish by means of experiments what is necessary to the primordial psychical requirements of the child; and then we shall witness the development of complex vital phenomena, in which the intelligence, the will and the character develop together, just as the brain, the stomach and the muscles of the rationally nourished child develop together.

Together with the first psychical exercises, the first coordinated cognitions will be fixed in the child's mind, and the known will begin to exist in him, providing the first germs of an intellectual interest, supplementing his instinctive interest. When this takes place, a state of things begins to establish itself which has some analogy with that mechanism of attention which the pedagogues of today take as the basis of the art of teaching. The transition from the known to the unknown, from the simple to the complex, from the easy to the difficult, is reproduced from a certain point of view, but with special characteristics.

The progression *from the known to the unknown* does not proceed from object to object, as would be assumed by the master who does not bring about the development of ideas from a centre, but merely unites them in a chain, without any definite object, allowing the mind to wander aimlessly, though bound to himself. Here, on the other hand, the known establishes itself in the child as a *complex system* of ideas, which system was actively constructed by the child himself during a series of psychical processes, representing in themselves an internal *formation*, a psychical growth.

To bring about such a progress we must offer the child a systematic, complex material, corresponding to his natural instincts. Thus, for instance, by means of our sensory apparatus we offer the child a series of objects capable of drawing his instinctive attention to colours, forms, and sounds, to tactile and baric qualities, etc. and the child, by means of the characteristically prolonged exercises with each object, begins to organise his psychical personality, but at the same time acquires a clear and orderly knowledge of things.

Thenceforth all external objects, for the reason that they have forms, dimensions, colours, qualities of smoothness, weight, hardness, etc. are no longer foreign to the mind. There is something in the consciousness of the child which prepares him to *expect* these things, and invites him to receive them with interest.

When the child has added a cognition to the primitive impulse which directs his attention to external things, he has acquired other relations with the world, other forms of interest; these are no longer merely those primitive ones which are bound up with a species of primordial instinct, but have become a discerning interest, based upon the conquests of the intelligence.

It is true that all these new conquests are fundamentally and profoundly based upon the *psychical needs* of the individual; but the intellectual element has now been added, transforming an impulse into a conscious and voluntary quest.

The old pedagogic conception, which assumed that to call the attention of the child to the unknown it is necessary to connect it with the known, because it is thus that his interest may be won for the new knowledge to be imparted, grasped but a single detail of the complex phenomenon we now witness after our experiments.

If the known is to represent a new source of interest directed towards the unknown, it is essential that it should itself have been acquired in accordance with the tendency of nature; then preceding knowledge will lend interest to objects of ever-increasing complexity and of lofty significance. The culture thus created ensures the possibility of an indefinite continuation in the successive evolution of such formative phenomena.

Moreover, this culture itself creates order in the mind; when the teacher, giving her plain and simple lesson, says: This is long, this is short, this is red, this is yellow, etc. she fixes with a single word the clearly marked order of the sensations, classifies, and "catalogues" them. And each impression is perfectly distinct from the other, and has its own determined place in the mind, which may be recalled by a word; thenceforth, new acquisitions will not be thrown aside or mixed together chaotically, but will be duly deposited in their proper places, side by side with previous acquisitions of the same kind, like books in a well-arranged library.

Thus the mind not only has within itself the propulsive force required to increase its knowledge, but also an established order, which will be steadily maintained throughout its successive and illimitable enrichment by new material; and as it grows and gains strength, it retains its "equilibrium". These continual exercises in comparison, judgment and choice carried out among the objects, further tend to place the internal acquisitions so logically into relation one with another, that the results are a singular facility and accuracy or reasoning power, and a remarkable quickness of comprehension: the law of "the minimum of effort" is truly carried out as it is everywhere where order and activity reign.

This internal co-ordination, like physiological adaptation, establishes itself as a result of the spontaneity of the exercises; the free development of a personality which grows and organises itself is that which determines such an internal condition, just as in the body of the embryo the heart, in process of development, makes a place for itself in the space of the diastinum between the lungs, and the diaphragm assumes its arched form as a result of pulmonary dilation.

The teacher directs these phenomena; but, in so doing, she is careful to avoid calling the child's attention to herself, since the whole future depends upon his concentration. Her art consists in understanding and in avoiding interference with natural phenomena.

That which has been clearly demonstrated as regards the nutrition of the newborn infant and the first co-ordinated activities of the spirit will be repeated at every period of life, with the necessary modifications induced by the increased complexity of the phenomena.

Continuing the parallel with physical nutrition, let us consider the growing infant which has cut its teeth, developed its gastric juice, and so gradually requires a more complicated diet, until we come to the adult man, nourishing himself by means of all the complications of modern kitchen and table; to keep himself in health, he should eat *only* the things which correspond to the intimate needs of his organism; and if he introduces over-rich or unusual, unsuitable or poisonous substances, the result will be impoverishment, self-poisoning, a "malady". Now it was the study of the child's nutrition during the period of suckling and during the first years of life which created alimentary hygiene, not only for the child but for the adult, and pointed out the perils to which all were alike exposed during the epoch when infantile hygiene was unknown.

There is a singular parallel in psychical life: the man will have an infinitely more complex life than the child; but for him, too, there should always be a correspondence between the needs of his nature and the manner in which his spirit is nourished. A *rule* of internal life will always promote the health of the man.

Turning to attention, the primitive fact of correspondence between nature and stimulus which is the fundamental of life should prevail, however modified, when dealing with older children, and should remain the basis of education.

I am prepared for the objections of "experts". Children must be accustomed to pay attention to everything, even to things which are distasteful to them, because practical life demands such efforts.

The objection is based on a prejudice analogous to that which at one time made good fathers of families say: "Children should be accustomed to eat everything". In just the same way, moral training is put outside its rightful sphere – a fatal confusion. Following ideas of this order, happily obsolete, fathers would allow their children to fast all day if they refused a dish they disliked at the midday meal, forbidding them anything but the rejected portion, which became ever colder and more disgusting, until at last hunger weakened the child's will and destroyed his caprice, and the plateful of cold food was swallowed. Thus argued such a father, in the various circumstances in which he may be placed throughout his life, my son will be ready to eat whatever comes to hand, and will not be greedy and capricious. In those days also, sweets were forbidden to children (whose organisms require sugar, because the muscles consume a great deal of this during growth), in order to teach them to overcome greediness, and an easy and convenient method of correcting naughty children was to "send them to bed without any supper".

Very similar methods are now adopted by those who insist that children should pay attention to things they dislike, in order to accustom them to the necessities of life. But as in the case of psychical nourishment hunger is never brought to bear upon the "cold and distasteful viands", the indigestible and heavy food weakens and poisons the unwilling recipient.

Not thus shall we prepare the robust spirit, ready for all the difficult eventualities of life. The boy who swallowed the cold soup and went fasting to bed was the one whose body developed badly, who was too weak to resist infection when he encountered it, and fell ill; and morally it was he who, having a store of unsatisfied appetites within him, looked upon it as the greatest joy of his liberty, when he became an adult, to eat and drink to excess. How unlike was he to the boy of today, who, rationally fed and made robust of body, becomes the *abstemious* man, who eats to live in health, and combats alcoholism and excessive and injurious feeding; the modern man, who can defend himself by so many means against infectious diseases, and who is so ready for effort that, without any compulsion, he braves the arduous exertion of sport and attempts and carries out great enterprises, such as the discovery of the Poles and the ascent of lofty mountains.

So, too, the man capable of braving the icy wastes of moral conflict, of undertaking spiritual ascents, will be he whose will is strong, whose spirit is well balanced, whose decisions are prompt and steadfast.

And the more a man's inner life shall have grown *normally*, organizing itself in accordance with the provident laws of nature, and forming an individuality, the more richly will he be endowed with a strong will and a well-balanced mind. To be ready for a struggle, it is not necessary to have struggled from one's birth, but it is necessary to be strong. He who is strong is ready; no hero was a hero before he had performed his heroic deed. The trials life has in store for us are unforeseen, unexpected; no one can prepare us directly to meet them; it is only a vigorous soul that can be prepared for everything.

When a living being is in process of evolution, it is essential to provide for the special requirements of the moment, in order to ensure its normal development. The foetus must be nourished with blood; the newborn infant with milk. If during its intrauterine life the foetus should lack blood rich in albuminous substances and oxygen, or if poisonous substances should be introduced into its tissues, the living being will not develop normally, and no after-care will strengthen the man evolved from this impoverished source. Should infant lack sufficient milk, the malnutrition of the initial stage of life condemns him to a permanent state of inferiority. The suckling "prepares himself to walk" by lying stretched out, and spending long, quiet hours in sleep. It is by sucking that the babe begins his teething. So, too, the fledgling in the nest does not prepare for flight by flying, but remains motionless in the little warm shell where its food is provided. The preparations for life are indirect.

The prelude to such phenomena of Nature as the majestic flight of birds, the ferocity of wild beasts, the song of the nightingale, the variegated beauty of the butterfly's wings, is the preparation in the secret places of a nest or a den, or in the motionless intimacy of the cocoon. Omnipotent Nature asks only peace for the creature in process of formation. All the rest she gives herself.

Then the childish spirit should also find a warm nest where its nutrition is secure, and after this we should await the revelations of its development.

It is essential, therefore, to offer objects which correspond to its formative tendencies, in order to obtain the result which education makes its goal: the development of the latent forces in man with the minimum of strain and all possible fullness.

7
Will

When the child chooses from among a considerable number of objects the one he prefers, when he moves to go and take it from the sideboard and then replaces it, or consents to give it up to a companion; when he waits until one of the pieces of the apparatus he wishes to use is laid aside by the child who has it in his hand at the moment; when he persists for a long time and with earnest attention in the same exercise, correcting the mistakes which the didactic material reveals to him; when, in the silence-exercise, he restrains all his impulses, all his movements, and then, rising when his name is called, controls these movements carefully to avoid making a noise with his feet or knocking against the furniture, he performs so many acts of the "will". It may be said that in him the exercise of the will is continuous; nay, that the factor which really acts and persists among his aptitudes is the will, which is built up on the internal fundamental fact of a prolonged attention.

Let us analyse some of the coefficients of will.

The whole external expression of the will is contained in *movement*: whatever action man performs, whether he walks, works, speaks or writes, opens his eyes to look, or closes them to shut out a scene, he acts by "motion". An act of the will may also be directed to the restriction of movement: to restrain the disorderly movements of anger; not to give way to the impulse which urges us to snatch a desirable object from the hand of another, are voluntary actions. Therefore the will is not a simple impulse towards movement, but the intelligent direction of movements.

There can be no manifestation of the will without completed action; he who thinks of performing a good action, but leaves it undone; he who desires to atone for an offence, but takes no steps to do so; he who proposes to go out, to pay a call, or to write a letter, but goes no farther in the matter, does not accomplish an exercise of the will. To think and to wish is not enough. It is action which counts. "The way to Hell is paved with good intentions".

The life of volition is the life of action. Now all our actions represent a resultant of the forces of impulse and inhibition, and by constant repetition of actions this resultant may become almost habitual and unconscious. Such is the case, for instance, with regard to all those customary actions, the sums of which constitute "the behaviour of a well-bred person". Our impulse might be to pay a certain visit, but we know that we might disturb our friend, that it is not her day for receiving, and we refrain; we may be comfortably seated in a corner of the drawing-room, but a venerable person enters, and we rise to our feet; we are not much attracted by this lady, but nevertheless we also bow and kiss her hand; the sweetmeat to which our neighbour helps herself is just the one we desired, but we are careful to give no sign of this. All the movements of our body are not merely those dictated by impulse or weariness; they are the correct expression of what we consider decorous. Without impulses we could take no part in social life; on the other hand, without inhibitions we could not correct, direct, and utilise our impulses.

This reciprocal equilibrium between opposite motor forces is the result of prolonged exercises, of *ancient habits* within us; we no longer have any sense of effort in performing these, we no longer require the support of reason and knowledge to accomplish them; these acts have almost become reflex. And yet the acts in question are by no means reflex actions; it is not Nature but habit which produces all this. We know well how the person who has not been brought up to observe certain rules, but has been hastily instructed in the knowledge of them, will too often be guilty of blunders and lapses, because he is obliged to "perform" there and then all the necessary co-ordination of voluntary acts, and there and then direct them under the vigilant and immediate control of the consciousness; and such a perpetual effort cannot certainly compete with the "habit" of distinguished manners. The will stores up its prolonged efforts outside the consciousness, or at its extreme margin, and leaves the consciousness itself unencumbered to make new acquisitions and further efforts. Thus we cease to consider as *evidences of will* those habits in which we nevertheless see the consciousness, as it were, hanging over and watchful of each act, that it may accord with the perfect rule of an external code of manners. An educated man who acts thus is merely a man *in himself*, merely a man of "healthy mind".

It is, in fact, only disease which can disintegrate the personality organised upon its adaptations, and induce a man of society to cease to act in a becoming manner; it is well known that a neurasthenic subject who begins to show the first symptoms of paranoia, may at first seem to be merely one who fails in good breeding.

But he, on the other hand, who remains within the limits of good breeding, is nothing more than a *normal* man. We will not venture to call him "a man of will"; the consciousness of such an one is always being put to the test, and the mechanisms stored up in the margin of consciousness no longer possess a "volitive value".

But the child is making his first trial of arms, and his personality is a very different thing from that just described. In comparison with the adult, he is an unbalanced creature, almost invariably the prey of his own impulses and sometimes subject to the most obstinate inhibitions. The two opposite activities of the will have not yet combined to form the new personality. The psychical embryo has still the two elements separate. The great essential is that this "combination", this "adaptation", should take place and establish itself as a supporting girdle at the margin of consciousness. Hence it is necessary to induce active exercise as soon as possible, since this is essential to such a degree of development. The aim in view is not to make the child a little precocious "gentleman", but to induce him to exercise his powers of volition, and to bring about as soon as possible the reciprocal contact of impulses with inhibitions. It is this "construction" itself which is necessary, not the result which may be achieved externally by means of this construction.

It is, in fact, merely a means to an end: and the end is that the child should act together with other children, and practise the gymnastics of the will in the daily habits of life. The child who is absorbed in some task, inhibits all movements which do not conduce to the accomplishment of this work; he makes a selection among the muscular co-ordinations of which he is capable, persists in them, and thus begins to make such coordinations permanent. This is a very different matter to the disorderly movements of a child giving way to un-coordinated impulses. When he begins to respect the work of others; when he waits patiently for the object he desires instead of snatching it from the hand of another; when he can walk about without knocking against his companions, without stamping on their feet, without overturning the table – then he is organizing his powers of volition, and bringing impulses and inhibitions into equilibrium. Such an attitude prepares the way for the habits of social life. It would be impossible to bring about such a result by keeping children motionless, seated side by side; under such conditions "relations between children" cannot be established, and infantile social life does not develop.

It is by means of free intercourse, of real practice which obliges each one to adapt his own limits to the limits of others, that social "habits" may be established. Dissertations on what ought to be done will never bring about the construction of the will; to make a child acquire graceful movements, it will not suffice to inculcate "ideas of politeness" and of "rights and duties". If this were so, it would suffice to give a minute description of the movements of the hand necessary in playing the piano, to enable an attentive pupil to execute a sonata by Beethoven. In all such matters the "formation" is the essential factor; the powers of will are established by exercise.

In education, it is of very great value to organise all the mechanisms useful in the production of personality at an early stage. Just as *movement*, the *gymnastics* of children, is necessary, because, as is well known, muscles which are not exercised become incapable of performing the variety of movements of which the muscular system is capable so an analogous system of gymnastics is necessary to maintain the activity of the psychical life.

The uneducated organism may be easily directed towards subsequent deficiencies; he who is weak of muscle is inclined to remain motionless, and so to perish, when an action is necessary to overcome danger. Thus the child who is weak of will, who is "hypobulic" or "abulic", will readily adapt himself to a school where all the children are kept seated and motionless, listening, or pretending to listen. Many children of this kind, however, end in the hospital for nervous disorders, and have the following notes on their school reports: "Conduct excellent; no progress in studies". Of such children some teachers confine themselves to such a remark as: "They are so good", and by this they tend to protect them from any intervention, and leave them to sink undisturbed into the weakness which threatens to engulf them like a quicksand. Other children, whose natural impulses are strong, are noted merely as creators of disorder, and are set down as "naughty". If we enquire into the nature of their naughtiness we shall be told almost invariably that "they will never keep still". These turbulent spirits are further stigmatised as "aggressive to their companions", and their aggressions are nearly always of this kind: they try by every possible means to rouse their companions from their quiescence, and draw them into an association. There are also children in whom the inhibitory powers are dominant; their timidity is extreme; they sometimes seem as if they cannot make up their minds to answer a question; they will do so after some external stimulus, but in a very low voice, and will then burst into tears.

The necessary gymnastic in all these three cases is free action. The constant and interesting movement of others is the best of incitements to the abulic; motion directed into the channel of orderly exercise develops the inhibitory powers of the too impulsive child, and the child who is too much in subjection to his inhibitory powers, when liberated from the bondage of surveillance and free to act privately on his own initiative – in other words, when he is removed from all external inducements to exercise inhibition, is able to find an equilibrium between the two opposite volitional forces. This is indeed the way of salvation for all men: that wherein the weak gain strength is that wherein the strong attain perfection.

The want of balance as between impulse and inhibition is not only a familiar and interesting fact in pathology; it is further met with, though in a minor degree, among normal persons, just as frequently as deficiencies of education are to be met with in the external social sphere.

Impulse leads criminals to commit evil actions against other men; but how often normal persons have to regret thoughtless acts and nervous outbursts which have sad consequences to themselves! For the most part the normal impulsive person harms himself only, compromises his career, and is unable to bring his talents to fruition; he suffers from a conscious servitude, as from a misfortune from which he might perhaps have been saved.

He who is pathologically the victim of his own powers of inhibition is certainly the more unhappy sufferer, he remains immobile and silent; but internally he longs to move. A thousand impulses which can find no outlet torture the soul which aspires to art, to work; and eloquent speech on his own misfortunes would fain flow from his lips to implore help from a physician, or comfort from some lofty soul; but his lips are sealed. He feels the horrible oppression of one buried alive. But how many normal persons suffer from something of the same kind! On some propitious occasions in their lives they ought to have come forward and shown their worth, but they were unable to do so. A thousand times they have thought that a sincere expression of feeling might have straightened out a difficult situation; but the heart has closed and the lips have remained mute. How passionately they have longed to speak to some noble soul who would have understood them, illuminated and comforted them! But when they have been face to face with this person, they have been unable to speak a word. The longed-for individual encouraged them, questioned them, urged them to express themselves, but the sole response to the invitation was an internal anguish. "Speak! Speak!" said impulse in the depths of their consciousness; but inhibition was inexorable as a resistless material force.

It is in the education of the will by means of free exercises wherein the impulses balance the inhibitions that the cure for such subjects might be found, provided such a cure could be undertaken at the age when the will is in the process of formation.

⋆ ⋆ ⋆

Such an equilibrium established as a mechanism at the margin of consciousness, which makes a man of the world "correct" in his conduct, is by no means that which constitutes the "person of will". It has been said above that the consciousness remains free for other voluntary acquirements. The most refined and aristocratic lady might nevertheless be a person "without will" and "without character", although she might have acquired the most rigorous mechanisms productive of a mechanical will directed solely to external objects.

There is a voluntary fundamental quality upon which not only are the superficial relations between man and man based, but on which the very edifice of society is erected. This quality is known as "continuity". The social structure is founded upon the fact that men can work steadily and produce within certain average limits on which the economic equilibrium of a people is constructed. The social relations which are the basis of the reproduction of the species are founded upon the continuous union of parents in marriage. The family and productive work: these are the two pivots of society; they rest upon the greatest volitive quality: constancy, or persistence.

This quality is really the exponent of the uninterrupted concord of the inner personality. Without it, a life would be a series of episodes, a chaos; it would be like a body disintegrated into its cells, rather than an organism, which persists throughout the mutations of its own material. This fundamental quality, when it embraces the sentiment of the individual and the direction of his ideation, that is to say, his whole personality, is what we have called *character*. The man of character is the persistent man, the man who is faithful to his own word, his own convictions, his own affections.

Now the sum of these various manifestations of constancy has an exponent of immense social value: persistence in work.

The degenerate, even before he gave way to criminal impulse, before he betrayed the inconstancy of his affections, before he broke his word, before he made havoc of all the convictions that ennoble the soul of man, had a certain stigma which marked him as one lost and disintegrated; this was laziness, incapacity to persist in work. Directly an honest and well-behaved man begins to suffer from brain-disease, before he shows any violent impulses, disorder in conduct, or signs of delirium, he has a premonitory symptom: he can no longer apply himself to work. Among the masses, it is justly thought that a girl will make a good wife when she is industrious, and a man is said to be an honest fellow and one who can offer good prospects to the girl who is to be his wife, when he is a good workman. This *goodness* is not a matter of ability; it implies steadiness, perseverance. For instance, a pseudo-artist of great skill in producing small artistic objects, but lacking the will to work, would not be considered a good match. Everyone knows that he is not only incapable of economic production, but that he is a suspicious and dangerous character, that he might become a bad husband, a bad father, a bad citizen. On the other hand, the humblest artisan who "works" undoubtedly contains within himself all the elements which make for happiness and security in life. This unquestionably was the meaning of the great Roman encomium: "She stayed indoors and spun the wool", that is to say, she was a woman of character, a worthy companion for the conquerors of the world.

Now the little child who manifests perseverance in his work as the first constructive act of his psychical life, and upon this act builds up internal order, equilibrium, and the growth of personality, demonstrates, almost as in a splendid revelation, the true manner in which man renders himself valuable to the community. The little child who persists in his exercises, concentrated and absorbed, is obviously elaborating the constant man, the man of character, he who will find in himself all human values, crowning that unique fundamental manifestation: persistence in work. Whatever task the child may choose it will be all the same, provided he persists in it. For what is valuable is not the work itself, but the work as a means for the construction of the psychic man.

He who interrupts the children in their occupations in order to make them learn some pre-determined thing; he who makes them cease the study of arithmetic to pass on to that of geography and the like, thinking it is important to direct their culture, confuses the means with the end and destroys the man for a vanity. That which it is necessary to direct is not the culture of man, but the man himself.

* * *

If persistence be the true foundation of the will, we nevertheless recognise *decision* as the act of will *par excellence*. In order to accomplish any conscious act whatever, it is necessary that we should decide. Now a *decision* is always the result of a *choice*. If we have several hats, we must decide which one we will put on when we go out; it may not in the least matter whether it be the brown hat or the grey, but we must choose one of them. For such a choice we must have our motives, whether they be in favour of the grey or the brown; but finally one of the motives will prevail and the choice will be made. Obviously, the habit of taking a hat and going out will facilitate our choice; we are almost unconscious which of the motives stirred and struggled within us. It is the question of a minute and leaves no impression of effort. Our knowledge as to which hat will be suitable for the morning or the afternoon, for the theatre or for sport, saves us from any mental conflict.

But this will not be the case if, for instance, we are about to spend a certain sum of money on a present. What shall we buy among the various objects from which it will be possible to choose? If we have no very definite knowledge of the things, our task may become an anxiety. We should like to choose something artistic, but we do not know much about art, and we fear to be deceived and so to cut a sorry figure; we know not what is customary and have no idea whether a piece of lace or a silver bowl would be suitable. We then feel the need of someone to enlighten us as to all these unknown details, and we go to ask advice. It does not, however, follow that we shall take the advice we receive. To tell the truth, the advice was to deal with our ignorance; we required an aid to knowledge rather than an incitement to an effort of the will. Volition is something which we jealously reserve for ourselves, and is a very different matter from the knowledge indispensable to a decision. The choice which we make after the advice of one of more persons will bear our own impress; it will be the decision of our *ego*.

The choice which the mistress of a house will make to prepare a dinner for guests is of the same nature; but there she has a perfect knowledge of the subject, and good taste, and the decision will be made with pleasure and without any extraneous aid.

But who does not know that in every case this making a decision is an *internal labour*, a genuine effort; so much so that persons of feeble will shall try to avoid it, as a thing irksome to them. If possible, the mistress of the house will leave the decisions to the cook, and to a dressmaker all the arguments necessary to make one of the many motives that come into play in the choice of a gown prevail over the rest; the dressmaker, seeing that a decision will only be reached after long hesitation, will say at a certain moment: "Choose this which suits you so well", and the lady will agree, more to evade the effort of a decision than because the garment pleases her. Our entire life is a continual exercise of decisions. When we go out of the house after having locked the door, we have a clear consciousness of this act, a certainty that the house is well protected, and we *decide* to step out and walk away from it.

The stronger we are in such exercises, the more independent we shall be of others. Clarity of ideas, the mechanism of the habit of decision, give us a sense of liberty. The heaviest chain, which may bind us in a humiliating form of slavery, is an incapacity to make our own decisions, and the consequent need to refer to others; the fear of making "a mistake", the sense of groping in the dark, of having to bear the consequences of an error we are not certain to recognise, makes us run behind another person like a dog on a chain. Finally, we shall fall into an extremity of dependence; we shall no longer be able to dispatch a letter or buy a pocket-handkerchief without asking advice.

But when an actual conflict arises in such a consciousness, and the decision has to be instantaneous, irresolution is the portion of one whose weakness has placed him in subjection to another stronger will, and then we behold a subjection which has almost imperceptibly become an incubus: the victim has taken the first step towards an abyss where the feeble in will run the risk of perdition. Thus the more the young are placed in subjection, without power to exercise their own wills, the more easily do they fall a prey to the perils of which the world is full.

That which gives strength to resist is not the *moral vision*, it is the *exercise of will power;* and this exercise is to be found in the routine of life itself. The mother of a family, much occupied in her mission of domestic work and accustomed to making decisions in all matters pertaining to the daily round, is more likely to gain the victory in the event of moral conflict than a childless woman who lives in an enervating atmosphere of domestic idleness, and has accustomed herself to accepting her husband's will as her own. Yet both these women might have the same moral vision. The first mentioned, if left a widow, might make herself conversant with business and carry on the undertaking managed by her husband; but the second in like circumstances would require tutelage, and would run every risk of disaster. To ensure moral salvation, it is primarily necessary to *depend* on oneself, because in the moment of peril we are *alone*. And strength is not to be acquired instantaneously. He who knows that he will have to fight prepares himself for boxing and duelling by strength and skill; he does not sit with folded hands, because he knows that he will then either be lost or he will have to depend, like the shadow of a body, on someone to protect him step by step throughout his life, which in practice is impossible.

"Ma solo un punto fu quel che ci vines" [22] says Francesca, in Dante's *Inferno*.

Temptation, if it is not to conquer, must not fall like a bomb against another bomb of instantaneous moral explosions, but against the strong walls of an impregnable fortress strongly built up, stone by stone, beginning at that distant day when the foundations were first laid. Persistent work, clarity of ideas, the habit of sifting conflicting motives in the consciousness, even in the minutest actions of life, decisions taken every moment on the smallest things, the gradual mastery over one's actions, the power of self-direction increasing by degrees in the sum of successively repeated acts, these are the stout little stones on which the strong structure of personality is built up. This may then be inhabited by morality, as by a princess who lives among the embattled towers and moats of a mediaeval fortress that is in a perpetual state of defence, always under arms, but with every probability of remaining the "lady", the *"chatelaine"*. If to "build up the house" which morality will inhabit, some mastery of the body is also necessary, such as abstinence from alcohol, which is the chief example of poison taken from without and tending to weaken, and movement in the open air, which facilitates material recuperation by freeing us from the poisons which we ourselves manufacture and which weaken us, how much more essential must be the continual exercise of the will as a vivifying means of psychical recuperation?

Our little children are constructing their own wills when, by a process of self-education, they put in motion complex internal activities of comparison and judgment, and in this wise make their intellectual acquisitions with order and clarity; this is a kind of "knowledge" capable of preparing children to form their own decisions, and one which makes them independent of the suggestions of others; they can then *decide* in every act of their daily life; they decide to take or not to take; they decide to accompany the rhythm of a song with movement; they decide to check every motor impulse when they desire silence. The *constant work* which builds up their personality is all set in motion by *decisions;* and this takes the place of the primitive state of *chaos,* in which, on the other hand, *actions* were the outcome of *impulses.* A voluntary life develops gradually

---

22 One single moment served to conquer us.

within them; and doubt and timidity disappear, together with the darkness of the primitive mental confusion.

Such a development of the will would be impossible if, instead of allowing order and clarity to mature in the mind, we should seek to encumber it with chaotic ideas, or with stores of lessons learnt by heart, and then prevent children from making decisions by deciding everything for them. Teachers who adopt these methods are justified in saying that "a child ought not to have a will of his own", and in teaching him that "there is no such plant as 'I will'". Indeed, they prevent the infantile will from developing. Under such conditions children are conscious of a power which inhibits all their actions; they become timid, and have not the courage to undertake anything without the help and consent of the person on whom they depend entirely. "What colour are these cherries?" a lady once asked a child, who knew quite well that they were red. But the timid, nervous child, doubtful as to whether it would be right or wrong to answer, murmured: "I will ask my teacher".

The volitive mechanism which prepares for decision is one of the most important mechanisms of the will; it is valuable in itself, and should be established and strengthened in itself. Pathology illustrates it for us apart from the other factor of the will, and thus places it before our eyes as a pillar of the great vault which supports the human personality. The so-called "mania of doubt" is one of the most frequent phases in the degenerative forms of psychopathy, and sometimes precedes certain obsessions, which urge the sufferer on irresistibly to the commission of immoral or harmful acts. But there may also be a mania of doubt, simple and genuine, which is confined to the impossibility of taking a decision, and which produces a serious state of distress, though it induces no moral lapses, and may even arise from a moral scruple. In a hospital for nervous disorders I once encountered a characteristic case of the "mania of doubt" which had a moral basis. The patient was a man whose business it was to go round the houses collecting refuse; he was seized with misgivings lest some useful object should have accidentally fallen into the rubbish baskets, and that he would be suspected of appropriating it. Hereupon the unhappy man, just when he was about to go off with his load, climbed all the stairs again, and knocked again at all the doors, asking whether something valuable might not perhaps have chanced to be in the baskets. Going away after assurances to the contrary, he would return and knock again, and so on. In vain he applied to the doctor for some means of strengthening his will. We told him repeatedly that there was nothing of any value in the baskets, that he might be quite easy on this point, and carry on his business without any preoccupations. Then a gleam of hope shone in his eyes. "I may be quite easy!" he repeated, going away. In a minute he was back again. "Then I may really be easy?" In vain we reassured him. "Yes, indeed, quite easy." His wife led him away, but from the window we saw the man stop at a certain point in the street, struggle with her, and come back in great agitation. Once more he appeared at the door to ask: "I may be quite easy then?"

But how often normal persons harbour in their minds the germs of such a mania! Here, for instance, is a person who is going out; he locks the door and shakes it; but when he has gone a few steps he is assailed by doubt: did he fasten the door? He knows that he did, he perfectly remembers having shaken it, but an irresistible impulse makes him go back to see if the door is really fastened. There are children who, before getting into bed at night, always look under it to see if there are any animals there – cats, for instance; they see there are none, and quite understand there are none. Nevertheless, after a while they get out again "to see if there is anything". These germs are carried about enclosed like tubercular bacilli in some tiny lymphatic gland; the whole organism is weak. But the mischief is hidden and causes no uneasiness, just as the pallor of the face may be concealed for a time by rouge.

If we consider that the will must manifest itself in actions which the body must carry out effectively, we shall understand that a formative exercise is necessary to develop it by means of its mechanisms.

There is a perfect parallel between the formation of the will and the co-ordination of movement of its physiological structure, the striated muscles. It is evident that exercise is necessary to establish precision in our movements. We know that we cannot learn to dance without preliminary exercises, that we cannot play the piano without practising the movements of the hand; but prior to this, the fundamental co-ordination of movements, that is to say, ambulation and prehension, must have already been established from infancy. It is not yet so evident to us that similar gradual preparations are necessary to develop the will.

In the purely physiological functions of the muscular apparatus, our voluntary muscles do not all act in the same manner, but rather in two opposite senses; some, for instance, serve to thrust the arm out from the body, others to draw it near; some serve to bend, others to straighten the knee; they are, that is to say, "antagonistic" in their action. Every movement of the body is the result of a combination between antagonistic muscles, in which now one, now the other prevails in a kind of collaboration by which the greatest diversity of movements is made possible to us: movements energetic, graceful, elegant. It is thus we are enabled to establish not only a noble attitude of the body, but a delightful motor correspondence with musical rhythm.

To bring about this intimate combination between antagonistic forces, all that is necessary is exercise in movement. True, we can *educate* movement; but this only after the natural co-ordination has already taken place; then we can "provoke" special movements as in sporting games, dances, etc. which movements must, however, be repeatedly executed by the performer himself in order to produce in him the possibility of new combinations of movement. Not only in the case of movements of grace and agility, but also in those of strength, it is necessary that the performer himself should act repeatedly. The will certainly comes into play here: the performer wishes to devote himself to sport, or to dancing, or to the arts of self-defence, to compete in matches, etc. . . . but in order to will this it is necessary that he should have practised continually, thus making ready the apparatus on which the volitive act will finally depend, and to which it will issue its commands. Movement is always voluntary, both when the first movements established by "muscular co-ordination" take place, and when exercises designed to produce fresh combinations of movements (skill) follow each other – as, in short, when the will acts like a commander whose orders are carried out by a well-organised, disciplined, and highly skilled army. Voluntary action, in respect of its "powers", increases in degree as its dependent muscles perfect themselves and so achieve the necessary conditions for seconding its efforts.

It would certainly never occur to anyone that, in order to educate the voluntary motility of a child, it would be well first of all to keep it absolutely motionless, covering its limbs with cement (I will not say fracturing them!) until the muscles became atrophied and almost paralysed;

and then, when this result had been attained, that it would suffice to read to the child wonderful stories of clowns, acrobats and champion boxers and wrestlers, to fire him by such examples, and to inspire in him an ardent desire to emulate them. It is obvious that such a proceeding would be an inconceivable absurdity.

And yet we do something of the same kind when, in order to educate the child's "will", we first of all attempt to annihilate it, or as we say, "break" it, and thus hamper the development of every factor of the will, substituting ourselves for the child in everything. It is by our will that we keep him motionless, or make him act; it is we who choose and decide for him. And after all this we are content to teach him that "to will is to do" *(volere e potere)*. And we present to his fancy, in the guise of fabulous tales, stories of heroic men, giants of will, under the illusion that by committing their deeds to memory a vigorous feeling of emulation will be aroused and will complete the miracle.

When I was a child, attending the first classes of the elementary schools, there was a kind teacher who was very fond of us. Of course, she kept us captive and motionless on our seats and talked incessantly herself, though she looked pale and exhausted. Her fixed idea was to make us learn by heart the lives of famous women, and more especially "heroines", in order to incite us to imitate them; she made us study an immense number of biographies, in order to demonstrate to us all the possibilities of becoming illustrious and also to convince us that it was not beyond our powers to be heroines, since these were so numerous. The exhortation which accompanied these narratives was always the same: "You, too, should try to become famous; would not you, too, like to be famous?" "Oh, no!" I answered one day, drily; "I shall never do so. I care too much for the children of the future to add yet another biography to the list".

★ ★ ★

The unanimous reports of the educationists from all parts of the world who attended the last pedagogic and psychological international congresses lamented the "lack of character" in the young as constituting a great danger to the race. But it is not that character is lacking in the race; it is that school distorts the body and weakens the spirit. All that is needed is an act of liberation; and the latent forces of man will then develop.

The manner in which we are to make use of our strong will is a higher question, which, however, can rest only upon one basis: that the will exists – that is, has been developed, and has become strong. One of the examples usually given to our children, to teach them to admire strength of will, is that of Vittorio Alfieri[23], who began to educate himself late in life, overcoming the drudgery of the rudiments by a great effort. He who had hitherto been a man of the world, set to work to study the Latin grammar, and perservered until he became a man of letters, and, in virtue of his ardent genius, one of our greatest poets. The phrase by which he explained his transformation is just the phrase every child in Italy has heard quoted by his teachers: "I willed, perpetually I willed, with all my strength I willed."

Now, before he made the great "decision", Vittorio Alfieri was the victim of a capricious society lady whom he loved. Alfieri felt that he was ruining himself by remaining the slave of his passion; an internal impulse urged him to raise himself; he felt the great man latent within him, full of powers not yet developed, but potential and expansive; he would have turned them to account, responded to their inner call, and dedicated himself to them; but then a scented note from the lady would summon him to join her in her box at the play, and the evening would be wasted. The power this lady exercised over him overcame his own will, which would gladly have resisted. Nevertheless, the rage and weariness he endured as he sat through the silly performances at the theatre caused him such acute suffering that at last he felt that he hated the fascinating lady.

His determination took a material form: he resolved to create an in-surmountable obstacle between himself and her; he accordingly cut off the thick plait of hair which adorned his head, the badge of gentle birth, without which he would have been ashamed to leave the house; then he had himself bound with ropes to his armchair, where he spent several days in such agitation that he was unable even to read a line; it was only the material impossibility of moving, and the thought of cutting a ridiculous

---

23 Count Vittorio Alfieri (1749-1803) was an Italian dramatist and poet, considered the founder of Italian tragedy.

figure, which kept him there, in spite of the impulse to hasten to the beloved one.

It was thus that he "willed, willed perpetually, with all his strength", and so left the man within him free to expand; it was thus he saved himself from futility and perdition, and worked for his own immortality.

And it is something of the same sort that we desire to bring about in our children by the education of the will; we wish them to learn to save themselves from the vanities that destroy man, and concentrate on work which causes the inner life to expand, and leads to great undertakings; we wish them to work for their own immortality.

This loving and anxious desire inclines us to draw them along shielded by us. But is there not within the child himself a power which enables him to save himself? The child loves us with his heart and follows us with all the devotion of which his little soul is capable; nevertheless, he has something within himself which governs his inner life: it is the force of his own expansion. It is this force, for instance, which leads him to touch things in order to become acquainted with them, and we say to him "do not touch"; he moves about to establish his equilibrium, and we tell him to "keep still"; he questions us to acquire knowledge, and we reply, "do not be tiresome". We relegate him to a place at our side, vanquished and subdued, with a few tiresome playthings, like an Alfieri in the box at the theatre. He might well think: Why does she, whom I love so dearly, want to annihilate me? Why does she wish to oppress me with her caprices? It is caprice which makes her prevent me from developing the expansive forces within me, and relegate me to a place among vain and wearisome things, merely because I love her.

Thus, to save himself, the child should be a strong spirit, like Vittorio Alfieri; but too often he cannot.

We do not perceive that the child is a victim and that we are annihilating him; and then we demand *everything* from his *nullity* by a *fiat*, by an act of our omnipotence. We want the adult man, but without allowing him to grow.

Many will think, when they read the story of Vittorio Alfieri, that they would have wished something more in their sons; they would have wished it to be unnecessary to set up material obstacles against temptation, such as the cutting off of the hair and the binding to the armchair with ropes;

and would have hoped that a spiritual force would have sufficed to resist it. Like one of our great poets who, singing of the Roman Lucrezia, reproves her for having killed herself; since she ought to have died of grief at the outrage, had she been even more virtuous than she was.

Now that father with the spiritual ideals would not, in all probability, ask himself what he himself had done to enable his son to become strong and rise to the level of spiritual aid. Very likely he is a father who did his utmost to break the will of his son and make him submissive to his own will. No earthly father can make the spirit rise to such heights; this can only be accomplished by the mysterious voice which speaks within the heart of man in the silence. A voice which is strident because it is raised against the laws of Nature, like the voice of the father who wishes to subdue another creature to himself, disturbs that "silence" where, in peace and liberty, the divine works are being accomplished. Without the "strong man" all is vain.

It is recorded that a priest once presented to Saint Teresa a young girl who wished to become a Carmelite nun, and who, according to him, had angelic qualities. Saint Teresa, accepting the neophyte, replied: "See, my father, our Lord has given this maiden devotion, but she has no judgment, and never will have any; and she will always be a burden to us."

One of the greatest of contemporary theologians, who during the proceedings to obtain the canonisation of Joan of Arc had made a profound study of her personality, says, in reference to the suggestion that she was simply the instrument of divine inspiration: "Let no one deceive himself. Joan of Arc was no blind and passive instrument of a supernatural power. The liberator of France had entire command of her personality; she gave proof of this by her independent action, both in decisions and in deeds."

I believe that the work of the educator consists primarily in protecting the powers and directing them without disturbing them in their expansion; and in the bringing of man into contact with the spirit which is within him and which should operate through him.

8
Intelligence

Let us pause a moment to consider what is the "key" by means of which we may bring about the realisation of the liberty of the child; that key which sets in motion the mechanisms essential to education.

The child who is "free to move about", and who perfects himself by so doing, is he who has an "intelligent object" in his movements; the child who is free to develop his inner personality, who perseveres in a task for a considerable time, and organises himself upon such a fundamental phenomenon, is sustained and guided by an intelligent purpose. Without this his persistence in work, his inner formation, and his progress would not be possible. When we refrain from guiding the subjugated child step by step, when, liberating the child from our personal influence, we place him in an environment suited to him and in contact with the means of development, we leave him confidently to "his own intelligence". His motor activity will then direct itself to definite actions: he will wash his hands and face, sweep the room, dust the furniture, change his clothes, spread the rugs, lay the table, cultivate plants, and take care of animals. He will choose the tasks conducive to his development and persist in them, attracted and guided by his interest towards a sensory material which leads him to distinguish one thing from another, to select, to reason, to correct himself; and the acquirements thus made are not only "a cause of internal growth" but a strong propulsive force to further progress. Thus, passing from simple objects to objects of ever-increasing complexity, he becomes possessed of a culture; moreover, he organises his character by means of the internal order which forms itself within him, and by the skill which he acquires. Therefore, when we leave the child to himself, we leave him to his intelligence, not, as is commonly supposed, "to his instincts", meaning by the word "instincts" those designated as animal instincts. We are so accustomed to treating children like dogs and other domestic animals, that a "free child" makes us think of a dog, barking, jumping, and stealing dainties. And so accustomed are we to regarding as manifestations of evil instincts the *rebellions* of the child treated as a beast, his obscure protests and desperations, or the protective devices he has to invent to save himself from such a humiliating situation, that, by way of elevating him we first compare him to plants and flowers, and then actually try to keep him as far as possible in the state of physical immobility of vegetables, subjecting him to the same sensations, reducing him to slavery. But he never becomes the "plant with angelic perfume" we would fain believe him to be; rather do signs of corruption gradually manifest themselves as his "human substance" mortifies and dies.

But when we leave the child "free as a man" in the palestra of his own intelligence, his type changes entirely.

It is of this type we must form new conceptions in discussing the question of "liberty".

That of intelligence should also, I believe, be the key to the problem of the social liberty of man. We have heard much talk of late years, of a very superficial kind, concerning "liberty of thought". The issue being obscured by prejudices akin to those prevalent concerning children, it has been supposed that man would be "liberated" were he "abandoned" to his own thoughts. But was he capable of "thinking"? Was not the epoch of such "freedom" also that of cerebral-neurasthenia? Was it not also that epoch when laws for extending social rights to illiterates were under discussion?

Now let us take an example: if we told a sick person to choose between disease and health, would this make him free to do so? If we offer an uneducated peasant good and bad paper money, leaving him "free to choose" which he will take, and if he chooses the bad notes, he is not free, he is cheated; if he chooses the good, he is not free, he is lucky. He will be free when he has sufficient knowledge not only to distinguish the good from the bad, but to understand the social utility of each. It is the giving of this "internal formation" which makes a man free, irrespective of a "social sanction" which is merely an external conquest of liberty. If the liberty of man were such a simple problem, we should only need to pass a law, enabling the blind to see and the deaf to hear, in order to restore "poor humanity" to health.

Our honesty ought to make us recognise one day that the fundamental rights of man are those of his own "formation", free from obstacles, free from slavery, and free to draw from his environment the means required for his development. In short, it is in education that we shall find the fundamental solution of the social problems connected with "personality".

Deeply instructive is the revelation made to us by the children, that "the intelligence" is the key which reveals the secrets of their formation, and is the actual means of their internal construction.

The hygiene of the intelligence thus assumes cardinal importance. When intelligence is recognised as the means of formation, the pivot of life itself, it can no longer be exhausted for dubious ends, or oppressed and suffocated without discernment.

At a not-far-distant day, the intelligence of children must become the object of treatment much wiser and more elaborate than that which we now bestow on their bodies, to adjuncts of which, such as teeth, nails and hair, we devote costly and laborious processes. When we reflect that a mother who is perfectly conscious of the dangers and remedies connected with the hair of her child, can oppress and enslave his intelligence quite unknowingly, we are at once obliged to admit that the new road leading to civilisation must needs be a long one, if such contrasts in our attitude to the superfluities and the essentials of life are still possible at the present day.

$$\star \star \star$$

What is intelligence? Without rising to the heights of the definitions given by the philosophers, we may, for the moment, consider the sum of those reflex and associative or reproductive activities which enable the mind to construct itself, putting it into relation with the environment. According to Bain,[24] the consciousness of difference is the beginning of every intellectual exercise; the first step of the mind is appreciation of "distinction". The bases of its perceptive functions towards the external world are the "sensations". To collect facts and distinguish between them is the initial process in intellectual construction. Let us try to infuse

---

24 Alexander Bain (1818 – 1903) was the founder of the journal Mind, the first journal on psychology.

a little more precision and clarity into the analysis of intelligence.

The first characteristic which presents itself to us as an indication of intellectual development is related to *time*. The masses are so much alive to this primitive characteristic, that the popular expression "quick" is synonymous with intelligence. To be rapid in reacting to a stimulus, in the association of ideas, in the capacity of formulating a judgment – this is the most obvious external manifestation of intelligence. This "quickness" is certainly related to the capacity for receiving impressions from the environment, elaborating images, and externalizing the internal results. All these activities may be developed by means of an exercise comparable to a system of mental "gymnastics": to collect numerous sensations, to put them constantly in relation – one with another, to deduce judgments therefrom, to acquire the habit of manifesting these freely; all this ought, as the psychologists would say, to render the conductive channels and the associative channels more and more permeable, and the "period of reaction" ever briefer. As in intelligent muscular movement, the repetition of the act not only renders it more perfect in itself, but more rapid in execution. An intelligent child at school is not only one who understands, but one who understands quickly. On the other hand, one who learns the same things, but who takes a longer time in so doing, say two years instead of one, is *slow*. Of a "quick" child, the people say that "nothing escapes him"; his attention is always on the alert, and he is ready to receive every kind of stimulus: as a sensitive scale will show the slightest variation in weight, so the sensitive brain will respond to the slightest appeal. It is equally rapid in its associative processes: "He understands in a flash" is a familiar saying to indicate accurate conception.

Now an exercise, which "puts in motion" the intellectual mechanisms can only be an "auto-exercise". It is impossible that another person, exercising himself in our stead, should make us acquire skill.

The sensory exercises arouse and intensify the central activities in our children. When, sense and stimulus duly isolated, the child has clear perceptions in his consciousness; when sensations of heat, cold, roughness, smoothness, weight and lightness, and a sound, an isolated noise, are perceived by him; when, in almost complete silence, he closes his eyes and waits for a voice to murmur a word; it is as if the external world had knocked at the door of his soul, awakening its activities. And further, when the multitudinous sensations are all contained in the richness of the environment, the two react harmoniously one upon the other, intensifying the activities that have been awakened: this is exemplified in the case of the child absorbed in colouring his designs, who will choose the most beautiful tints while music is being played; or in that of another who, contemplating the gay and gracious environment of the school and the flowering plants, will sing his song to perfection.

The first characteristic which manifests itself in our children after their process of auto-education has been initiated, is that their reactions become ever more ready and more rapid: a sensory stimulus which might before have passed unobserved or might have roused a languid interest, is vividly perceived. The relation between things is easily recognised, and thus errors in their use are quickly detected, judged, and corrected. By means of the sensory gymnastics the child carries out just this primordial and fundamental exercise of the intelligence, which *awakens and sets in motion* the central nervous mechanisms.

When we see these external manifestations of our quick and active children – sensitive to the slightest call, ready to run swiftly towards us without relaxing the attention they give to their own movements and to all the external objects they encounter – and compare them with the torpid children in the ordinary schools – clumsy in their movements, indifferent to stimuli, incapable of spontaneous association of ideas – we are led to think of the civilisation of our own days as compared with that of olden times. The civil environment of bygone years, as compared with our own was more leisurely: we have learnt how to save time. The stagecoach was once the means of transport, whereas now we travel in motorcars and even in aeroplanes; the voice was the medium of speech from a distance, whereas now we speak through the telephone; men killed each other one by one, whereas now they kill each other *en masse.* All this makes us realise that our civilisation is not based upon "respect for life" and "respect for the soul", but rather is it based upon "respect for time". It is solely in an external sense that civilisation has pursued its course. It has become more rapid, it has set in motion *machinery.*

But man has not had the same preparation to keep up with it: individuals have not *accelerated* themselves methodically; the children of this bewildering environment are not new men, more active, readier, and more intelligent. The transformed human personality has not yet arisen ready to meet all eventualities and to utilise for his own benefit the external conquests of his environment. Torpid man saves time and money in this civilisation; but his soul remains defrauded and oppressed. If he does not rise to the task of reforming himself in harmony with the new world he has created, he runs the risk of being some day overthrown and crushed by it.

★ ★ ★

The swift reactions among our children are not merely an external manifestation of the intelligence. They are related not only to the *exercise*, but also to the *order* which has been established within: and it is this intimate work of re-arrangement which is in itself a more exact indication of intellectual formation.

Order is, in short, the true key to rapidity of reaction. In a chaotic mind, the recognition of a sensation is no less difficult than the elaboration of a reasoned discourse. In all things, social as well as others, it is organisation and order which make it possible to proceed rapidly.

"To be able to distinguish" is the characteristic sign of intelligence: to *distinguish is* to arrange and also, in life, it is to prepare for "creation".

Creation finds its expansions in *order*. We find this conception in the Genesis of Scripture. God did not begin to create without preparation; and this preparation was the introduction of order into chaos. "And God divided the light from the darkness. And he said: Let the waters be gathered together into one place, and let the dry land appear." The consciousness may possess a rich and varied content; but when there is *mental confusion*, the intelligence does not appear. Its appearance is exactly like the kindling of a light which makes it possible to distinguish things clearly. "Let there be light."

Thus we may justly say that to help the development of the intelligence is to help to put the images of the consciousness in order.

We ought to think of the mental state of the little child of three years old, who has already looked upon a world. How often he has fallen asleep utterly weary from having seen so many things. It has not occurred to anyone that for him to walk is, in fact, to work; that seeing and hearing, when the organs are not as yet accommodated, so that he is obliged to be perpetually correcting the errors of his senses, and verifying with his hand what he cannot as yet appraise correctly with his eye, is a great exertion. Hence the little one who is overtaxed by stimuli, in places where these abound, cries or falls asleep.

The little child of three years old carries within him a heavy *chaos*.

He is like a man who has accumulated an immense quantity of books, piled up without any order, and who asks himself: "What shall I do with them?" When will he be able to arrange them in such a fashion as to enable him to say: "I possess a library"?

By means of our so-called "sensory exercises" we make it possible for the child to *distinguish* and to *classify*. Our sensory material, in fact, analyses and represents the attributes of things: dimensions, forms, colours, smoothness or roughness of surface, weight, temperature, flavour, noise, sounds. It is the qualities of the objects, not the objects themselves which are important; although these qualities, isolated one from the other, are themselves represented by objects. For the attributes long, short, thick, thin, large, small, red, yellow, green, hot, cold, heavy, light, rough, smooth, scented, noisy, resonant, we have a like number of corresponding "objects" arranged in graduated series. This gradation is important for the establishment of order; indeed, the attributes of the objects differ not only in quality, but also in quantity. They may be more or less high or more or less low, more or less thick or more or less thin; the sounds have various tones; the colours have various degrees of intensity; the shapes may resemble each other in varying degrees; the states of roughness and smoothness are by no means absolute.

The material for the education of the senses lends itself to the purpose of distinguishing between these things. First of all it enables the child to ascertain the *identity* of the two stimuli by means of numerous exercises in matching and fitting. Afterwards *difference* is appreciated when the lessons direct the child's attention to the external objects of a series: light, dark, long, short.

At last he begins to distinguish the *degrees of the various attributes*, arranging a series of objects in gradation, such as the tablets which show the various degrees of intensity of the same chromatic tone; the bells which produce the notes of an octave, the objects which represent length in decimal proportions, or thickness in centimetric proportions, etc.

These exercises, which are so attractive to children, are, as we have seen, repeated by them indefinitely. The teacher puts the seal upon each acquisition with a word; thus the classification is complete, and finally has its schedule: that is, it becomes possible to recall the attribute and its *image* by a name.

Now as we have no possible means of distinguishing things other than by their attributes, the classification of these entails a fundamental order of arrangement comprehending everything. Henceforth the world is no longer a chaos for the child; his mind bears some resemblance to the orderly shelves of a library or a rich museum: each object is in its place, in its proper category. And each acquisition he makes will be no longer merely "stored", but duly "allocated". This primitive order will never be disturbed, but only enriched by fresh material.

Thus the child, having acquired the power of distinguishing one thing from another, has laid the foundations of the intelligence. It is unnecessary to repeat what an internal impulse the acquired order contributes towards the seeking after objects in the environment; henceforth the child "recognises" the objects which surround him. When he discovers with so much emotion that the sky is blue, that his hand is smooth, that the window is rectangular, he does not in reality discover the sky, nor the hand, nor the window, but he discovers their position in the order of his mind by arrangement of his ideas. And this determines a stable equilibrium in the internal personality, which produces calm, strength, and the possibility of fresh conquests, just as the muscles which have co-ordinated their functions enable the body to maintain its equilibrium, and to acquire that stability and security which facilitate all movements. This order conduces to an economy of time and strength; like a well-arranged museum, it saves the time and strength of the inquirers. The child can therefore perform a greater quantity of work without fatigue, and can react to stimuli in a briefer space of time.

★ ★ ★

To be able to distinguish, classify, and catalogue external things on the basis of a secure order already established in the mind – this is at once intelligence and culture. This is, indeed, the popular conception; when an educated person can recognise an author by his style, or the characteristics of the literary compositions of a period, he is pronounced "versed (*intelligente*) in literature". In the same way we say of one who can recognise a painter by the manner in which he lays his colours on the canvas, or fix the period of a sculptor from the fragment of a bas-relief, that he is "versed (*intelligente*) in art". The scientist is of the same type. He is able to observe things, and to give due value even to their minutest details; hence the differences between the characteristics of things are clearly perceived and classified. The scientist distinguishes objects in accordance with the orderly content of his mind. A seedling, a microbe, an animal or the remains of an animal, are not enigmas to him, though in themselves they may be strange to him. We may say the same of the chemist, the physicist, the geologist, the archaeologist.

It is not the accumulation of a direct knowledge of things, which forms the man of letters, the scientist, and the connoisseur; it is the prepared order established in the mind which is to receive such knowledge. On the other hand, the uncultivated person has only the direct knowledge of objects; such a person may be a lady who spends a great part of the night reading books, or a gardener, who spends his life making material distinctions between the plants in his garden. The knowledge of such uncultured minds is not only disorderly, but it is confined to the objects with which it comes into direct contact, whereas the knowledge of the scientist is infinite, because, possessing the power of classifying the attributes of things, he can recognise them all, and determine now the class, now the relationships, now the origins of each; facts much more profound than the actual things could of themselves reveal.

Now our children, after the manner of the connoisseur of art and the man of science, recognise objects in the external world by means of their attributes and classify them; hence they are sensitive to all objects; everything possesses a value for them. Uncultured children, on the other hand, pass blind and deaf close to things, just as an ignorant man passes by a work of art or listens to a performance of classical music without recognition or enjoyment.

The educational methods now in use proceed on lines exactly the reverse of ours; having first abolished spontaneous activity, they present objects with their accumulation of attributes directly to the child, calling attention to each attribute, and hoping that from all this mass the mind of the child will be able to abstract the attributes themselves, without any guidance or order. Thus they create in a passive being an artificial chaos, more limited than that which the natural world would offer.

The "objective" method now in use, which consists in presenting an object and noting all its attributes – that is, describing it, is nothing but a "sensory" variation on the customary mnemonic method[25]; instead of describing an absent object, a present object is described; instead of the imagination alone working to effect its reconstruction, the senses intervene: this is done so that the distinctive qualities of the object itself should be better remembered. The passive mind receives images, which are limited to the objects presented; and which are "stored up" without any order. As a fact, every object may have infinite attributes; and if, as often happens in object-lessons, the origins and ultimate ends of the object itself are included among these attributes, the mind has literally to range throughout the universe. If, for instance, in an object lesson on coffee, which I heard given in a Kindergarten school, the object is described and the attention of the children directed to its size, its colour, its shape, its aroma, its flavour, its temperature; and then if the teacher goes on to describe the plant, and the manner in which the substance was brought to Europe across the ocean, and finally, lighting a spirit-lamp, boils the water, grinds the berries and prepares the beverage, the mind has been led to wander in infinite spaces, but the subject has not been exhausted. For it would be possible to go on to describe the exciting effects of coffee, caffeine, which is extracted from the berry, and many other things. Such an analysis would spread like spilt oil until finally dispersed, and the outcome would be of no use in any way. If, indeed, we should ask a child so instructed: "What is coffee, then?" he might well reply: "It is such a long story that I cannot remember it". A notion so vague (I cannot certainly say so complete!) fatigues and encumbers the mind and can never transform itself into a dynamic excitation of similar associations. The efforts of the child will be, at most, efforts of memory to recall the history of coffee. If associations are formed in his mind, they will be inferior associations of contiguity: his mind will wander

---

25 Mnemonic systems are special techniques to improve memory.

from the teacher who is speaking to the ocean that was traversed, to the dining-table at home on which coffee appears in cups every day; in other words, it will stray aimlessly as does the idle mind when it "allows itself" to wander from the continuity of its passive associations.

In this kind of *reverie* to which the minds of children give themselves up, there is no sign of internal activity, far less of any individual difference. Children subjected to the object-lesson system always remain purely receptive beings; or, if we prefer to put it so, storehouses in which new objects are continually deposited.

No activity is thus aroused and directed towards the object, in order to recognise its qualities in such a manner that the child himself forms an idea of it; nor can the possibility of connecting other objects with the first by their common characteristics arise in his mind. For in what particular characteristic does any object resemble the others. In its use?

When we associate the images of different objects by similarity, we should extract from the whole the qualities, which the objects themselves have in common. If, for instance, we say that two rectangular tablets are alike, we have first extracted from the numerous qualities of these tablets such facts as that they are of wood, that they are polished, smooth, coloured, of the same temperature, etc. the quality relating to their *shape*. They are alike in *shape*. This may suggest a long series of objects: the top of the table, the window, etc.; but before such a result as this can be achieved, it is necessary that the mind should first be capable of abstracting from the numerous attributes of these objects the quality of *rectangular shape*. The work of the mind in this quest must necessarily be *active*; it analyses the object, extracts a determined attribute therefrom, and under the guidance of this determined attribute makes a synthesis associating many objects by the same medium of connection. If this capacity for the selecting of single attributes among all those proper to the object be not acquired, association by means of similarity, synthesis, and all the higher work of the intelligence becomes impossible. Moreover, this is intellectual work in reality, because the essential quality of the intelligence is not to "photograph" objects, and "keep them one upon the other" like the pages of an album, or juxtaposed like the stones in a pavement. Such a labour of mere "deposit" is an outrage on the intellectual nature. The intelligence, with its characteristic orderliness and power of discrimination, is capable of distinguishing and extracting the dominant characteristics of objects, and it is upon these that it proceeds to build up its internal structures.

Now our children, whose minds are thus ordered in relation to the classification of attributes by the pedagogic aid they have received, are led, not only to observe objects according to all the attributes they have analysed, but also to distinguish identities, differences and resemblances; and this work renders the extraction of one of the qualities corresponding to one of the sensory groups which have been considered apart, easy and spontaneous. That is to say, it will be easy for the child thus to recognise the various qualities of an object, to note, for instance, that certain objects are alike in form, or alike in colour; because "forms" and "colours" have already been grouped into very distinctive categories, and they therefore recall series of objects by similarity. This classification of attributes is a kind of loadstone; it is an attractive force of a determined group of qualities; and the objects which have this quality are attracted thereto and united one with another; this is association by similitude, almost of a mechanical kind. Books are of the shape of prisms, one of our children might say; and such a pronouncement would be the conclusion arrived at by a very complex mental process, were it not that prismatic forms already existed as a well-defined series in his mind, attracting to itself all the surrounding objects which possess the same character. Thus the whiteness of sheets of paper, interrupted by dark signs, may be attracted by the colours systematised in the mind into a synthetic whole, which might make the child say: Books are sheets of white printed paper.

It is in this *active* work that individual differences may manifest themselves. What will be the group of attributes which will attract similar objects? And what will be the prevailing characteristic chosen for the purpose of association by similarity? One child will note that a curtain is light green; another that the same curtain is light in weight; one will be struck by the whiteness of a hand, another by the smoothness of its skin. For one child the window will be a rectangle; to another it is something through which the blue of the sky may be seen. The choice of prevailing characteristics made by children becomes a "natural selection" harmonizing with their own innate tendencies.

In like manner, a scientist will choose the characters *most useful* to his associations. An anthropologist may choose the shape of the head to distinguish the human races, and another might choose the cutaneous pigment – either will serve the purpose. Each anthropologist may have the most accurate knowledge of the external characteristics of men; but the important matter consists in finding a characteristic which will serve as a basis for classification: that is to say, a characteristic on which it will be possible to group numerous characteristics in the order of similitude. Purely practical persons would consider man from the utilitarian rather from the scientific point of view; a maker of hats would single out the dimensions of the head from among other human characteristics; an orator would consider man from the point of view of his susceptibility to the spoken word. But *selection* is the fundamental necessity which enables us to realise things; to emerge from the vague into the practical, from aimless contemplation into the sphere of action.

Every created thing in existence is characterised by the fact that it has *limitations*. Our own psycho-sensory organisation is founded upon a selection. What are the functions of the senses, but to respond to a determined series of vibrations and to no others? Thus the eye limits light and the ear sounds. In forming the contents of the mind the first step is, therefore, a selection, necessarily and materially limited. Nevertheless, the mind imposes still further limits on the selection possible to the senses, fashioning it upon the activity of internal choice. Thus attention is fixed upon determined objects and not upon all objects; and the volition *chooses* the actions, which are really to be performed from among a multitude of possible actions.

It is in like fashion that the lofty work of the intelligence is accomplished; by an analogous action of attention and internal will, it abstracts the dominant characteristics of things, and thus succeeds in associating their images and keeping them in the foreground of consciousness. It ceases to consider an immense amount of ballast which would render its context formless and confused. Every superior mind distinguishes the essential from the superfluous, rejecting the latter, and thus, it is enabled to achieve its characteristic, clear, delicate and vital activities. It is capable of extracting that which is useful to its creative life, and thus finds in the cosmos the means of salvation. Without this characteristic activity, the intelligence cannot construct itself; it would be like an attention that wanders from thing to thing without ever fixing upon anyone of them, and like a will that can never decide upon any definite action.

"It is possible to suppose", says James, "that a God could, without impairing his activity, simultaneously behold all the minutest portions of the world. But if our human attention should be thus dissipated, we should merely contemplate all things vacuously, without ever finding occasion to do any particular act."

It is one of the marvellous phenomena of life that it is impossible to realise anything without determining limits; that mysterious law which ordains that every living being has its "form" and "stature", unlike the minerals, which are indefinite in form and dimensions, is repeated in the psychical life. Its development, its auto-creation, is nothing but a determination ever more precise, a progressive "concentration"; it is thus that from the primitive chaos our internal characteristic form is gradually shaped and chiselled.

The capacity for forming a conception of a thing, for judging and reasoning, has always this foundation. When, after having noted the usual qualities of a column, we abstract the general truth that the column is a support, this synthetic idea is based upon a selected quality. Thus in the judgment we may pronounce: columns are cylindrical; we have abstracted one quality from among the many others we could have adduced, as, columns are cold, they are hard, they are a composition of carbonate of lime, etc. It is only the capacity for such a selection, which makes reasoning possible. When, for example, in the demonstration of the theorem of Pythagoras, children handle the various pieces of the metal insets, they should start from the point at which they become aware that a rectangle is equal to the rhomb, and a square is equal to the same rhomb. It is the perception of this truth which makes it possible to go on to the following reasoning: therefore the square and the rectangle are equal to each other. If it had not been possible to determine this attribute, the mind could not have arrived at any conclusion. The mind has succeeded in discovering an attribute common to two dissimilar figures; and it is this discovery, which may lead to a series of conclusions by means of which the theorem of Pythagoras will be finally demonstrated.

* * *

As in the case of will, decision presupposes a methodical exercise of the impulsive and inhibitory forces, only to be performed by the individual himself, until habits have been established; likewise in the case of the intelligence, the individual must exercise himself in his activities of association and selection, guided and aided by external means, until he has developed, by the definitive elimination of certain ideas and the choice of others, "mental habits" characteristic of the individual, characteristic of the "type". Because, underlying all the internal activities the mind can construct, there is, as the phenomena of attention show us, the individual tendency, the "nature".

There is, undoubtedly, a fundamental difference between understanding and learning the reasoning of others, and being able "to reason", between learning how an artist may see the external world according to his prevailing interest in colour, harmony and form, and actually seeing the external world about a fulcrum which sustains one's own aesthetical creation. In the mind of one who "learns the things of others" we may find, as in a sack of old clothes hanging over the shoulders of a hawker, solutions of the problems of Euclid, together with the images of Raphael's works, ideas of history and geography, and rules of style, huddled together with a like indifference and a like sensation of "weight". While, on the other hand, he who uses all these things for his own life, is like the person who is assisted in attaining his own welfare, his own relief, his own comfort by those same objects which are merely burdens when in the sack of the hawker. Such objects are, however, no longer huddled together without order and without purpose in a closed bag, but set out in the spacious rooms of a well-ordered house. The mind which constructs may contain a great deal more than that mind in which pieces of knowledge are heaped up as in the bag; and in that mind, as in the house, the objects are clearly divided one from another, harmoniously arranged, and distinctive in their uses.

Between "understanding" because another person seeks to impress upon us the explanation of a thing by speech, and "understanding" the thing of ourselves, there is an immeasurable distance; the two are comparable to the impression made in soft wax, which will subsequently be effaced and replaced by other impressions, and the form chiselled in the marble by an artist as his creation. He who understands of himself has an unforeseen impression; he feels that his consciousness has been liberated, and something luminous shines forth within him. Understanding, then, is not a matter of indifference; it is the beginning *of something;* sometimes it is the beginning of a life, which renews itself within us. Perhaps no emotion is more fruitful for man than the intellectual emotion. He who makes a discovery rich in results certainly enjoys the greatest of human felicities; but even he who merely "understands" gets a lofty enjoyment which will rise superior to and overcome the most acute suffering. Indeed, he who is oppressed by a misfortune, if he can be brought to differentiate his own case from that of another, or to see a reason for his affliction, experiences relief, and a "sense of salvation". Amidst the confused darkness in which he was plunged, a consoling ray of intellectual light has reached him. The difficult matter, indeed, is to find the way of escape in the hour of darkness. When we reflect that a dog may die of grief on the grave of his master, and that a mother can survive on the grave of her only son, we see at once that it is the light of *reason* which makes the difference between the two. The dog *cannot reason on the matter;* it may die because no light can penetrate the darkness of its intelligence to overcome the depression of its grief.

But the thought of a universal justice, the living memory of the lost one, which remains to us, saves the human being. And by degrees, not forgetfulness, which alone can save the animal, but the connection, which the intelligence establishes with the universe, restores calm to the suffering soul. Such comfort could never be derived from the dry lesson of a professor, from memorizing the theory of a savant who is not in sympathy with the state of our soul. When we say, "to give ourselves a reason", "to derive strength from a principle", we imply that the ever-inquiring intelligence should be left at liberty to perform its work of reconstruction and salvation.

Now if intelligence in "comprehending" may actually prove our salvation when in danger of death, what a source of enjoyment it should prove to man!

When we talk of "the opening of the mind", we mean a creative phenomenon, which is not the weak result of an impression violently made from without. The opening of the mind is the *active comprehension* which accompanies great emotions, and which is therefore felt as a spiritual event.

I once knew a motherless girl, who was so much depressed by the arid teaching of her school, that she had become almost incapable of study and even of understanding the things which were taught her. Her life of solitude, lacking in natural affection, was a further aggravation of her mental fatigue. Her father decided that she should live for a year or two in the open country like a little savage; he then brought her back to town, and placed her under the private direction of a number of "professors". The girl studied and learned, but remained passive and weary. Every now and then her father would say: "Is your mind opening again?" and the girl always replied: "I do not know. What do you mean?" Owing to a curious coincidence in my life, this girl was confided to my sole care; and it was thus that I, when I was still a medical student, made my first pedagogic experiment upon which I cannot linger now, though it would be worthy of interest. One day we were together, and when she was at work on organic chemistry she broke off, and looking at me with beaming eyes, said: "Here it is now! I *do* understand!" She then got up and went away, calling out aloud: "Father, father! My mind has opened!" I not then knowing the girl's history, was astonished and agitated. She had taken her father's hand, and was saying: "Now I can tell you, yes, yes; I did not know what it meant before; my mind has opened." The joy of father and daughter and their union at that moment made me think of the joys and well-springs of life which we destroy by enslaving the intelligence.

Indeed, every intellectual conquest is a well-spring of joy to our free children. This is the "pleasure" to which they are now most susceptible, and which makes them scorn lower pleasures; it is after having tasted of this that our little ones despise sweetmeats, toys, and vanities.

It is this which makes them sublime to the eyes of those who contemplate them.

Their pleasure is that lofty pleasure which distinguishes man from the brute, and can save us even from the desolation of grief and darkness.

When our method is reproached for seeking to promote the "pleasure" of the child, and that this is immoral, it is the child and not the method which is insulted. For the essence of this reproach is the calumny against the child, who is considered by all as on a level with the beasts, and whose "pleasure" is supposed to lie solely in gluttony and idleness, and worse. But none of these could keep the child's "pleasure" alive for hours and days and years. It is only when he has laid hold on "humane pleasure" that he persists in it, and lives with a joy which is comparable to that of the young girl who ran to her father to proclaim the end of the darkness in which she had languished for years.

May it not perhaps be that those "crises", which are today but the intellectual illuminations of genius when it discovers a truth, represent a natural phenomenon of psychical life? May not the manifestation of the genius be but the manifestation of a "vigorous life", saved from perils by its exceptional individuality, and therefore itself alone capable of revealing the true nature of man? His type would then be the common one, and all men, in a greater or less degree, would seem to be of the same "species". The paths the child follows in the active "construction" of his individuality are indeed identical with those followed by the genius. His characteristics are absorbed attention, a profound concentration, which isolates him from all the stimuli of his environment, and corresponds in intensity and duration to the development of spiritual activities. As in genius, this concentration is not without results, but is the source of intellectual crises, of rapid internal developments, and above all, of an "external activity" which expresses itself in work.

We may say, then, that the genius is the man who has burst his bonds asunder, who has maintained his liberty, and who has upheld before the eyes of the multitude the standard of the humanity conquered by him.

Nearly all the manifestations of those men who liberated themselves from the external bondage of their times are to be noted in our children. Such, for instance, is that sublime "spiritual obedience", at present still unknown to the majority of mankind, with the exception of monks, who, however, often recognise it only in theory, and contemplate it only in the examples given by the saints; such again are those means necessary to the construction of a strong internal life which form part of the preparation for the cloistered life in the methodical "meditations" of those about to enter upon it. No persons, with the exception of monks, practise meditation. We can hardly distinguish meditation from methods for "learning" intellectually. We know, for example, that to read a great

number of books consecutively dissipates our powers and our capacity
for thought; and that to learn a piece of poetry by heart means to repeat
it until it is engraven on our minds: and that all this is not "meditation".

He who commits a verse of Dante to memory and he who meditates
upon a verse of the gospel, performs a totally different task. The canto will "adorn" the mind on which it is impressed for a certain time,
without leaving any lasting trace upon it. The verse which has been the
subject of meditation will have a transforming and edifying effect. He
who meditates clears his mind as far as possible of every other image,
and tries to concentrate upon the subject of meditation in such a manner
that all the internal activities will be polarised thereby: or, as the monks
say, "all the powers of the mind".

The expected result of the meditation is "an internal fruit of strength";
the soul is strengthened and unified, it becomes active; it can then act
upon the seed around which it has concentrated and cause it to become
fruitful.

Now the method chosen by our children in following their natural
development is "meditation", for in no other way would they be led to
linger so long over each individual task, and so to derive a gradual internal maturation therefrom. The aim of the children who persevere in
their work with an object is certainly not to "learn"; they are drawn to it
by the needs of their inner life, which must be organised and developed
by its means. In this manner they imitate and carry on their "growth".
This is the habit by which they gradually co-ordinate and enrich their
intelligence. As they meditate, they enter upon that path of progress,
which will continue without end.

It is after an exercise of meditation on the objects that our children
become capable of enjoying "the silence exercise"; and then, having
been rendered delicately susceptible to impressions, they try to make no
noise when they move, to refrain from awkward actions, because they
are enjoying the fruit of the "concentration" of the spirit.

It is thus that their personality is unified and strengthened. The exercise, which serves as the means to this end is designed gradually to
perfect the accuracy with which they perceive the external world, observing, reasoning and correcting the errors of the senses in a sustained and
spontaneous activity. It is they who act, they who choose the objects,

they who persevere in their work, they who seek to win from their environment the possibility of concentrating their minds upon it. Each one of them moves in obedience to the motor power within him. They are not disturbed by a teacher, by a being obviously superior to themselves, who intimidates the shrinking poverty of those who are beginning life by her lofty intellectual riches, who darkens rather than illuminates, who wearies rather than refreshes; but they live in peace with her who, almost a priestess, is yet a servant. As in some ideal convent, humility, simplicity and work make up the environment where he who meditates will some day feel within himself the clearness of vision, the intuition, almost the sensibility, which make one ready to receive the truth.

To a different end, but by the same road, amidst the silence, the simplicity and the humility of the monastery, the spirit prepares itself to receive the faith at the outset of life.

Many years ago, when I first received the impression that our children revealed general principles of life which in practice we are only privileged to encounter among the intellectual and spiritual *elite* of society; and that for this reason they were at the same time the revealers of a form of unconscious oppression which weighed down humanity, deforming the inner life, I spoke at length upon the matter to an intellectual lady, who was much interested in my "theories", and very anxious that I should make them the subject of an elaborate philosophical treatise; but she could not bring herself to accept the idea that it was a question of an experimental process. When I spoke of the children, she showed some impatience: "Oh, yes, I quite understand all about these children; in intelligence they are so many geniuses, and in goodness so many angels." But when, after some persuasion, I succeeded in making her come and *see* for herself, she took my hands and looked earnestly in my face: "Have you never thought," she asked, "that you might die at any moment . . . Write at once, anyhow, in all haste, as you would write a will, a simple description of the facts, that you may not carry away this secret with you to the grave." Nevertheless, I was in excellent health.

★ ★ ★

If we examine the mental labours of men of genius to whom we owe discoveries which have opened new paths to thought, and have given us new sources of well-being and social progress, we shall have to admit that in themselves they cannot be described as extraordinary processes inaccessible to mediocrity. "Genius coincides with the possession in a very high degree of the power of association by similarity. This is the essential quality of genius", says Bain. Even at the "central point" of discovery, it is only by accurate observation and a very simple process of reasoning, of which most persons would consider themselves capable, that the discovery is made. At most it is due to a marshalling of "evidences" which, however, passed unnoticed by all but the discoverer.

We may say that genius has the faculty of isolating a fact in the consciousness, and of so distinguishing it from all others that it is as if a single ray of light should fall upon a diamond in a dark room. This single idea, then, causes a complete revolution in the consciousness, and is capable of constructing something infinitely great and precious for all humanity.

But it is the intense significance of ordinary things, and not the abnormal, which is the main factor; it is the isolation in a homogeneous field, not the intrinsic value of the thing, which determines the marvellous phenomenon. Perhaps within countless thousands of chaotic perceptions the gem had existed, stored up amidst a multitude of useless and cumbrous objects, and had never succeeded in arresting attention; meanwhile inertia continued to allow new objects to penetrate continually within the distended and impotent walls. After a discovery, many will perceive that they themselves held the same truth within them; but in this case it is not the truth itself that has value, but the man who is capable of appreciating it and bringing it into relation with action.

But very often it is not the case that the newly discovered truth already exists in the chaos of obscure consciousness; and then the new light, simple though it be, can find no way by which to penetrate into the mind.

It is rejected as something strange and fallacious; and a certain lapse of time is necessary, a certain co-ordination of the intelligence, to enable the "novelty" to enter. Yet some day it will be considered clear as crystal. It was not the "nature" of man which shrank from it, but his "errors". These errors not only make man incapable of production, but are in themselves hostile to receptivity. Thus it often happens that a sort of unconscious ingratitude persecutes the pioneers of salvation, which is the fruit of spiritual darkness.

What was the argument of Christopher Columbus? He thought: "If the earth is really round, he who starts from a certain point and advances steadily, will return to the point of departure." This was the *sum* of the intellectual work which enriched mankind with a new world.

That a great continent should have lain in the track of Columbus, and that he should have encountered this and not death, was the destiny due to the chance of environment. The environment sometimes rewards "small reasonings" of this kind in a surprising manner.

It was certainly not a great labour of human intelligence which brought about these great results; it was the triumph of this idea over the whole consciousness, and the heroic courage of the man which gave it its value. The great difficulty for the man who had conceived the idea, was to persevere until he could persuade others to help him in his enterprise, to give him ships and followers. It was the *faith* and not the *idea* of Columbus which triumphed.

That simple and logical reasoning kindled within him something infinitely more precious than intelligence, and enabled a single man of humble origin, and almost uneducated, to present a world to a queen.

We are told that Alessandro Volta's wife was ill with fever, and that he, in accordance with the practice of his day, was preparing the usual febrifuge, a broth of skinned frogs; it was a rainy day, and when he hung up the dead frogs on the iron bar of the window, he noticed that their legs contracted. "If dead muscles contract, it must mean that some external force has penetrated them." This was the simple argument of the "genius", the "great discoverer". And seeking this force, Volta, by means of his batteries was able to wrest from the earth electricity, which is, literally as well as figuratively, the "gleam" of an immense progress. Laying due weight upon a little fact, such as that of a dead being having moved, considering it soberly without any fanciful additions, and fixing the mind upon the resulting problem: Why does it move? – such was the lengthy process by which one of the greatest conquests of civilisation was achieved.

Akin to this was Galileo's discovery, when, standing in Pisa Cathedral, he watched the oscillations of a hanging lamp. He observed that the oscillations were all completed in the same space of time, and the isochronism of the pendulum was the beginning of the measurement of time for all men, and of the measurement of worlds for the astronomer.

How simple, too, is the story of Newton, who felt an apple fall upon him as he lay under a tree, and thought to himself: "Why did that apple fall?" Such was the simple origin of the theory of the gravity of bodies, and that of universal gravitation.

When we study the life of Papin,[26] we marvel at the culture, which placed him on a level with the most learned men of his times: as physician, physiologist and mathematician, he was distinguished and honoured by the universities of England and Germany. Nevertheless, what gave him his value to humanity, and hence his greatness, was the fact that this attention had been arrested by the sight of the lid of a saucepan of boiling water raised by the steam. "Steam is a force which could lift a piston as it lifts the cover of a saucepan, and become the motor power of a machine." Papin's famous saucepan is a kind of magic wand in the history of mankind, which thenceforth began to work and travel without fatigue. How wonderful are such stories of great discoveries arising from humble beginnings, and working miracles throughout the world!

These, in their origins, resemble those living creatures, born of two imperceptible microscopic cells, the fusion of which inevitably tends to the creation of complex lives. To perceive exactly and to connect the things perceived logically is the work of the highest intelligence. But this work is characterised by a peculiar power of attention, which causes the mind to dwell upon a subject in a species of meditation, the characteristic mark of genius; the outcome is an internal life rich in activities, just as the germinative cells are the fruit of internal existences. It would seem that such mentalities are distinguished from those of the ordinary type, not by their form, but by their "force". It is the vigorous life from which those two small intellectual sparks arise, which makes them so marvellous. If they had not sprung from strong, independent personalities, capable of persistent effort and heroic self-sacrifice, those little intellectual works would have remained as things inert and negligible. Hence all that strengthens the spiritual man may lead him in the footsteps of the genius.

---

26 Denis Papin (1647 – 1712) pioneer in the field of steam power.

Thus, as regards the intelligence in itself, the work it has to accomplish is a small matter, but it is clearly defined, and stripped of superfluous complications. Simplicity is the guide to discovery; simplicity which, like truth, should be naked. Very little is necessary; but this little must constitute a powerful unity; the rest is vanity.

And the greater this vanity, that is to say, the futile encumbrance of the mind, the more will the light of the spirit be darkened and its forces dissipated, making it difficult or impossible not only to reason and act, but even to perceive reality, to see.

★ ★ ★

It would be interesting to make a rapid survey of those collective individual errors by which the progress of a new discovery of a simple kind, offering relief to suffering humanity, has been impeded; errors which have even caused persistent denial of the existence of obvious facts, merely because these were not generally known.

Let us consider for a moment the discovery of the cause of malaria. This discovery, due to the Englishman Ross, in connection with birds, and to the Italian Grassi, in connection with man, consists in having found out that the plasmodium of malaria, which produces the malady, is inoculated in man and in the various animals subject to it by a special kind of mosquito. Let us inquire what was the state of science prior to this discovery. In 1880 Laveran[27] had described an animal microorganism, which preyed upon the red corpuscles of the blood producing an attack of fever with the cycle of its existence. Subsequent studies confirmed and elucidated this fact, and the *Plasmodium malariae* became a matter of common knowledge. It was known that animal micro-organisms unlike vegetable micro-organisms, after a cycle of life in which reproduction takes place by scission – that is, by subdivision of a single body into several other bodies equal to the first – give place to *sexual forms*, masculine and feminine, which are separate, and incapable of scission, but are designed for *fusion into one another*, after which the organism recommences its cycle of scissions until it again reaches the sexual forms.

---

27 Charles Louis Alphonse Lavaran (1845 – 1922) discovered that a parasite was the cause of malaria.

Laveran had found that in the blood of sufferers who recover spontaneously from malarial fever there are a great number of corpuscles which have no longer the rounded forms of the plasmodia, but are crescent-shaped and rayed. He took these to be transformations of the plasmodia, "modified in form" and "incapable of producing disease", and pronounced them to be "degenerate" organisms, almost as if they had been deformed and exhausted by the "excess of work" they had previously performed. These organisms were described as "Laveran's degenerative forms". After the discovery of the transmission of malaria in 1900, Laveran's "degenerative forms" were recognised as the sexual individuals of the reproductive cycle: individuals which were incapable of conjugation in the blood of man, and could only produce new organisms in the body of the mosquito. We may well wonder: Why did not Laveran simply recognise those sexual forms, and why did he not seek for the period of conjugation in the plasmodia, which were animal micro-organisms? If he had borne in mind the complete cycle of the protozoa, he would have recognised them. But evidently Morel's theories of the degeneration of man had made a much livelier impression on his imagination; and his leap from these remote theories to his interpretation of the plasmodia seemed an achievement of "genius". It may be said that this "feat of genius", this visionary generalisation, prevented Laveran from seeing the truth. A form of *arrogance* and *levity* is apparent in such errors.

Moreover, we are astonished by something still more serious: how came it that hundreds and thousands of students throughout the world accepted Laveran's error with their eyes shut, that not one among so many took into consideration on his own account the cycle of the protozoa, and that not one was sufficiently independent to set about studying the phenomenon for himself? What is this mental form of inertia? and why does it produce itself in man? All these disciples, heedless of the problem presented to their minds by the sexual form of the plasmodium, left it alone although it had not yet been solved, and certainly had no intuition of the fame, the progress in science, and the benefit to humanity which would have been the outcome, had the problem constituted an obstacle which had arrested their attention, saying: "Solve me".

They passed on indifferently, commending Laveran's "effort of genius", repeating with him: They are degenerate forms. A futile effort, which only increased a crowd of persons who had resigned their own individuality all unconsciously.

Another biological acquisition was the assurance that the circulatory system of the blood is a closed system of vessels, and that the enclosing epithelium is not permeable by non-incisive solid bodies such as vegetable microbes, and still less by rounded protozoa, which are much larger than microbes and soft in substance. This wellknown and clearly demonstrated fact ought to have suggested a problem to the minds of students: How do the protozoa of malaria enter the circulatory current of the blood? But ever since the days of Hippocrates, Pliny, Celsius and Galen it had been held that this fever was caused by the "poisonous atmosphere" of marsh lands, the bad air of the morning and the evening, so much so that even a few years before the discovery of the real cause of malaria, eucalyptus trees were planted in the belief that they would filter and disinfect the air. How was it that no one asked himself how it was possible that the plasmodia could enter the *current of the blood* from the *air*? What was the species of torpor which took possession of the intelligence of persons who had specialised in intellectual work? Here was a colossal *sum* of intelligence, without any individuality.

Until Ross[28] discovered that birds are inoculated with malaria by a particular kind of mosquito.

And then, behold! we have at last the fundamental argument from which the knowledge of the truth sprang forth: "If birds are inoculated with malaria by mosquitoes, then the same thing must happen to man."

A simple argument, which sped like an arrow to the final discovery. Nothing seemed more *incredible* than the fact that in the malarial regions good air and fertile soil were to be found, that it was possible to breathe that air morning and evening and remain in perfect health, so long as one was not bitten by mosquitoes, and that the innumerable peasants who were wasted by malarial anaemia would be saved and restored if they protected themselves by mosquito-netting. But after the first stupefaction, when men were convinced of the facts, there was an outcry from

---

28 Ronald Ross (1857 – 1932) was a physician, who worked in the British Army.

all the intelligent: How was it possible that we did not find it out before? Was not the cycle of the protozoa a wellknown fact? Did not everyone declare that the system of circulation was closed and impervious to micro-organisms? Was it not natural to think that only a blood-sucking insect could inoculate it?

How many students *felt* that glory had passed close to them, and were amazed and saddened by the knowledge, like the disciples of Emmaus, who said to each other when the Master disappeared before they recognised Him: "Did not our hearts burn within us when He spoke and expounded the Scriptures to us?"

Many must have thought: We worked so laboriously only to encumber our minds, and yet but one thing was needful: we should have been humble and simple, but independent. Instead, we filled our souls with darkness, and the ray that would have made us see, could not penetrate to us.

Let us take some grosser errors. As far back as the days of the Greek civilisation it was known empirically that "stones can fall from the sky". Falls of aerolites are recorded in the most ancient Chinese chronicles. In the Middle Ages and in modern times intimations of the fall of aerolites have increased in frequency. Remarkable facts are indeed recorded in history in connection with similar phenomena: the meteorite which fell in 1492 served the Emperor Maximilian I of Germany as a pretext to excite Christendom to a war against the Turks. Nevertheless, men of science did not admit the phenomenon until the eighteenth century. One of the largest meteorites on record was that which fell near Agram[29] in 1751; it weighed about forty kilogrammes, and was deposited and catalogued in the court mineralogical museum at Vienna. This is what Stutz, a German savant, had to say on the subject in 1790: "Those ignorant of natural history may believe that iron has fallen from the sky, and even educated men in Germany may have believed this in 1751, taking into account the universal ignorance then prevalent as to natural history and physics; but in our times it would be unpardonable to admit even the plausibility of such fables."

In the same year 1790, an aerolite weighing ten kilogram fell in Gascony. It was observed by a large number of persons, and an official

---

29 Today Agram is known as Hraschina near Zagreb in Croatia.

report, signed by three hundred witnesses, was sent to the Academy of Paris. The reply was that "it had been very amusing to receive a legal document dealing with such an absurdity".[30]

When, a few years later, Chladni of Wittenberg, the founder of scientific acoustics, began to admit the phenomenon and to believe in the existence of aerolites, he was stigmatised as "a man who was ignorant of every law and who did not consider the damage he was doing in the moral world"; and one savant declared that "if he had himself seen iron fall from the sky at his own feet, he would not have believed it."

This was incredulity greater than that of St. Thomas, who said: "Unless I can touch I will not believe." Here were pieces of iron weighing ten and forty kilogrammes, which could be touched, but the savant said: "Even if I touch them, I will not believe."

It is, therefore, not enough to *see in order to believe*; we must *believe in order to see*. It is faith which leads to sight, not sight which produces faith. When the blind man in the gospel uttered the anxious cry: "Make me to see", he asked for "faith", because he knew that it is possible to have eyes and not to see.

The fact of being insensible to evidence is little considered in psychology, much less is it taken into account in pedagogic laws. And yet many similar facts, though of an inferior psychological order, are notorious, as for instance, that stimuli will appeal in vain to the senses if the internal co-operation of attention be lacking. A thousand experiences of this kind enter in to make up the sum of common knowledge. It is not enough that an object should be before our eyes to make us see it; it is necessary that we should fix our attention upon it; an internal process, preparing us to receive the impression of the stimulus, is essential.

In a loftier and purely spiritual sphere something of the same kind takes place: an idea cannot enter triumphantly into the consciousness, if it is not accompanied by a preparation of faith. Lacking this, it may knock violently and brutally, with clamorous insistence, without being able to penetrate. It is necessary that the field of consciousness should

---

30 But a great physicist, unable to share this *amusement,* wrote: "It is sad to see a municipality giving credence to the babble of the vulgar in a protocol, and to see authentic testimonies to an occurrence which is obviously impossible."

be not only free, but "expectant". He who is bewildered by a chaos of ideas cannot accept a truth which arrives unexpectedly in the unprepared field.

This fact is not only analogous to other psychical facts of less importance, such as that of sensory perception in relation to attention; it is also analogous to the spiritual facts which are so well known in the field of religion. In vain will a fact, however remarkable, be explained or even *demonstrated* where there is no *faith*; it is not evidence but faith which opens the mind to truth. The very senses are useless as a medium if the internal activity does not open the doors to receive it. When the most striking miracles of Christ are related in the gospel, the narrative always concludes with: "And *many* of those who saw, believed". The parable of the invitation to the feast, to which those who were absorbed in their own affairs could not respond, seems to indicate a fact similar to this intellectual fact, that the "preoccupations" of complicated pre-existing ideas prevent the new and obvious truth that presents itself, from entering in. It is for this reason that we need the Precursor to make ready for the Messiah. And for this reason the Messiah, and also new ideas, are readily received by the "simple", by those who are not "laden with heavy preoccupations", but have preserved the natural characteristics of the spirit: to be pure and always "expectant".

When in 1628 Harvey [31] discovered the circulation of the blood, physiology was almost unknown, and medicine was in the full tide of empiricism. It is well known that the Faculty of Medicine of Paris refused to believe in circulation, in *spite of experiments,* and that it persecuted and calumniated Harvey. "That which pleases me in my son," said Diafoirus, "and in which he follows my example, is, that he remains faithful to the opinions of our ancient teachers, and that he has always refused either to *understand* or to *listen* to the arguments and experiments of the pretended discoveries of our century, especially as regards the circulation of the blood." [32]

---

31 William Harvey (1578 – 1657) was a British biologist and physician.

32 Thomas Diafoirus is a doctor from the play *Le Maladie Imaginaire* by Molière. He is portrayed as a pedantic man who loves to use elaborate scientific terminology but is not overly concerned with his patients' actual health.

⋆ ⋆ ⋆

The history of the discovery of germinative foliations in the embryonic development of vertebrates forms one of the most impressive of human documents. In 1700 the theory of *preformation* was vigorously upheld amongst the many ideas relating to generation: that is to say, it was believed that the germs contained little organisms completely formed which would eventually unfold and increase the parts of infinitesimal dimensions which were packed one within the other. This theory applied to every living creature, animal, vegetable and human. It had led, by its own logical development, to the more far-reaching theory of "mutual inclusion" – that is, the doctrine that, as all living organisms are *preformed*, they must of necessity all have existed from the Creation, the one included, or wrapped up, in the other. All humanity must have lain in the ovaries of Eve. When in 1690 Van Leeuwenhoek [33] discovered spermatozoa by the aid of the microscope, the idea was evolved that each male cell contained a complete microscopic man, the *homunculus*; and then it was announced that not Eve, but Adam had contained all humanity within himself. Hence the two contradictory theories which in the eighteenth century kept their adherents sharply divided, the theories of the ovulists and those of the animalculists, and the dispute seemed to offer little hope of a possible decision. The names of famous scientists and philosophers were associated with these dissensions; those, for instance, of Spallanzani and of Leibnitz, who applied the principles of generation even to the soul. "Thus I should think," said Leibnitz, "that the souls which will one day become human souls, were present in the germ; that they have always existed as organised bodies in their progenitors from Adam onwards – that is, from the beginning of things."[34]

Haller, an ovulist who had great authority as a physiologist, in a famous work, *Elementa physiologiae* upheld the principle vigorously: "*Nulla est epigenesis. Nulla in corpore animale pars ante aliam facia est et omnes simul creatae existunt*" (nothing is created anew, no part of the human body is made before any other part, all are created at the same time).

---

33 Antoni van Leeuwenhoek (1632 – 1723) was a Dutch scientist, who – amoung other things – worked in the field of microbiology.
34 From Haeckel's "Anthropogenie".

Making a calculation based on Biblical cosmogony of the number of human beings who were packed in the ovaries of Eve, he reckons them at two hundred thousand millions. Such was the state of thought when in 1759 K. F. Wolff [35] published some of his studies in the work *Theoria generationis*, where he maintained, on the strength of experiments and microscopic observations made on the embryos of fowls, that new organisms are not pre-formed, but that they create themselves entirely, starting from nothing – that is, from a microscopic cell, simple as are all primitive cells. He described the simple process by which the real evolution of individuals is brought about: from a single cell, by division, two, and then four and then eight, are formed, and so on. And the cells thus germinated divide themselves into two or three tiny folds or "primitive folioles" from which all the organs are evolved, beginning with the alimentary canal. "This assertion," says Wolff, "is not a fanciful theory; it is description of facts collected by means of the most trustworthy observations."

All the scientists of his day knew and made use of the microscope; all might have taken an egg, that is the embryo of a fowl, as a subject for observation; they were not indifferent to the problem of individual genesis, but in their case it had merely excited the most complex efforts of the imagination, and had divided them into factions, as adversaries in a battle of thought. Could anyone of them attempt to experiment and observe save at the risk of destroying himself together with his adversaries, as Samson destroyed himself with the Philistines? The possibility that there might be some truth in what had been seen and described, and that it might recur, should indeed have induced someone to venture upon a road which, if it proved to be the right one, would have been a glorious path to a future of discoveries and distinctions. But no. A dense fog obscured all minds, and the dazzling truth could not pierce it; thus all progress in embryology was precluded.

Fifty years had passed, and Wolff, poor and persecuted, had died at Petrograd, an exile from his native land, when Pander and Ernest von Baer grappled anew with the theory of "blastodermic foliation". Then the scientific world *perceived* the truth and accepted the evidence, inaugurating

---

35 Caspar Friedrich Wolff was a German physician.

those studies in embryology which shed so much lustre on the nineteenth century.

Why was it necessary that fifty years should elapse before men could see what was evident? What had happened in these fifty years? The work of Wolff, dead and forgotten, can have had no influence whatever. The fact was merely that men saw *subsequently* what it had been previously *impossible for them to see*. A kind of internal maturity must have come about in them, by virtue of which their spiritual eyes were opened and they saw. When *those eyes were closed*, evidence was useless. Fifty years earlier a direct attack would have spent itself on insuperable obstacles; but with the lapse of time the subject presented itself and was simply and universally accepted, not only without a struggle, but without any excitement.

This fact might be arguable in relation to the internal maturation of the masses; but it is beyond question in its relation to the individual. When an obvious truth cannot be seen, we must retire and leave the individual to mature. A struggle "to bring about perception of evidence" would be bitter and exhausting. But when maturity comes, we shall find the seer filled with enthusiasm and bearing fruit like the vines of the Land of Promise.

When in 1859 Charles Darwin expounded the theory of evolution in his book, *The Origin of Species*, he recognised the great influence it had had upon the thought of his day, for he wrote in his notebook: "My theory will lead to a philosophy." His conception of the struggle for life and of the natural selection of characteristics, so widely adopted by the thinkers of this day, popularised the principles of Lamarck as to the casual formation of new characteristics in a species by adaptation to environment; Darwin's conception carried these principles along with it – and almost fused them in its own content. These principles, excluding both creation and its finalities, implicitly denied the immortality of the soul. The effect of such a revolution may be imagined: for many centuries the soul had been the *object of life*, and when the fundamental faith of existence was shaken, the life of the conscience itself was convulsed. It may be supposed that there was an anxious search for contradictions in the destructive theory, if on no other grounds than that of the instinct to preserve ancient beliefs, which lies deeply rooted in the human race.

But let us take into consideration the two revolutionary principles which so greatly impressed and fired the consciousness of the university students of several generations. One principle was: "There can be no function without an organ." The other principle which created much enthusiasm among studious youths was: "The function creates the organ." What! There is no function without an organ, nor can the function even *exist without* the organ; and yet, on the other hand, the function without the organ can exist so vigorously as to *create!* No such glaring and tangible contradiction had ever existed in any theory.

And it cannot be said that Darwinism and the principles of Lamarck were hastily studied and confused in a varied series of philosophical theories, for Darwinism had isolated itself as a victorious idea which drives out all other ideas, as the light of day disperses the darkness of night. And students dwelt upon it, anxious to construct a new morality and a new conscience; therefore, these two principles were not studied coldly and languidly. Moreover, they *penetrated together* into the consciousness and excited enthusiasm *each on its own account*; on such a triumphant contradiction it was proposed to destroy a world and create another.

The final conclusion of thought then was this: "We are mere beasts, there is no substantial difference between the animals and ourselves; we are apes, but our more remote ancestors were earthworms." With what ardour did professors from their chairs analyse the psychology of men to prove that! Try as we may, we can find nothing in ourselves which we do not share with animals and with what enthusiasm did their pupils applaud them! When professors of psychiatry removed the brains of pigeons and monkeys by vivisection, and, after curing the creatures exhibited them at international psychological congresses, devoting the most sincere attention to the study of their psychical reactions, observing the attitudes of their bodies, their activity of perception, and similar things – all really believed that an animal without a brain could throw light upon the psychology of man!

When we think that this was the epoch of *positivism* – that is to say, of those who could not believe without touching, we are profoundly impressed by this reflection: The intelligence then is threatened by dangers like the spirit. It may be obscured, it may contain a contradiction, and "error", without perceiving it, and as a result of a single unnoticed error it may rush into a species of delirium, a mortal aberration. Like the spirit, it has its way of salvation and it *needs to be sustained* lest it should perish.

The support it requires is *not that of the senses*. Like the spirit, it needs a continual purification which, like the fish of Tobias, heals the eyes of their blindness. That "self-care" which the hygiene of today prescribes for the body, and which makes us spend so much time even on cleaning and polishing our nails, should be extended to the inner man that this may preserve its health and its integrity.

This should be the object of "the education of the intelligence". To educate the intelligence is to save it from its peculiar perils of disease and death: it is to "purge it of its offences". We shall not educate the intelligence if we weary it by making it learn things. This is patent in these days of ours when the victims of nervous disorders and lunacy abound, and when, even among those who are considered healthy, the material consequences of madness may explode threatening the whole of humanity with ruin.

Our care of the child should be governed, not by the desire "to make him learn things", but by the endeavour always to keep burning within him that light which is called the intelligence. If to this end we must consecrate ourselves as did the vestals of old, it will be a work worthy of so great a result.

9
Imagination

The creative imagination of science is based upon truth

If a century ago someone had told the men who were travelling in stage-coaches and using oil-lamps that some day New York would blaze with light at midnight; that men would ask for succour in mid-ocean and that their message would be understood on land; that their flight in the air would surpass that of the eagle – our good forefathers would have smiled incredulously. Their imaginations would never have been able to conceive these things. To them, modern men would have seemed almost like men of another species.

This is because the imagination of modern men is based upon the positive researches of science, whereas the men of past ages allowed their minds to wander in the world of unreality.

This single fact has changed the face of the world.

When man loses himself in mere speculations, his environment will remain unchanged, but when imagination starts from contact with reality, thought begins to construct works by means of which the external world becomes transformed; almost as if the thought of man had assumed a marvellous power: the power to create.

It is thus we imagine the thought of God; all creation is the divine thought, which has the property of realizing itself. God thought: and behold! light, the order of creation, living things, appeared.

Modern man, by the method of positive science, seems to have found the secret trace of thought which puts him in the divine path, which gives him the revelation of his true nature, as indicated in the words of Scripture: "Let us make man in our image and likeness."

Thus human intelligence said: "Let there be light" – and there was a magic effulgence which comes and goes at a touch. "Let man fly in the air and rise far above all the birds of creation" – and it was so. "Let the voices of shipwrecked mariners travel mysteriously and without sound and reach distant places" – and it was so. "Let things multiply, plants in their varieties, so that all men may have the means of life more abundantly" – and it was so.

The imagination has created when it has started from creation: that is when it has first taken in existing truth. Only then has it accomplished marvellous things.

Like the tiny bird which hid under the wing of an eagle about to soar and when it had been thus borne up to an immense height, disengaged itself from the eagle and began to fly still higher by its own efforts – so too is man, who at first holds fast to Nature, attaches himself to her by means of the most severe speculations, and with her soars aloft in search of truth; then he disengages himself from her and his imagination creates over and above Nature herself. In this manner man seems to reflect divine attributes; the marvellous and miraculous issue from him in such grandiose form that the man of the past, the wren without the eagle, could not even have conceived it.

Original sin is an allegory of this eternal story, of the man *who wished to act for himself,* to substitute himself for God, to emancipate himself from Him and to create. Whereupon he fell into impotence, slavery and misery.

The mind that works by itself, independently of truth, works in a void. Its creative power is a *means* for working upon *reality.* But if it confuses the means with the end, it is lost.

This kind of *sin* of the intelligence, so akin to original sin, the sin of confounding the means with the end, recurs in every form as a "force of inertia" which pervades the psychical life. Thus man confounds the means, which is simpler, easier and more comprehensible, with the end in many of his functions. Thus, for example, when nutrition is made a pretext for gluttony, and the appetite an end in itself, the body, instead of renewing itself in health and purity, is poisoned. Man is guilty of a like sin against the intelligence when he employs his creative activity of thought for its own sake, without basing it upon truth; by so doing he creates an unreal world, full of error and destroys the possibility of creating in reality, like a god, producing external works.

Thus positive science represents to us the "redemption" of thought; its purification from original sin, a return to the *natural laws* of psychical energy. Scientists are like those men of the Bible story who, after Israel had come out of Egypt, were permitted to explore the Land of Promise, and who came back with such a huge cluster of grapes that it took two men to carry it and the people saw it with amazement.

So have the scientists of today penetrated into the Promised Land of truth, where lies the secret which enables man to scrutinise Nature; and they have come out therefrom bearing marvellous fruits for all men to see. The secret is a simple one: it consists of an exact method based on observation, prudence and patience. All men might be allowed to share the secret, for indeed such virtues correspond to the "occult", the intimate needs of their spiritual life.

It may be asked: Why should only explorers enter in, while the people remain outside, passively enjoying the fruits of their labours?

Is it because the method of positive science, which puts man in the way of knowing the truth, of gathering up realities – and hence of building up his own imagination thereupon – is a monopoly, the privilege of the chosen few?

That method which denotes the redemption of the intelligence ought to be the method by which all new humanity is moulded – the formative method of the new generation.

In the Bible story the explorers were the messengers, and the witnesses to the existence of the Promised Land, into which all the people were to enter. And so it is here: all men should come under the influence of the scientific method; and every child should be able to experiment at first hand, to observe and to put himself in contact with reality. Thus the flights of the imagination will start from a higher plane henceforth, and the intelligence will be directed into its natural channels of creation.

Truth is also the basis of artistic imagination

The work of the intelligence is not limited to the exact observation and the simple logical reasoning upon which great scientific discoveries may be founded. There is a more exalted work, confronting which none can say, as in the presence of certain scientific discoveries: "I might also have been able to do this."

Dante, Milton, Goethe, Raphael, Wagner, are mighty mysteries, miracles of intelligence which cannot be classed with the simple processes of observation and reasoning. Nevertheless every man has his share of artistic imagination, he has the instinct to create the beautiful with his mind; and from this instinct duly developed come all the vast treasures of art, scattered almost like crumbs of gold wherever there was an intensity of civil life, wherever the intelligence had time to mature in peace. In every province which has preserved traces of ancient peoples we find local artistic types of work, of furniture, of poetic songs and popular music. This multiform creation of the inner man, then, enfolds him and protects his spirit in its intellectual needs, just as the iridescent shell encloses the mollusc.

In addition to the work of observing material reality, there is a creative work which lifts man up from earth and transports him into a higher world which every soul may attain within its individual limits.

Yet no one can say that man *creates* artistic products out of nothing. What is called *creation is* in reality a composition, a construction raised upon a *primitive material* of the mind, which must be collected from the environment by means of the senses. This is the general principle summed up in the ancient axiom: *Nihil est in intellectu quod prius non fuerit in sensa* (There is nothing in the intellect which was not first in the senses). We are unable to "imagine" things, which do not actually present themselves to our senses; even language would be lacking to us to explain things lying beyond those customary limits by which our consciousness is bounded. The imagination of Michelangelo was unable to picture God otherwise than as a venerable old man with a white beard. When we try to imagine the eternal torments of hell, we talk of fire; we think of Paradise as a place of light. Those born blind and deaf can form no definite idea of sensations they have never been able to perceive. It is well known that persons blind from their birth imagine colours by comparing them to sounds: for instance, they imagine red as the sound of a trumpet, blue as the sweet music of the violin. The deaf, when they read descriptions of delicious music, imagine the classic beauty of a painted picture. The temperaments of poets and artists are pre-eminently sensorial. And all the senses do not contribute in equal measure to give a type to the individual imagination; but certain senses are often predominant. Musicians are auditive and are inclined to describe the world from the sounds it conveys to them; the warbling of the nightingale in the silence of a wood, the patter of the rain in the solitude of the countryside, may be as springs of inspiration for great musical composers; and some of them, describing a tract of country, will dwell only on its silences and noises. Others again, whose susceptibilities are predominantly visual, are impressed by the forms and colours of things. Or it may be the motion, the flexuosity, the impetus of things; the tactile impressions of softness and harshness, which make up the descriptive content of imaginative types in whom the tactile and muscular sensations predominate.

There are persons who have had non-sensorial impressions, and they are persons whose spiritual life was of very great intensity. They have *internal impressions* which cannot be accounted as fruits of the imagination, but must be accepted as realities simply perceived. That they are realities is affirmed not only by the introspection of normal subjects, but by the effect upon their internal personality. "The revelations vouchsafed by God," says Saint Teresa[36], "are distinguished by the great spiritual benefits with which they enrich the soul; they are accompanied by light, discernment, and wisdom." But if such persons wish to describe these impressions which do not penetrate by means of the senses, they are obliged to borrow the language of sensorial impression. "I heard a voice," says the Blessed Raymond of Capua[37], "which was not in the air and which pronounced words that reached my spirit, but not my ear; nevertheless I understood it more distinctly than if it had come to me from an external voice. I could not reproduce this voice, if I can call that a voice which had no sound. This voice formed words and presented them to my spirit." The Life of Saint Teresa abounds in similar descriptions, in which she tries to convey by the inappropriate language of the senses what she saw, not with her eyes, but with her soul.

The difference between these internal impressions, which occur in others as well as in saints (and certainly do not constitute saintliness), and the hallucinations of the insane, is clearly marked. In the madman, an excitement of the cerebral cortex reproduces old images deposited by the sensorial memory, which project themselves into the

---

36 Theresia of Avila (1515 – 1582).
37 Raymond of Capua (1330 – 1399) Member of the Dominican Order.

external world whence they were taken with external sensorial characteristics; so that the sufferer really believes that he sees his phantasms with his actual eyes, and that he hears the voices which persecute him; he is the victim of a pathological condition; the whole personality reveals signs of his organic decadence, the concomitants of his psychical disintegration.

Setting aside then direct spiritual impressions of very rare occurrence, not to be looked upon even as aids to sanctity, impressions which may form suitable subjects of study for specialists such as teleologists or the members of the English Society of Psychical Research, but which do not enter into educational conceptions, there remains for our consideration but a single material of construction for intellectual activities: that of the senses.

Imagination can have only a sensory basis.

The sensory education which prepares for the accurate perception of all the differential details in the qualities of things, is therefore the foundation of the observation of things and of phenomena which present themselves to our senses; and with this it helps us to collect from the external world the material for the imagination.

Imaginative creation has no mere vague sensory support; that is to say, it is not the unbridled divagation of the fancy among images of light, colour, sounds and impressions; but it is a construction firmly allied to reality; and the more it holds fast to the forms of the external created world, the loftier will the value of its internal creations be. Even in imagining an unreal and superhuman world, the imagination must be contained within limits which recall those of reality. Man creates, but on the model of that divine creation in which he is materially and spiritually immersed.

In literary works of the highest order, such as the *Divina Commedia*, we admire the continual recurrence to the mind of the supreme poet of material and tangible things which illustrate by comparison the things imaged:

> As doves
> By fond desire invited, on wide wings
> And firm to their sweet nest returning home,
> Cleave the air, wafted by their will along;

Thus issued from that troop where Dido ranks,
They, through the ill air speeding.
(Dante's Inferno, Canto V in the translation of Francis Cary.)

And as a man with difficult short breath
Forespent with toiling, 'scaped from sea to shore,
Turns to the perilous wide waste, and stands
At gaze; e'en so my spirit, that yet fail'd
Struggling with terror, turn'd to view the straits
That none hath passed and lived.
(Dante's Inferno, Canto I in the translation of Francis Cary.)

As sheep that step from forth their fold by one
Or pairs, or three at once; meanwhile the rest
Stand fearfully, bending the eye and nose
To ground, and what the foremost does, that do.
The others, gathering round her if she stops,
Simple and quiet, nor the cause discern;
So saw I moving to advance the first
Who of that fortunate crew were at the head,
Of modest mien, and graceful in their gait.
(Dante's Purgatorio, Canto III in the translation of Francis Cary.)

As through translucent and smooth glass or wave
Clear and unmoved, and flowing not so deep
As that its bed is dark, the shape returns
So faint of our impictured lineaments
That on white forehead set, a pearl as strong
Comes to the eye; such saw I many a face
All stretch'd to speak.
(Dante's Paradiso, Canto III in the translation of Francis Cary.)

Dante's metaphors are profuse and marvellous, but every lofty writer
and every great orator perpetually links the fruits of the imagination
with the observation of fact; and then we say that he is a genius full of
imagination and knowledge, and that his thought is clear and vital.

"As a pack of hounds, after vainly pursuing a hare, returns in mortification to the master with hanging heads and drooping tails, so on that tumultuous night did the mercenaries return to Don Rodrigo's stronghold.[38]

Imagery is confined to actual figures; and it is this measure and this *form* which give power to the creations of the mind. The imaginative writer should possess a rich store of perceptive observations and the more accurate and perfect these are, the more vigorous will be the form he creates. The insane talk of fantastic things, but we do not therefore say that they have a great deal of "imagination"; there is a vast gulf between the delirious confusion of thought and the metaphorical eloquence of the imagination. In the first case there is a total incapacity to perceive actual things correctly, and also to construct organically with the intelligence; in the second, the two things are coexistent as forms closely bound up one with the other.

The value of imaginative speech is determined by these conditions: that the images used should be *original*, that their author should himself link together the actual and the created images, his own skill making him susceptible to their just and harmonious association. If he repeats or imitates the images of others, he achieves nothing. Hence it is necessary that every artist should be an observer; and so, speaking of the generality of intelligences, it may be said that in order to develop the imagination it is necessary for everyone first of all to put himself in contact with reality.

The same thing holds good in art. The artist "imagines" his figure; he does not copy it, he "creates" it. But this creation is in fact the *fruit* of the mind which is rooted in the observation of reality. The painter and the sculptor are, *par excellence*, types of visual susceptibility to the forms and colours of their environment, capable of perceiving its harmonies and contrasts; and it is by refining his powers of observation that the artist finally perfects himself and succeeds in creating a masterpiece. The immortal art of Greece was above all an art based on observation; the scanty clothing which was the fashion of his day enabled the Greek artist

---

38 From *I promessi sposi* (*The engaged couple*). A very well known 19th century Italian historical novel by Alessandro Manzoni.

to contemplate the human form freely; and the exquisite sensibility of his eye enabled him to distinguish the beautiful body from that which lacked harmony, until, under the impulse of genius, he was able to create the ideal figure conceived by the fusion of individual beauties chosen from details in the sensorial storehouse of the mind. The artist, when he creates, certainly does not compose by putting together the parts which are to form the whole as in a mosaic; in the ardour of inspiration he sees the complete *new figure* born of his genius; but details he has accumulated have served to nourish it, as the blood nourishes the new man in the bosom of his mother.

Raphael continually visited the Trastevere, a popular quarter where the most beautiful women in Rome were to be found, in order to seek the ideal Madonna. It was here he became acquainted with the Fornarina and his models. But when he painted the Madonna he reproduced "the image of his soul". We are told that Michelangelo would spend entire evenings gazing into space; and when they asked him at what he was gazing, he replied: "I see a dome". It was after this form, so marvellously created within him, that the famous cupola of St. Peter's in Rome was fashioned. But it could never have been born, even in the mind of Michelangelo, if his architectural studies had not prepared the material for it.

No genius has ever been able to create the absolutely new. We have only to think of certain forms much used in art, and heavy and grotesque as the human fancy which is incapable of rising above the earth. It seems to me amazing that the figure of the winged angel should still persist and that no artist should have yet improved upon it. To represent a being more diaphanous than man and without corporeal weight, we have robust beings whose backs are furnished with colossal wings covered with heavy feathers. Strange indeed is this fusion in a single creature, of such incompatible natural features as hair and feathers, and this attribution to a human being of six limbs – arms, legs and wings, as to an insect. This "strange conception" continues to be so materialised, not certainly as an artistic idea, but as the result of poverty of language. Indeed, we talk of angels "flying" because our language is human and earthly, and we cannot imagine the attributes of angels. Few indeed are the artists who in pictures of the Annunciation represent the Angel as a luminous, delicate and evanescent figure.

The more perfect the approximation to truth, the more perfect is art.

When, for instance in a drawing-room, someone pays us a compliment, if this is founded upon one of our real qualities and touches it closely, we feel legitimate satisfaction, because what has been said is relevant and we may conclude that the person *has observed us* and feels a sincere admiration for us. We accordingly think of such a person: He is subtle and intellectual; and we feel disposed to reciprocate his friendliness. But if the compliment praises us for qualities we do not possess, or distorts or exaggerates our true attributes, we think with disgust: What a coarse creature! and feel even more coldly to him than before.

Dante's sublime sonnet must certainly have touched the heart of Beatrice profoundly:

> My lady looks so gentle and so pure
> When yielding salutation by the way,
> That the tongue trembles and has nought to say,
> And the eyes, which fain would see, may not endure.
> And still, amid the praise she hears secure,
> She walks with humbleness for her array;
> Seeming a creature sent from Heaven, to stay
> On earth, and show a miracle made sure.
> She is so pleasant in the eyes of men
> That through the sight the inmost heart doth gain
> A sweetness which needs proof to know it by;
> And from between her lips there seems to move
> A soothing essence that is full of love,
> Saying for ever to the spirit: "Sigh!"
> (Dante's Vita nuova, Ch. XXVI in the translation of Dante Gabriel Rossetti.)

A very different impression must have been made on the self-respect and delicate sensibility of a feminine soul by this other sonnet, which is clumsy and bombastic because it is full of inappropriate and exaggerated metaphors:

> Your salutation and your glances bright
> Deal death to him who greets you on your way;

Love my assailant, heedless of my plight,
Cares nought if what he does shall heal or slay.

Straight to the mark his arrow flew apace
Piercing my heart and cleaving it in twain;
I was as one who sees Death face to face;
No word I spake – so great my burning pain.

As through the window of the lordly tower
The missile hurtles, shattering all within,
So did the arrow enter through my eye;
Bereft of life and spirit in that hour
I stood there, to a man of brass akin,
That mocks with semblance of humanity.
(Guinizelli.)[39]

If, then, the true basis of the imagination is reality, and its perception is related to exactness of observation, it is necessary to prepare children to perceive the things in their environment exactly, in order to secure for them the material required by the imagination. Further, the exercise of the intelligence, reasoning within sharply defined limits, and distinguishing one thing from another, prepares a cement for imaginative constructions; because these are the more beautiful the more closely they are united to a form, and the more logical they are in the association of individual images. The fancy which exaggerates and invents coarsely does not put the child on the right road.

A true preparation digs the beds where the waters which well up from intellectual creation will flow in smiling or majestic rivers, without overflowing and so destroying the beauty of internal order.

In the matter of causing the springing up of these rushing waters of internal creation we are powerless. "Never to obstruct the spontaneous outburst of an activity, even though it springs forth like the humble trickle of some almost invisible source", and "to wait" – this is our task. Why should we delude ourselves with the idea that we can "create an

---

39 Guinizelli, Guido (ca. 1230 – 1276) was an Italian poet.

intelligence", we who can do nothing but "observe and await" the blade of grass which is sprouting, the microbe which is dividing itself?

We must consider that creative imagination must rise like an illuminated palace on dark foundations deeply imbedded in the rock, if it is to be anything but a house of cards, an illusion, an error; and the salvation of the intelligence is "to be able to plant the feet on firm ground".

Imagination in children

It is a very common belief that the young child is characterised by a vivid imagination and therefore a special education should be adopted to cultivate this special gift of nature.

His mentality differs from ours; he escapes from our strongly marked and restricted limits and loves to wander in the fascinating worlds of unreality, a tendency which is also characteristic of savage peoples.

This childish characteristic, however, gave rise to the generalisation of a materialistic idea now discredited: "Ontogenesis sums up philogenesis", that is the life of the individual reproduces the life of the species; just as the life of man reproduces the life of civilisation, so in young children we find the psychical characteristics of savages. Hence the child, like the savage, is attracted by the fantastic, the supernatural and the unreal.

Instead of indulging in such flights of scientific fancy as these, it would be much simpler to declare that an organism as yet immature like that of the child, has remote affinities with mentalities less mature than our own, like those of savages. But even if we refrain from interfering with the belief of those who interpret childish mentality as "a savage state", we may point out that just as this savage state is transient and must be superseded, education *should help the child* to overcome it; it should not *develop the savage state*, nor *keep* the child therein.

All the forms of imperfect development we encounter in the child have some resemblance to corresponding characteristics in the savage; for instance, in language, poverty of expression, the existence only of concrete terms, and the generalisation of words by means of which a single word serves several purposes and indicates several objects, the absence of inflections in verbs causing the child to use only the infinitive. But no one would maintain that "for this reason" we ought to restrict the child artificially to such primitive language, to enable him to pass through his prehistoric period easily.

And if some people remain permanently in a state of imagination in which unrealities predominate, our child, on the contrary, belongs to a people for whom the delights of the mind are to be found in the great works of art and the civilizing constructions of science, and in those products of the higher imagination which represent the environment in which the intelligence of our child is destined to form itself. It is natural that in the hazy period of his mental development the child should be attracted by fantastic ideas; but this must not make us forget that he is to be our continuator, and for that reason should be superior to us; and the least we ought to give him this end is the maximum at our disposal.

A form of imagination supposed to be "proper" to childhood and almost universally recognised as creative imagination, is that spontaneous work of the infant mind by which children attribute desirable characteristics to objects which do not possess them.

Who has not seen a child riding upon and whipping his father's walking-stick, as if he were mounted upon a real horse? There we have a proof of "imagination" in the child! What pleasure it gives to children to construct a splendid coach with chairs and armchairs; and while some recline inside, looking out with delight at an imaginary landscape or bowing to an applauding crowd, other children, perched on the backs of chairs, beat the air as if they were whipping fiery horses. Here is another proof of "imagination".

But if we observe rich children, who own quiet ponies and drive out habitually in carriages and motorcars, we shall find that they look with a touch of contempt at the child who is running about whipping a stick in great excitement; they would be astonished to see the delight of children who imagine themselves to be drawn along by stationary armchairs. They would say of such children: "They are very poor; they act thus because they have no horses or carriages." An adult resigns himself to his lot; a child creates an illusion. But this is not a proof of imagination, it is a proof of an unsatisfied desire; it is not an activity bound up with gifts of nature; it is a manifestation of conscious, sensitive poverty. No one, we may be sure, will say that in order to educate a rich child we should take away his pony and give him a stick. Nor is it necessary to prevent the poor child from being content with his stick. If a poor man, a beggar, had nothing but dry bread to eat, and if he placed himself by the grated window of a rich underground kitchen because when he smelt its savoury odours he imagined himself to be eating excellent dishes together with his bread, who could prevent him? But no one would say that in order to develop the imaginative activity of the fortunate persons for whom the actual dishes were destined, it would be well to take away their meat and give them bread and fragrance.

A poor mother who was devoted to her little child offered him the piece of bread which was all she had to give in this manner: she divided it into two portions, and gave them to him in succession, saying: "This is the bread, this is the meat". The child was quite content. But no mother would deprive her child of food in order to develop his imagination in this way.

And yet I was once seriously asked by someone if it would be injurious to give a piano to a child who was continually practising with his fingers upon the table, as if he were playing the piano. "And why should it be injurious?" I asked. "Because, if I do so, he will learn music, it is true, but his imagination will no longer be exercised, and I do not know which would be best for him."

Some of Fröbel's games are based upon similar beliefs. A wooden brick is given to a child with the words: "This is a horse". Bricks are then arranged in a certain order, and he is told: "This is the stable; now let us put the horse into the stable". Then the bricks are differently arranged: "This is a tower, this is the village church, etc." In such exercises the objects (bricks) lend themselves to illusion less readily than a stick used as a horse, which the child can at least bestride and beat, moving along the while. The building of towers and churches with horses brings the mental confusion of the child to its culmination. Moreover, in this case it is not the child who "imagines spontaneously" and works with his brains, for at the moment he is required to see that which the teacher suggests. And it is impossible to know whether the child really thinks that the stable has become a church, or whether his attention has wandered elsewhere. He would, of course, like to move, but he cannot, because he is obliged to contemplate the kind of cinematograph of which the teacher speaks in the series of images she suggests, though they exist only in the shape of pieces of wood all of the same size.

What is it that is thus being cultivated in these immature minds? What do we find akin to this in the adult world which will enable us to understand for what definitive forms we prepare the mind by such a method of education? There are, indeed, men who really take a tree for a throne, and issue royal commands: some believe themselves to be God, for "false perceptions", or the graver form, "illusions", are the beginning of false reasoning and the concomitants of delirium. The insane produce nothing nor can those children, condemned to the immobility of an education, which tends to *develop* their innocent manifestations of unsatisfied desires into mania, produce anything either for themselves or others.

We, however, suppose that we are developing the imagination of children by making them accept fantastic things as realities. Thus, for instance, in Latin countries, an ugly woman, the Befana, who comes through the walls and down the chimneys, bringing toys for the good children and leaving only lumps of coal for the naughty ones, personifies Christmas. In Anglo-Saxon countries, on the other hand, Christmas is an old man covered with snow who carries a huge basket containing toys for children, and who really enters their houses by night. But how can the *imagination* of children be developed by what is, on the contrary, the fruit of our imagination? It is we who imagine, not they; they *believe*, they do not imagine. Credulity is, indeed, a characteristic of immature minds which lack experience and knowledge of realities, and are as yet devoid of that intelligence which distinguishes the true from the false, the beautiful from the ugly, the possible from the impossible.

Is it, then, *credulity* we wish to develop in our children, merely because they show themselves to be credulous at an age when they are naturally ignorant and immature? Of course credulity may exist in adults; but it exists in *contrast* with *intelligence* and is neither its foundation nor its fruit. It is in periods of intellectual darkness that credulity germinates; and we are proud to have outlived these epochs. We speak of credulity as a mark of the uncivilised.

Here is a piquant anecdote of the seventeenth century. The Pont Neuf in Paris was the main highway for foot-passengers and a meeting-place for loungers. Many mountebanks and charlatans mingled with the crowd. There was one of these charlatans who was making a fortune; he sold an ointment from China which enlarged the eyes, decreased the size of the mouth, lengthened noses that were too short, and shortened those that were too long. De Sartine, Chief of the Police, called up this charlatan to have him imprisoned and said to him:

"Mariolo, how do you manage to attract so many people and gain so much money?"

"Sir," replied the other, "how many persons, do you suppose, cross the bridge in one day?"

"From ten to twelve thousand," replied De Sartine.

"Well, sir, how many intelligent persons do you suppose there are among them?"

"A hundred," replied the official.

"That's a liberal allowance," said the charlatan, "but let us leave it at that. I will rely on the other nine thousand nine hundred for my living."

The situation has so far changed between those days and our own that there are now more intelligent and fewer credulous persons. Education, therefore, should not be directed to credulity but to intelligence. He who bases education on credulity builds upon sand.

I know of an incident which is perhaps reproduced in our society thousands of times. Two girls of noble family had been educated in a convent, where, to safeguard them from the seductions and vanities of the life for which they were destined, the nuns had persuaded them that the world is full of deceit, and that if when people praise us, if we could conceal ourselves and listen to what they say when we have disappeared, we should hear very chastening things. When they were of an age to be presented in Society, the two youthful princesses made their first appearance at an evening reception to which their mother had invited a great many guests. All lavished praises on the charming young girls. In the drawing-room there was an alcove concealed by a large curtain. Curious to hear what would be said of them when they disappeared, the two agreed to slip out and hide behind the curtain. Scarcely had the attractive objects of the general admiration vanished when the praises, which had been kept within due bounds in their presence, were redoubled. The two girls told me that they experienced an indescribable revulsion of feeling at the moment; they thought that everything the nuns had made them believe was false; they renounced religion there and then and made up their minds to throw themselves into the pleasures of society. "We afterwards had to reconstruct our lives ourselves, embrace the truths of religion afresh, and understand for ourselves the emptiness of social brilliance."

Credulity gradually disappears with experience, and as the mind matures *instruction* helps towards this end. In nations as in persons, the evolution of civilisation and of souls tends to diminish credulity; knowledge, as is commonly said, dispels the *darkness* of ignorance. In the void which is ignorance, the fancy easily wanders, just because it lacks the support which would enable it to rise to a higher level. Thus the Pillars of Hercules disappeared when the Straits of Gibraltar became the gates of the oceans; and no Columbus could now persuade the Red Indians, whom the great American spirit of democracy receives into its civilizing schools, that the heavens are obedient to him, darkening the sun at his command; for eclipses are phenomena as well known to them as to the white races.

Is this illusory imagination, based upon credulity, a thing we ought "to develop" in children? We certainly have no wish to see it persist; in fact, where we are told that a child "no longer believes in fairy-tales", we rejoice. We say then: "He is no longer a baby". This is what *should* happen and we await it: the day will come when he will no longer believe these stories. But if this maturation takes place, we ought to ask ourselves: "What have *we* done to help it? What support did we offer to this frail mind to enable it to grow straight and strong?" The child overcomes his difficulties *in spite* of our endeavour to keep him in ignorance and illusion. The child overcomes himself and us. He goes where his internal force of development and maturation lead him. He might, however, say to us: "How much you have made us suffer! The work of raising ourselves was hard enough already and you oppressed us." Would not such conduct be much as if we compressed the gums to prevent the teeth from coming because it is characteristic of babies to be toothless, or prevented the little body from standing erect because at first the characteristic of the infant is that it does not rise to its feet? Indeed, we do something of the same sort when we deliberately prolong the poverty and inaccuracy of childish speech; instead of helping the child by making him listen intently to the distinct enunciation of speech sounds, and watch the movements of the mouth, we adopt his rudimentary language and repeat the primordial sounds he utters, lisping and perverting the consonants in the manner habitual to those making first efforts to articulate words. Thus we prolong a formative period full of difficulty and exertion for the child, thrusting him back into the fatiguing infant state.

And we are behaving in exactly the same manner today with regard to the so-called education of the imagination.

We are amused by the illusions, the ignorance, and the errors of the immature mind, just as at no very remote date we were amused to see an infant *laugh* when it was tossed up and down, a proceeding now condemned by infantile hygiene as wrong and dangerous in the extreme. In short, it is *we* who are amused by the Christmas festivities and the credulity of the child. If we confess the truth, we must admit that we are somewhat like the fine lady who took a superficial interest in a hospital for poor children, but who kept on declaring: "If there were to be no more sick children, I should be quite unhappy." We too might say: "If the credulity of children were to cease, a great pleasure would be taken from our lives."

It is one of the careless errors of our day to arrest artificially a stage of development for our amusement; as in the ancient courts the bodily growth of certain victims was arrested to make them dwarfs and the pastime of the king. Such a statement may seem severe but it rests on an actual fact. We are unconscious of it, it is true; yet we speak of it continually when we say among ourselves with lofty scorn of the age of immaturity: "Really, we are not children." If we would refrain from prolonging the child's immaturity in order to be able to contemplate his inferior state in immobility, and would, on the contrary, allow free growth, admiring the marvels of his progression ever on the road of higher conquests, we should say of him with Christ: "He who would be perfect must become as a little child."

If what is called infant imagination is the product of "immaturity" of the mind, combined with the poverty in which we leave the child and the ignorance in which he finds himself, the first thing to do is to enrich his life by an environment in which he will become the owner of something, and to enrich his mind by knowledge and experience based on reality. And having given him these, we must allow him to *mature in liberty*. It is from freedom of development that we may expect the manifestations of his imagination.

To enrich the child, who is the poorest among us, because he has nothing and is the slave of all – this is our first duty towards him. It will be said: Must we, then, give horses, carriages and pianos to all children? By no means. Remedies are never direct when a complex life is in question. The child who has nothing is the one who dreams of things the most impossible of attainment. The destitute dream of millions, the oppressed of a throne. But he who possesses something attaches himself to that which he possesses to preserve and increase it reasonably.

A person without employment will dream of becoming a prince; but a teacher in a school dreams of becoming a headmaster. Thus the child who has a "house" of his own, who possesses brooms, rubbers, pottery, soap, dressing-tables and furniture, is happy in the care of all these things. His desires are moderated, and the peace he derives from them opens up a life of expansion to his internal creative activities.

* * *

It is "living among real possessions of his own" which calms the child and assuages those desires, which consume his precious powers in the vanity of illusion. Such a result is not to be achieved by *imagining* that he is living among possessions of his own. Some teachers in charge of a model orphanage once said to me: "We too make our children perform the exercises of practical life which you describe; come and see." I went. Some of the authorities were also present, and a university professor of pedagogy.

Some children seated at a little table with playthings were laying the table for a doll's meal; their faces were quite without expression, I looked in amazement at the persons who had invited me; they seemed quite satisfied; they evidently thought that there was no difference between laying a table in play and laying it for an actual meal; for them imaginary life and real life were the same thing. May not this subtle form of error be instilled in infancy and afterwards persist as a mental attitude? It was perhaps this error, which caused a famous Italian pedagogue to say to me: "Liberty a new thing? Pray read Comenius. You will find that it was already discussed in his times." I replied: "Yes, many talk of it, but the liberty I mean is a form of liberty actually realised." He seemed not to understand the difference. I ought to have asked: "Do you not believe that there is any difference between him who talks of millions and him who possesses them?"

To be contented with the imaginary, and to live as if what we imagine actually existed; to run after illusion, and "not to recognise" reality, is a thing so common that scarcely is it apprehended, and the cry of alarm raised: "Awake to truth, o man!" when the consciousness becomes aware of a kind of gnawing parasite which has wormed itself subtly into our intelligence.

The power to imagine always exists, whether or not it has a solid basis on which to rest, and materials with which to build; but when it does not elaborate from reality and truth, instead of raising a divine structure it forms incrustations, which compress the intelligence and prevent the light from penetrating thereto.

How much time and strength man has lost and is losing by this error! Just as vice, which is an exercise of function without purpose, wastes the body until it becomes diseased, so imagination unsustained by truth consumes the intelligence until it assumes characteristics akin to the mental characteristics of the insane.

Fable and religion

I have frequently heard it said that the education of the imagination on a basis of fancy prepares the soul of the child for religious education; and that an education based on "reality", as in this method we would adopt, is too arid and tends to dry up the founts of spiritual life. Such reasoning, however, will not be accepted by religious persons. They know well that faith and fable are "as the poles apart", since fable is in itself a thing without truth, and faith is the very sentiment of truth, which should accompany man even unto death. Religion is not a product of fantastic imagination, it is the greatest of realities, the one truth to the religious man. It is the fount and basis of his life. The man without religion is not certainly a person without imagination, but rather one who lacks internal equilibrium; compared with the religious man he is less calm, less strong in adversity; not only this, but he is more unsettled in his own ideas. He is weaker and more unhappy; and it is in vain that he catches at imagination to create a world for himself outside reality. Something within him cries aloud in the words of David: "My soul is athirst for God." And if he hopes to reach the goal of his real life by the help of imagination alone, he may feel his feet giving way among quicksands at a supreme moment of effort.

When an apostle seeks to win a soul to religion, where man may plant his faltering feet on a rock, he appeals to understanding, not to imagination, for he knows that his task is not to create something, but to call aloud to that which is slumbering in the depths of the heart. He knows that he must shake off the torpor from a feeble life as he would shake the snow from a living body buried in a drift, not build up a puppet of ice which will melt under the rays of the sun.

It is true that fantastic imagination penetrates religion, but in the guise of error. In the Middle Ages, for instance, epidemics were ascribed, with great simplicity, to a direct act of divine chastisement; today they are attributed to the direct action of microbes. Papin's steam engines suggested diabolical intervention. But these are precisely the kind of prejudices which, like all fantasies, swarm in the void of ignorance.

All religion is not thus constructed like a fantastic castle erected on a basis of ignorance. Otherwise we should see savage people religious and civilised people without religion; whereas savages have a frail and fantastic religion mainly constructed upon the terror inspired by the mysterious activities of Nature, and civilised people have a positive religion, which becomes stronger as it becomes purer, the science of truth, penetrating into Nature, serves to exalt and illustrate its mysteries.

And, above all, today, when there is a movement in favour of eliminating religion altogether from the school, can we propose to introduce it by cultivating *fable?* It is such a simple matter to open the door directly to religion itself and allow its radiance to penetrate, warming and invigorating life.

But it should enter like the sun into creation, not like the Befana from the chimney-top.

Fable could prepare to some extent for pagan religion, which split up the divinity into innumerable minor gods symbolizing the external world; this being apprehended by the senses, may lend itself to illusion; but fable could certainly never prepare for Christianity, which brings God into contact with the inner life of man, "one and indivisible", and teaches the laws of a life which is "felt" by men. If the positive sciences be extraneous to religion, it cannot be said that it is the study of reality in itself which alienates us therefrom. Hitherto the positive sciences have studied the "external world" in its analytical details, and if they could have made a "sympathetic" religion, that religion might be the pagan creed. Indeed, so far science has brought a very perceptive breath of paganism among us. But when it shall have succeeded in *penetrating the inner man* and there make manifest the laws of life and the realities of existence, a great Christian light will surely shine upon men; and may be children, like the angels over Bethlehem, will sing the hymn invoking peace between science and faith.

Saint John in the desert "made straight the way of the Lord" and purged men of the grossest errors. And thus a method which gives internal equilibrium and disperses the grossest errors which suffocate the spiritual energies, makes ready for the reception of truth and the recognition of the "way of life".

The education of the imagination in schools for older children

What is the method adopted in the ordinary elementary schools for the education of the imagination?

The school is, in most cases, a bare, naked place where the grey colour of the walls and the white muslin curtains over the windows preclude any alleviation for the senses. The object of this depressing environment is to prevent the distraction of the scholar's attention by stimuli and concentrate it upon the teacher who speaks. The children, seated, listen motionless hour after hour. When they draw, they have to reproduce another drawing exactly. When they move, it is in obedience to an order given by another person. Their personalities are appraised solely by the standard of passive obedience; the education of their wills consists of the methodical renunciation of volition.

"Our usual pedagogy," says Claparède, "oppresses children with a mass of information which can never help them to direct their conduct; we make them listen when they have no desire to hear; speak, write, narrate, compose and discourse when they have nothing to say; we make them observe when they have no curiosity, reason when they have no desire to discover anything. We incite them to efforts which are supposed to be voluntary without the preliminary acquiescence of their *ego in* the task imposed, that inner consensus which alone gives moral value to submission to duty."

The children thus reduced to slavery use their eyes to read, their hands to write, their ears to hear what the teacher says. Their bodies, indeed, are stationary; but their minds are unable to dwell upon anything. They must be continually exerting themselves to run after the mind of the teacher, who, in his turn, is urged on by a programme drawn up at random, and which is certainly regardless of childish tendencies. The mind has to pass from thing to thing. Images, fugitive and uncertain as dreams, appear from time to time before the eyes of the child. The teacher draws a triangle on the blackboard and then erases it; it was a momentary vision represented as an abstraction; those children have never held a concrete triangle in their hands; they have to remember, by an effort, a contour around which abstract geometrical calculations will presently gather thickly; such a figure will never achieve anything within them; it will not be *felt*, combined with others, it will never be an inspiration. It is the same with everything else. The object would seem to be fatigue for its own sake, that fatigue which has engrossed almost the sum of effort of experimental psychology.

In this environment where free exercise is prohibited, as also the choice of work and meditation, where every sentiment is oppressed, and from which every external stimulus, which might enrich the intelligence with spontaneous acquisitions is eliminated, an attempt is made to excite the imagination by giving "compositions" to be written. This means that the child has to *produce* without having the necessary material; to give without possessing; achieve internal activities which he is prevented from developing. And *production* is to come from the *exercise of production;* "constant practice in composition" is to develop the imagination; from the sterility of the void the most complex products of the intelligence are to be evolved!

It is well known that "composition" represents the great difficulty of our schools. All teachers have declared that children are "poor in ideas", that they have "disorderly minds", that they are "absolutely without originality". The examination in written composition has always been the most painful of all; everyone knows the expression of the child who hears the title of an obligatory theme dictated, and who in a few hours must hand in a written composition, a product of the imagination; it is with anguish, with oppression of the heart, with cold hands and eyes anxiously interrogating the clock in terror of the fleeting hour, under the distrustful surveillance of a teacher who for the occasion is transformed into a spy-warder like those in penal prisons, that he undergoes his torture to the end. Woe to him if he does not hand in his composition! He will be ruined, for this is the principal test, the one in which he is *free* to manifest his own worth, to give the true individual fruit by which others will measure his intelligence. It is in this way that our young generations often find neurasthenia and even suicide. Scholars cannot answer as did the greatest poet of our times,

Carducci, when he was requested to write an ode on the occasion of the death of a personage: "It is inspiration, not an occasion, which would make me write an ode."

It is interesting to study the methods by which, in "modern schools", where some elements of psychical hygiene have penetrated, attempts are made to help the pupils by diminishing their exhausting effort and leading them on gradually to composition. Composition (we must pass over the contradiction in terms for the moment) is "taught". The teacher gives collective lessons in composition, just as she would explain arithmetic: this is called "collective oral composition".

We will allow specialists in this method to speak, giving a passage containing a preparation of teachers for such lessons:

Method to be followed in the manner of indicating the theme

"Let us take, by way of illustration, the following brief narrative, which consists of three phases: 1. Ernesto did not know his lesson; 2. The teacher scolded the child severely; 3. Ernesto wept and promised to do better. If we indicate the narrative by the words: 'Ernesto did not know his lesson' (first fact, cause), the pupil will go on easily to the effect, consisting of the two other phases which, logically and in chronological order, follow the cause. If, on the other hand, we give as the theme the indication corresponding to the second phase: 'The teacher scolded the child', we oblige the pupil to go back to the cause and to make the third phase follow upon the second. We place the pupil in a more difficult position if we give as the theme; 'Ernesto wept and promised to do better', since he will then be obliged to go back to the second and thence to the first phase.

Hence the first phase in every brief narrative ought to serve to indicate the theme.

Method – The teacher should write the theme on the blackboard, and invite the pupils to think of (not to say) a possible consequence of the fact indicated in the theme. The teacher must let it be understood that the pupils are to work independently, without the help of suggestion.

Let us see:

Louisa threw a piece of wool into the fire (theme). Think of a possible consequence, say what happened in consequence.

The wool caused a bad smell. Very good. You repeat the narrative:

Louisa threw a piece of wool into the fire. The wool caused a bad smell. Can anyone add another little thought, another possible consequence?

The teacher reproved Louisa. A pupil opened the window. The teacher repeats the exercise using the themes A., B., C. and causing the result arrived at with the collaboration of the scholars to be written in their exercise-books.

A theme may be proposed and the pupils may be left free to develop it without any further explanations.

Theme A. Louisa threw a piece of wool into the fire (The wool caused a bad smell. The teacher reproved Louisa. A companion opened the window to allow the bad odour to escape.)

Theme B. Ernesto upset the ink on the floor (The floor was stained. The teacher reproved the child. Ernesto promised to be more careful.)

Theme C. Elisa read the story well. (The teacher praised her and gave her a good mark. Elisa was very much pleased.)

Theme D. Mario made a blot on his copy-book. (The teacher did not correct his exercise; she scolded him. The boy went home crying.)

After all this collective practice the teacher gives a free theme such as the following: 'Maria knew her lesson well'. In developing it, the children are expected to follow the above examples: that is to say, they are to indicate in two sentences the logical effects of such a cause (the teacher gave her ten marks and praised her; then she told her to persevere in her industry).

Sometimes the teaching has a psychological purport rather than a logical one. In such a case the "little thoughts" are not linked together as cause and effect, but by the display of psychical activities in three spheres: "knowing, feeling, and willing". Examples:

Amelia made me smell some ammonia (fact perceived). – What a horrible smell! (sentiment). – I will not smell it again (volition).

Gigi pulled my hair (fact perceived). – It hurt me (sentiment). I pulled my companion's hand away quickly (volition)." [40]

With methods such as these it is obvious that every possibility of inspiration and creation will be destroyed. The child has to follow phrase by phrase what the teacher indicates; thus every spark of aptitude for original composition is quenched. Not only does the child remain *empty of material* wherewith to create, as in the past, but the very capacity for creation disappears, so that if tomorrow material should be formed in his

---

40 Diritti della Scuola; Year XIV, No. 16, p. 232.

mind, he would no longer have the impulse to utilise it and his thought would be fettered by his school routine.

Intellectual education carried on by the teacher on such a system makes one think of a chauffeur who should shut off the motor of an automobile and try to propel it by the strength of his arms. He would in this case be a porter, and the automobile a useless machine. When, on the other hand, the motor is working, the internal force moves the car and the chauffeur only has to guide it that it may go safely along the street, not run into obstacles or rush into ditches, and not injure anyone upon its course. This *guidance* is the only thing necessary; but the real progression is due solely to the internal impulse, which no one can create.

It was thus that the first Italian literary Renaissance came about, when the "new sweet style" arose with Dante as the spontaneous expression of feeling:

> *Count of me but as one*
> *Who am the scribe of Love, that when he breathes*
> *Take up my pen and as he dictates, write.*
> *(Dante's Purgatorio, Canto XXIV in the translation of Francis Cary.)*

The child must create his interior life before he can express anything; he must take spontaneously from the external world constructive material in order to "compose"; he must exercise his intelligence freely before he can be ready to find the logical connection between things. We ought to offer the child that which is necessary for his internal life, and leave him free to produce. Perhaps it would not then be impossible to meet a child running with sparkling eyes to write a letter, or walking and meditating as he cultivates a nascent inspiration.

We ought to tend and nourish the internal child, and *await* his manifestations. If imaginative creation comes late, it will be because the intelligence is not sufficiently mature to create until late; and we should no more force it with a fiction than we would put a false moustache on a child because otherwise he will not have one till he is twenty.

10

The Moral Question

When we said, to begin with, that positive science had only given the "reform" of physical life, together with the modern rules of hygiene, as its contribution to society, we were unjust to positive science. It has considered not only physical life, but moral life.

It is enough to think of those studies in bacteriology which refer to the vehicles of infectious maladies in the environment, in order to recognise therefrom a primary token of the important place which is assigned to the community of human interests, and this is now affirmed with an emphasis never before displayed. Microbes multiply chiefly in damp and dirty places; underfed people are more prone to illness than others, and so are those who are overtired. Therefore illness and early death must be the heritage of the poor who, underfed and overtired, live in damp and dirty places? No. It is a question of vehicles. Microbes spread in all directions from the sources of infection by means of dust, insects and all the usual objects of life, in fact, by all the means of transport. They exist in inconceivable and fabulous numbers; and every sick person is an almost incredible source of illness and death. One single person would suffice to contaminate the whole of Europe.

The means of transport allow microbes to cross oceans and continents in every sense. We need only observe the transatlantic lines and those of the railways of the world, in order to realise the lines of communication between the maladies which afflict humanity in all the places of the earth. We need only study the industrial changes of matter in order to follow in detail the daily path of the microbes, which put all classes of society into intimate communication. The rich lady wears linen on her person which comes from the hands of the poor, and is constantly in their keeping; she cannot put food into her mouth unless it is offered to her by the poor who have handled it over and over again.

The air, which is breathed by the rich may contain in its dust the desiccated germs which a consumptive workman has scattered on the ground. There is no way of escape. Statistics prove this: the death rate from infectious diseases is tremendously high in all countries, among both rich and poor, although the poor die in a double proportion to the rich. How can we deliver ourselves from this scourge? Only on condition that there be no more sources of infection, that is to say, that there be no longer any unhealthy places in the world, and no underfed people constrained to work beyond their strength. The only way by which the individual may escape is that by which all humanity may be saved. This is a great principle, which seems to ring like a trumpet call: Men, help one another, or you will die.

It is a fact that science has inaugurated "works of sanitation" as its practical contribution to the fight against mortality; towns have been opened out, water has been laid on, houses have been built for the poor and labour has been protected. All the environment tends to ameliorate the "conditions of life" of the population. No works of charity, no expression of love or of pity, has ever been able to do so much. Science has shown us that those works which were called "charitable", and were looked upon merely as a moral virtue, represented the first step, although a restricted and insufficient one, towards the real salvation of the health of humanity. It was that which had to be done in order to fight against death. But, in order to reach the goal, such work should be universal and should constitute a "reformation" of society. Then it becomes "social progress", when there will be no benefactors or benefited, but merely humanity which has increased its own well-being. This principle: All men are brothers; let them love and help one another and let not the right hand know what the left hand doeth, will have been translated into practice.

In sentimental times poverty was a stimulus to which the rich man reacted. The poor did not really tend to educate the rich man's feelings. If, in those times, the poor man had said, "Give me necessities, or thou shalt die", the rich man would have been indignant. He was very far from realizing that the poor man was his brother, with whom he shared his rights, as well as the danger of death.

Today science has put things on a different footing. it has "realised" that charity benefits both rich and poor, and has constituted a principle of civilisation that which formerly was a "moral principle" entrusted to sentiment.

In the case of morals, too, hygiene has penetrated, and has given individual rules of life. It is through hygiene that debauchery has become less common, that those epicurean feasts, which were celebrated in ancient times are replaced today by hygienic meals, the value of which consists in the wise proportion between the needs of the body and the food which is prepared. The rich more than by the poor reject wine and alcohol. We eat in order to keep ourselves in good health, and therefore without excess and without poison. This is what the ancient morality preached when it fought against the vice of gluttony and proclaimed fasting and abstinence to be virtues. No one in those times could have imagined that the day would come when millionaires would voluntarily substitute lemonade for wine, and that great banquets would disappear entirely, leaving only the accounts of them as a "curiosity" of the past. Nay, more: none of these modern ascetics are proud of their virtue, they seem to respond with simplicity to the gospel precept:

"When ye fast, be not as the hypocrites, of a sad countenance . . . but anoint thine head, that thou appear not unto men to fast, but unto thy Father which seeth in secret."

If one of the ancient preachers could talk to these ascetics, he would also be much edified by their conversation. What has become of those pleasantries, which formed "life" and "delight" and "gaiety" in the time of Marguerite of Valois? The tales of Boccaccio could not now be discussed in English society, or in any modern aristocratic society even of much lower social rank than that which surrounded Marguerite of Valois. Nowadays people are afraid of uttering an incorrect word, even of hinting at the most innocent functions of the body, or of naming those parts of their clothing which come in contact with the skin. They only talk about elevated things, and only those people who instruct us are looked upon as brilliant conversationalists; those who, in speaking of their travels, tell us about the customs of the people, or who, speaking of politics, tell us of the current situation. Excessive laughter, jokes and violent gestures are not permitted. Everyone keeps his limbs quiet, even avoiding those vivacious and inoffensive gestures which are the natural accompaniment of conversation; the tone of voice is so modulated as to be scarcely audible. The ancient preacher would say, "These people have carried out St. Paul's exhortation to an exaggerated degree: 'But fornication and all uncleanness, let it not once be named among you, as becometh saints; neither filthiness nor foolish talking, nor jesting, which are not convenient'."

And among these evolutions of manners we find that it is once more hygiene which, making itself the guide of fashion, has by degrees simplified clothes, done away with pomatum and rouge, abolished crinolines, modified stays and shoes, caused long-trained dresses to disappear from the streets and has introduced uniformity in clothing. If a man who lived in ancient times were to appear among us, he would ask: "Why are the people doing penance? I see men without any ornaments and with their hair cut short; and women who, with an edifying renunciation of vanity, go along the street without wigs and without patches on their faces, with their hair simply knotted up; I see countesses dressed in inexpensive costumes, in simple, dark, monastic dresses, almost like those of the poor. The carriages are dark, like funeral cars, and the servants wear mourning livery. Carnival no longer enlivens the streets. Everyone goes about silently and gravely."

Who could ever have persuaded the people of old times, who used to preach against excessive vanity, that such a picture as this does not represent a time of penance, but ordinary daily life?

These modern people, on their side, are far from thinking that they are condemned to a life of suffering; on the contrary, they look back with horror on the society of the past; they would never go back to those days when men were enslaved by grand dresses and by rouge, poisoning themselves with debauchery and dying of infectious diseases. They have freed themselves from a great many useless bonds and have realised a higher enjoyment of life. All the comfort which makes life so delicious today would have been an incomprehensible secret to the nobility of past centuries. It is the secret of life.

Possibly, at one time, monks and those who were living in the world thought of each other in a similar way. Those who had renounced the bondage of the world and all its vanities possessed a secret of life which was full of hitherto unknown delights, and they looked with horror upon the so-called pleasure of their century; while those unconscious men who were slaves from the tops of their bewigged heads to their feet compressed in narrow boots, called the ways of death "life and enjoyment".

Positive science has made yet another contribution penetrating directly into the sphere of morality. By statistical methods of sociology the social problems of immorality and crime have been opened up and external facts have been studied; and criminal anthropology has revealed the "inferior types" who by hereditary taint are those who have a predisposition to all the moral infection of their surrounding. Morel's theories concerning degeneration and the resulting theories of Lombroso[41] concerning criminals, have undoubtedly brought light into this chaos, wherein opinion as to human goodness and wickedness was divided. Forms of "degeneration" are chiefly rooted in the nervous system, and all the abnormal personalities produced thereby "deviate" from the ordinary type. They have a different intelligence and different morality. False perceptions, false reasoning, illusions, anomalies of the will, such as impulses, irresolutions and crazes, the deficient moral sense on which the abnormal intelligence builds up systematic delusions, which are interpreted as philosophical principles, place these persons in a category apart as extra-social beings.

The general nervous weakness and the wandering intelligence, which preclude an interest in work make of these persons individuals incapable of production, who therefore try to live upon the productions of others. This fundamental fact, which tends to unite a dislike of productive labour with impulses towards rapine, causes them to make use of all those surrounding causes which prepare the external means for crime. These men are "bad". But if we observe more closely, we see that it is not wickedness with which we have to deal but morbid conditions and social errors. If such were the case, these bad men, who from no fault of their own were born in these unhappy conditions, and who are driven to perdition by society, are really "victims". Their whole history, when closely investigated, reveals this fact. They are hunted and neglected from babyhood. Incapable of making themselves beloved owing to mental deficiency, volitive disorders, to the anomaly of the affections and also to lack of physical attraction, they pass from maternal persecution to that

---

41 Cesare Lombroso (1835 – 1909) was an Italian criminologist. He thought that criminality was innate and could be determined by measuring jaws, eyes, ears, etc. Evolution would by and by eliminate this kind of people. The theory is dated.

of the school, and finally to that of society, bringing on themselves every kind of punishment.

The first picture, which Morel[42] drew of these "dead ones of the race" was an impressive one. According to his original theory, containing a synthesis which, if not very exact, yet sums up the phenomenon with comprehensive clearness, when a cause of degeneration acts upon a man, he may have defective children, whose deficiency increases in the two or three following generations, until it is extinguished in the final sterility of exceedingly debased individuals. According to Morel, madmen, criminals, epileptics and idiots form the sad series in the extinction of man. The man who dies leaving strong descendants, does not really die but is renewed in them, youth succeeding to age. It is only the degenerate who dies, for his kind is "extinguished", the few miserable generations whom he produces represent a "living agony". This "dying species", which lives among the healthy, exhibiting its weakness, its delusions, its convulsions, irritability and egoism, is finally driven into those tombs of the living, lunatic asylums and prisons.

What a living picture, and what a warning to man! One "fault" may be a mortal one to him, for, like the Biblical curse, it transmits itself to generations, and leads to eternal perdition.

How terrible it is to think of punishment falling on the innocent head of a child! And how evident it is that our present life is not everything, but that it has a continuation, when we shall reap the true rewards or the true punishments of our existence. The choice lies to a great extent in our own hands. Shall we have a beautiful, healthy, prolific son, or a deformed, unhealthy, barren son, incapable of loving and understanding us? The hygiene of generation is the most important part of moral hygiene. If the salvation of the individual life can be obtained only by caring for the hygienic life of the whole of humanity, it is only by rigorously following the laws of health and the laws of life that the salvation of the species can be obtained. Alcoholism, all poisons, overwork, constitutional maladies, dissipation of nervous force,

---

42 Social Degeneration was a widely influential concept at the interface of social and biological science in the 19th century. From the 1850s, it became influential in psychiatry through the writings of Bénédict Morel, and in criminology with Cesare Lombroso.

vice and idleness, are all *causes* of degeneration. It was science which went on preaching these things for the salvation of mankind and by these means propagated virtue. But above all, it inculcated the great principle of "pardon", which hitherto had been one of the mysteries of religious morality.

A few years ago, no one, however pitiful and generous, could have looked upon the delinquent with the same justice and pity as science has done. It has pointed out that we are *all* responsible for this victim of social causes, that we must all accuse ourselves of the sins committed by the inferior individual and exert ourselves for his regeneration by all the means in our power. It was only the saints who had an intuition of this truth, when they offered their merits for all men in common and accepted responsibility for the offences of all. "You will hold yourselves accountable," said St. John Chrysostom,[43] "not only for your own salvation, but for universal salvation; he who prays must take upon himself the burden of the interests of the whole human race."

It is certain that if a Tages[44] had cleansed our whole race of its deformities, and if an analogous morality had rendered us indifferent to the illnesses, weaknesses and sufferings of humanity, regenerative science would not have been able to arise. It is only by recognizing the effects that we can go back to the unhealthy causes and save humanity from danger. The *causes* of death are as invisible and intangible as microbes; man may drink poison when he thinks he is drinking nectar. Woe to us if the diseased and degenerate did not exhibit themselves to us as an advance guard, to testify to the unconscious errors, which threaten us with perdition. Science does not exactly limit itself to tending the sick like the *personnel* of a hospital, but it penetrated by that goodly door and made its way in a contrary direction towards a normal humanity, unconscious of its danger. The ultimate result of science is not the care of the sick but universal health. We owe the hygienic "comfort" which ensures our

---

43 St. John Chrysostom (347 – 407) was archbishop of Constantinople. He is known as a preacher and one of the church fathers of Christianity.

44 Tages was a founding prophet of Etruscan religion who is known from reports by Latin authors of the late Roman republic and Roman empire. He revealed a cosmic view of divinity and correct methods of ascertaining divine will concerning events of public interest.

health and diminishes general mortality to so great an extent, to the fact that sick people were collected together and tended.

When Christ showed the way of salvation to men He pointed to those who were rejected by society, in whom the obvious effects of evil could be seen, because the causes of evil are too subtle and are not always directly visible: "You hear with your ears and do not understand; you behold with your eyes and do not see."

But, on the other hand, the extreme consequences are obvious, and it is enough that the "will" of man should agree to gather them in charitably and without repugnance in order to obtain salvation. St. Matthew says that at the Last Judgment those who are lost will be separated from those who are saved, and that the King will call the latter to His right hand, saying, "Come, ye blessed of my Father, inherit the kingdom prepared for you from the foundation of the world. For I was an-hungered, and ye gave me meat: I was thirsty, and ye gave me drink . . . I was naked, and ye clothed me . . . . I was in prison, and ye came unto me." "And when," replied the just, "saw we thee, o Lord, an-hungered or thirsty or naked? When saw we thee sick or in prison and came unto thee?" and the King shall answer and say unto them, "Inasmuch as ye have done it unto the least of these my brethren, ye have done it unto me." Then shall he say also unto them on the left hand, "Depart from me, ye cursed, into everlasting fire . . . for I was an-hungered, and ye gave me no meat: I was thirsty, and ye gave me no drink . . . sick and in prison, and ye visited me not." Then shall they answer him, saying, "When saw we thee an-hungered, or athirst, or a stranger, or naked, or sick, or in prison, and did not minister unto thee?" Then shall he answer them, saying, "Inasmuch as ye did it not to one of the least of these, ye did it not to me."

This is the fundamental difference between heathen and Christian morality; between intellectual Greek philosophy and practical modern science; between the aesthetic ideal and the ideal of "life".

★ ★ ★

Positive science, therefore, has made us realise a part of Christianity. We might almost say that the monastic orders practically represented, throughout the centuries and the different civilisations, the only form of life which is really life – that which science has revealed today.

They alone, at a period of disorderly excess, had a dietary which begins to be generally recognised as hygienic; they ate coarse bread, fresh fruit, milk fresh from the cow, many vegetables, little meat, ate frugal but regular repasts. Withdrawing from the polluted air of crowded cities, they chose large, spacious houses in the open country or, at any rate, rather isolated – if possible, standing on a height. Their luxury was not heavy padded furniture, but large grounds where it was possible to live in the open air. Loose clothing, comfortable sandals or bare feet, woollen gowns, physical exercise, agricultural work, travelling, made them almost the precursors of the modern life of sport. Every convent spread benefactions all around – received the poor, tended the sick, as if to show that this freer and more privileged life was but a phase, which must necessarily be accompanied by help to humanity. They represented the social and intellectual *elite*; it was the Benedictines who preserved manuscripts and treasured the arts; it was the followers of Saint Bernard who practiced agriculture, and it was the sons of Saint Francis who preached peace.

Or it might be said that modern society, guided by positive study of the laws of life and of the means of saving it, has encountered the religious laws which reveal the paths of life; and realises a form of civilisation which recalls and, in some ways, reproduces the ancient oases of the spirit.

If, however, we were to risk a parallel between modern society and a convent, what kind of convent would the former be?

Here is a monastery where the brethren eat according to rule, wear hygienic clothing, are correct in their language, never indulge in noisy quarrels, have all their interests in life in common, and dispense their charities coldly, as if they were a custom or an obligation of their order; they meditate on eternal life, on salvation and rewards and punishments in a future life, but without being touched by these thoughts. The real truth is that they have lost their faith, and that they do not love one another; ambition, anger, envy and even hatred, drive away internal peace; and corruption begins to filter in under these other sins; a sign of a deeper decadence now begins to show itself, for chastity has been lost. That which is, *par excellence*, the standard of Christianity, the sign of respect for life, the consecration of the purity which leads to eternal life, has been overthrown together with faith. The love of man is not compatible with the excesses of the beast. It is through purity that an ardent love to all mankind, comprehension of others and intuition of truth, arise like a perfume. It is that ardent fire called charity or love, which keeps life kindled, and gives value to all things. "Though I bestow all my goods to feed the poor, and though I give my body to be burned," says St. Paul, "and have not charity, it profiteth me nothing. And though I have the gift of prophecy and understand all mysteries and all knowledge, and have not charity, I am nothing. Though I speak with the tongues of men and of angels and have not charity, I am become as sounding brass or a tinkling cymbal."[45]

In "degenerate" convents the greatest and most elevated acquirements, and the highest level of perfection reached, are lost; just as a person punished by degradation first loses the last and highest acquisitions, and only keeps the lower.

In social convents, on the other hand, the ultimate attainment has not yet been reached; that is the difference and the contrast. The social elevation towards Christianity is only on its first steps. Love is lacking, and thence chastity; and all this is absent owing to the arid void left by the absence of faith and the oppression of spiritual life. Positive science has not yet touched the inner man, and the social environment does not therefore realise in its "force of universal civilisation" the loftier human acquisitions.

When we occupy ourselves with the "moral education" of our children, we ought to ask ourselves if we really love them and if we are sincere in our wishes for their "morality".

Let us be practical. Fathers and mothers, what can you hope for from your children? The European war is far less dangerous to their bodies than the spiritual risks, which they run. We must imagine a much greater war, a universal one, to which all young men are called, and where the survivors are pointed out as absolutely exceptional. Therefore you are educating your sons for death. What, then, is the use of troubling so much about them? Is it not useless to take care of their soft hair, and their rosy nails, and the fresh and bewitching beauty of their vigorous little bodies, if they are to die before long?

---

45 Corinthians, 13.

Ah! all those who love children must fight in this deadly war, and struggle for peace!

The creed which Mme. d'Héricourt[46] set forth in her book, *La femme affranchie*, about the time of the French Revolution, is very eloquent.

"Mothers, you admonish your children, saying: Do not tell lies, because this is unworthy of a person who respects himself. Do not steal: would you like it if people stole your things? It is a dishonest thing to do. Do not oppress those of your companions who are weaker than yourself, and do not be rude to them, for that would be a cowardly act." These are excellent principles.

But when the child has become a young man his mother says, "He must sow his wild oats". And sowing his wild oats means that he must perforce be a seducer, an adulterer, and a frequenter of brothels. What? Is this mother, who told her boy not to tell lies, the same person who permits him, now that he is a man, to betray a woman like herself? And, although she taught her child not to steal another child's toy, she thinks it lawful for her son to rob a woman like herself of her life and her honour. And she who advised him never to oppress the weak, now permits him to range himself among the oppressors of a human being whom society had made into a slave.

These mothers acquiesce in the degrading fact, which perverts all humanity. There is a strong social movement today against the white slave traffic.

These are excellent things. But the question, which lies at the root of all these questions, is a spiritual question. It is not the white slaves who are the "lost" human beings; they are the victims of a universal act of perdition and slavery. If such a grave spiritual danger is hanging over us, what external hygiene can save us, unless it be preceded by a direct struggle against this danger? The really "lost" are those who persist in a state of death without perceiving it.

If anyone perceives the danger, he may by this mere fact find himself in the way of salvation. The so-called white slaves, held in scorn by society and oppressed by punishment, cry vengeance in the sight of the universe, and cover mankind with shame; but they are not the really lost – they are

---

46 Jenny d'Héricourt (1809 – 1875) was a feminist activist, writer and physician-midwife.

not the only slaves. He who is lost is the innocent, well-educated young man who, without remorse, unconscious of his own degradation, takes advantage of a human being who is made a slave for him, and moreover, covers her with contempt without hearing the voice of conscience which admonishes him: "Why beholdest thou the mote which is in thy brother's eye? Cast out the beam which is in thine own eye." This man, who seeks, perhaps, to protect his own body from disastrous consequences although very often it is not possible to escape them, and therefore risks for nothing suicide of his own person and of his species; and who only cares to seek a social position for himself and an honoured family – this is the man who is really lost in darkness and reduced to slavery.

And his mother is also a slave, for she cannot follow her son whom she brought up with so much care for his body, though she desires his moral good with all the passionate love of her heart; she is a slave when her son is forced away from her to go perhaps to death or to the ruin of his physical health, and to descend into moral degradation while she can do nothing but watch him, silent and immovable. She excuses herself sadly saying that her dignity and purity forbid her to follow her son in these paths. It is as if she were to say, "There is my son, wounded and bleeding; but I cannot follow him because the road is muddy and I might dirty my boots." Where is the heart of a true mother? How can maternal sentiment fall so low? "She only is dignified and pure," cries Madame d'Héricourt, "who is capable of bringing up her son in such a way that he will never have anything shameful to confess to his mother."

The mother who has lost all her authority is herself lost.

Maternal dignity, on the other hand, is great and powerful. Behold in ancient times the Roman matron, Veturia, the mother of Coriolanus! Having heard that her son, a traitor to his country, was coming to attack Rome in command of an alien army, she went bravely out from the protecting walls of the city, advanced towards the powerful leader of the hostile host and asked him, "Art thou my son, or art thou a traitor?" At those words Coriolanus renounced his unworthy undertaking.

In the same way, in these days, the true mother should pass beyond the walls of prejudice and the frontiers of slavery, and have sufficient dignity to be able to confront her son, saying to him: "Thou shalt not be a traitor to humanity!"

What pressure can have been brought to bear on a woman to have made her lose the sacred right of saving her son? And what can have so weakened affection as to lead a youth to despise the maternal authority in order to make himself a young man?

It is this death of the soul and not external facts which will pronounce our sentence.

* * *

If positive science, which has limited itself to the study of the external causes of maladies, or the causes of degeneration, and has confined itself to the inculcation of physical hygiene – that is to say, the protection of material life – has contributed so largely to morality, how much more may we hope for moral elevation from a positive science which concentrates upon the protection of the "inner life" of man?

And if the first part, scrupulously following the truth by exact research, has arrived at the social realisation of Christian principles, we may presume that its continuation, conducted with the same loyalty and exactitude of research, will in like manner succeed in filling up the voids which still exist in modern civilisation.

This is, I believe, the clearest and most direct reply to those who ask what can be hoped for in the morality and religion of the new generations from our "over-positive" method of education.

If experimental medicine, by going back to the causes of disease, has succeeded in solving the problems which concern health, an experimental science which concentrates upon the study of normal man's psychical activities should lead to the discovery of the superior laws of life and of the health of mankind.

This science has not yet been established and awaits its investigators; but we may foresee that if universal hygiene, which gives humanity a guide to physical life, has come from medical research, then this new science should produce a hygiene which will give to all men practical guidance in moral life.

And if positive medicine arose in the hospitals where sick people were collected by private and public generosity, with charitable intentions and under the guidance of empiricism, this science should, above all, concentrate and find its experiences in schools: that is to say, in the places where all children are gathered together for their social elevation and with the empirical guidance of education.

What was the elevated note of scientific medicine which gradually superseded the empirical method? While empirical medicine believed in blood-letting and blistering, scientific medicine elevated and illustrated the ancient principle which had been forgotten and which contained all the new wisdom in a synthesis: the medicinal force of nature, *vis medicatrix naturae*. A natural power of fighting and conquering illness exists in the living organism and it is to this that we must look in order to construct rational medicine; he who believes that the doctor and the medicine cure the sick is an empiricist; but he who knows that it is "only the organism" that can produce the cure and that therefore we must protect and assist the force which nature gives for our salvation, is a scientist.

Now the sum of treatments necessary to protect the natural forces of defense and reorganisation in positive medicine are much more minute and are diffused in much vaster fields than the old empiricism.

The great number of specialists who replace the single type of doctor of the last century is sufficient to emphasise the enormous difference in practice, which the new tendency involves.

It is interesting also to give a glance at the progress which has been made in medicine; it has begun to cure diseases; and thence it has gone on to discover the laws of normal physical life and to show the healthy how to preserve their health. When it reached this point, it found that the same measures which are necessary for preserving health are the best for curing disease; because it is the same source of life which gives health and the *vis medicatrix naturae*. Thus, for example, the rational diet of today is not only a hygienic measure which all should adopt in order to keep themselves in health, but the most important factor in the cure of illness. Dietetics, whether for the victims of gout, pellagra, fever, tuberculosis, or diabetes, is of primary importance; Lithia salts, caffeine and creosote are useless in comparison. The modern tendency is to reject these poisonous remedies altogether and to substitute the natural remedies of rest, medical gymnastics, hydropathical treatment, and, above all, climatic treatment. Psychiatry and neuro-pathology have introduced the treatment of work: that is a course of orderly intelligent activity to give occupation to individuals who begin to show signs of mental failure. By degrees, as progress is made in this direction, the conception of "natural healing" will triumph – the ever clearer conception, that is to say, of the forces which sustain life.

It is only Nature which can do everything and, if the doctor is to become useful, he must follow in her footsteps and serve her with increasing fidelity.

It is natural that investigation should lead to attempts at interpreting these forces upon which health depends, and these studies of "immunity" have been the most brilliant, widely diffused and scientific of all medical studies.

When Metchnikoff[47] believed he had discovered that the leucocytes in the blood absorb and digest microbes and thus save man from infection, it seemed as if a ray of clear and simple light had illuminated all the mystery. But no sooner was his theory promulgated than it was demolished by the successive studies in which it was subjected to destructive criticism, because the leucocytes are not always able to absorb living microbes; certain "conditions" of the organism are requisite in order that they may have this power, and so the knotty point was merely shifted. Moreover, it is not the actual microbes which cause disease but their toxins. Thus the theories of toxins seemed to be the true guide for researches; but then we entered into a sea of complications, and it is obvious that only "aspects" and "attributes" of immunity are accessible to us, but that the substance, the last word, underlying all those aspects which research has revealed is: mystery.

For this reason, there is silence today as to questions of immunity; that which was once familiar as a popular idea remains among the obscure studies which, not even the students of the university should approach.

Nevertheless, it is "impossible" that the medical science founded upon natural forces should develop, unless the imperative necessity be recognised of studying the mystery of life which conceals its source but continually expands its forces.

The invisible but real source of health and healing is always there

---

47 Eli Metchnikoff (1845 – 1916) was a Russian biologist, known for his research of the immune system.

at the climax of all efforts; and the palpitating energy which springs inexhaustibly therefrom is the only reality which makes evident this revival of the living. This medical science and this mystery cannot but form a unity.

It is probable that this will be brought about by that science which studies the health and the maladies of the soul. If this should discover that the soul, too, is corruptible, subject to disease and death, that it has its laws of health and its *cis medicatrix naturae*, treatments tending to respect and aid this precious force of life should multiply immeasurably; and at the same time the mysterious source whence it gushes should impose itself on modern medicine as the question of immunity has done. Then life, morality and religion will be indissolubly united.

★ ★ ★

Let us now turn to children of two and a half and three years old who touch everything, but especially those objects which they evidently prefer, the most simple objects, as for example a square block of paper, a square inkstand, or a round, shiny bell. All things which "are not meant for them".

Then the mother comes and takes them away; half caressing and at the same time tapping the little hands, she calls out, "Don't touch! Naughty!" I was once present at one of these many family scenes, which pass unnoticed. The father, who was a doctor, was sitting at the writing-table; the mother was holding in her arms a very small child, who was stretching out its little hands to the various objects upon the table. The doctor said, "That child is incorrigibly naughty although it is so young. However much its mother and I try to cure it of this fault of touching my things, we never succeed." "Naughty! naughty!" repeated the mother, holding its little hands tightly while the child threw itself back, howling and throwing its feet about as if it wished to kick.

When children are three or four years older, the struggle becomes more severe: they want to *do* things. Those who observe them carefully discover that they have some "tendency". They wish to imitate what their mother does. If their mother is a housewife, they willingly follow her into the kitchen; they wish to share her work, to touch her things, and they try furtively to knead and cook, and wash clothes and sweep the floor. The mother feels wearied by them; she keeps on repeating, "Be quiet; leave it alone. Don't tease me. Go away." Then the child makes a great noise, throws himself on the ground and kicks; but then he begins again to do as much as he can without being seen, as quickly as possible; and by trying to wash things in a hurry, he gives himself a bath; trying to conceal some contraband ragout he makes the floor dirty. The mother's anger, cries and reproofs increase; and the child reacts with naughtiness and tears; but begins again almost at once.

Where the mother does not do her own work, the child, if intelligent, is still more unfortunate. He looks for something which he cannot find and cries for no reason; he flies into a passion for which no one can account. Some fathers lament this, almost with despair. "My child is very intelligent, but so naughty! nothing will satisfy him. It is no use buying toys for him; he is really overdone with them, nothing is of any use."

The mother asks anxiously, "What do you advise me to do when the child is naughty and when he gets into passions? He is so naughty, he never keeps still; I cannot contend with him any more."

It is rare to hear a mother say, "My baby is good – it is always asleep." Who has not heard some poor mother shout in a threatening voice to the crying babe in her arms, "Be quiet, be quiet, I tell you!" and then, naturally, the child is frightened and redoubles its cries.

This is the first contest of the man who enters the world: he has to struggle with his parents, with those who have given him life. And this occurs because his infantlife is "different" from that of his parents; the child has to form himself, whereas his parents are already formed. The child must move about a great deal, to co-ordinate his movements, which are not yet under control; the parents, on the other hand, have their voluntary mobility organised and can control their movements; perhaps also they are often tired after their work. The child's senses are not yet fully developed; his powers of accommodation are insufficient, and need help from touching and feeling in order to take account of objects as well as of spaces; and his eyes are rectified by the experience of his hands. The parents, on the contrary, have developed senses and have already corrected the primitive illusions of these; their powers of accommodation are perfect if they have not spoilt them by abuse; in every way cerebral activity leads the senses to receive an exact impression;

they have no need to touch. Children are anxious to get knowledge of the external world; their parents know it too well already.

Therefore they do not understand each other.

Parents want their children to do as they do, and any diversity is called "naughtiness". Think of the mother who drags her child along with her; he has to run while she walks; his legs are short while hers are long; weak, while hers are strong; he has to bear the weight of his body and his disproportionately large head, while the mother has a head and body which are proportionally lighter and smaller. The child is tired and stands and cries, and the mother exclaims, "Come on, you naughty little thing! I won't have any nonsense. Do you want me to carry you, lazy-bones? No, I won't give in to you."

Or again, we see mothers who, when their children sit down on the ground – or lay themselves flat on their stomachs with their feet in the air and support themselves on their elbows, while they look round them, call out, "Off the ground! You are making yourself dirty, naughty child."

All this may be translated in this way: "The child is different from the adult. The formation of his body is such that his head and his body are enormously large in comparison with his small, slender legs, because they are the part, which will grow most. Hence the child cannot endure walking and prefers to lie at full length, which is the healthiest position for him. He has a wonderful tendency towards development; he gets his first ideas of external life and assists his senses of sight and hearing by touching, in order to realise the forms of objects and distance. He moves continually, because he must co-ordinate and adapt his mobility. Hence he moves a great deal, walks very little, throws himself on the ground and touches everything, and these are signs that he is alive and that he is growing." No – all this is looked upon as naughtiness.

This is evidently not a moral question. We do not seek for means to correct these depraved tendencies of the man who is but just born. No, it is not a moral question. It is, however, a question of life.

The child seeks to live and we want to hinder him. In that sense it does become a moral question, as regards ourselves, since we have begun to examine those errors on our part which do harm and infringe the rights of others. Moreover, our own egotism is concealed beneath our errors of treatment; what we really resent in the child is that he gives us trouble; we struggle against him in order to protect our own comfort, our own liberty. How often at the bottom of our hearts we have felt that we have been unjust, but have stifled this impression. The little rebel does not accuse us or bear us malice. On the contrary, just as he persists in his "naughtinesses" which are forms of life, so does he persist in loving us, in forgiving us everything, in forgetting our offences, in longing to be with us, to embrace us, to sit upon our knees, to fall asleep on our bosom. This, too, is a form of life. And we, if we are tired or satiated, repulse him, masking this excess of selfishness under a hypocritical pretence of concern for the child himself: "Don't be so silly!" Insult and calumny are always on our lips in the eternal refrain: "Naughty, naughty." And yet the figure of the child might stand for that of perfect goodness, which "thinketh no evil, delighteth not in iniquity, beareth all things, believeth all things, hopeth all things." As to us – no, we cannot always say as much of ourselves.

If the struggle between the adult and the child could be brought to an end in "peace", and the adult, accepting the conditions of infant life, would seek to help the child, the former would be able to advance towards one of the most sublime enjoyments which Nature can bestow: that of following the natural development of the child, and seeing the man evolved. If the opening rosebud has become a commonplace of poetry, how much greater is the poetry of the infant soul in its manifestations? Now this ineffable gift, which was placed beside us in order that the miracle might accompany us and comfort us, we trample under foot in our wrath, blaspheming as if demented.

★ ★ ★

When the child desires to touch and to act, in spite of "punishments of every kind", he persists in exercises necessary "to his development", and displays a strength of will in the matter against which we are often powerless; he shows the same persistence as in breathing, in crying when he is hungry, and in raising himself when he wants to walk. Thus the child turns to external objects which respond to his needs: if he finds them, he displays his powers in muscular or sensory exercises and then he is joyous; and if he does not find them, he is restless as when his desires are unsatisfied. Toys are too light to satisfy arms which require to make the efforts necessary in lifting and moving objects; they are too complex to satisfy senses which need to analyse a single sensation. They are vanity and in themselves they represent simulacra and parodies of actual life. And yet they form the world of our children in which they are constrained to "consume" their potential powers in a continuous exasperation which incites them to destroy things.

Happily, children do not hear the pronouncement of the common formula, that children have an "instinct" for destruction. Nor are they familiar with the other axiom which contradicts this: That the instinct of "property", in other words, selfishness, is strongly developed in them. On the contrary, the child has merely the overpowering instinct to "grow", and therefore to raise and to perfect himself; in every period of life he seeks instinctively to prepare himself for the next period. This fact is very much more comprehensible than the strange instincts we calumniously attribute to him.

Just try the experiment of allowing children to act for themselves; they are at once "transformed". In the Guerrieri Gonzaga Children's House it sufficed to provide a comb to transform the naughtiest, most rebellious of the children, the one whom the teacher designated as in need of "taming", into a lively and attractive little girl, who combed the hair of her companions most carefully with evident delight. We had only to say to an awkward, lethargic child, who came forward holding out her arms to have her sleeves pulled down for her: "Do it yourself", and there was a flash of intelligence in her eyes, her weary face was lighted up by an expression of satisfied pride and amazement, and she began to pull down her sleeves with positive delight. When these children were given a little basin and a piece of soap, how carefully they emptied and replaced the receptacle, fearing to break it, and how caressingly they handled the soap laying it down very gently! It seemed as if the task had been confided to a mechanism of moving figures with an accompaniment of music: the figures were the children, the music was their own joy.

These children, occupied in dressing, cleaning, washing, combing, cleansing and arranging their environment, work *themselves.* As a result, they love useful objects so much that they will preserve a piece of paper for years and instead of knocking against furniture and breaking objects, they perfect their movements.

But we place ourselves beside these lives, which are hastening trium-phantly to their salvation and seek to bind them to ourselves, in spite of the struggle which has begun and the fear we have already provoked. We approach them gently and seductively; and because when a child breaks things he is obviously grieved and, therefore, would endeavour to cor-rect and perfect his movements, we spare him this grief, which would be in the nature of "an act of repentance on the part of the muscles which have transgressed", and give him unbreakable objects: plates, basins and drinking vessels made of metal; toys made of stuff, woolly bears and India rubber dolls. Henceforth his "errors" will be concealed. Every er-ror of the muscles will pass unnoticed by the child: he will no longer feel the pain of evil-doing, repentance, and effort to perfect himself. He will be able to sink into error; behold him, clumsy, heavy, without expression in his face, a stuffed bear in his arms! He is now bound fast to vanity and error and has lost all consciousness thereof.

The adult hems him in ever more closely: he does everything for the child, dresses him, even feeds him. But the child's desire is not to be dressed and materially nourished: his deep desire is to "do", to exercise his own powers intelligently and thus to rise to his higher level. With what subtle insinuations does the adult seek to confound him! You are exerting yourself, and why? That you may be washed? That you may put on your pinafore? You can have all this done for you without any effort. You will find it all done with greater perfection and ease. Without moving a finger you shall have a hundred times more done for you than you could accom-plish for yourself, even with all the exertion of which you are capable. You need not even put the bread into your mouth, you shall be spared even this trouble, and you will take in nourishment all the more copiously.

The devil was less cruel when he tempted Christ in the wilderness, showing Him all the kingdoms of the world and the glory of them. "All these things will I give thee if thou wilt fall down and worship me." But the child has not the power to answer like Christ: "Get thee hence, Satan; for it is written: Thou shalt worship the Lord thy God, and Him only shalt thou serve." The child ought to obey God, who has prescribed that his nature shall demand action; and that he should conquer his world as he has conquered life, to the end that he may elevate himself, and not to the end that he may acquire external splendour and comfort. When tempted, however, he cannot resist. He ends by possessing the objects, the pretty, ready-made things; his soul makes no progress; he loses sight of the goal. Behold the child clumsy, unsteady, inept and enslaved! Those incapable muscles encase a captive soul. He is oppressed far more by this fatal inertia than by the physical contests, which initiated his relations with the adult. Often he has fits of rage like the sinner; he bites the bear that he cannot break, cries desperately when he is washed and has his hair combed, rebels and struggles when he is dressed. The only movements allowed by the devil are those of anger. But gradually he sinks into the depression of impotence. Adults say: "Children are ungrateful; they have none of the higher feelings as yet; they care only for their own pleasure."

Who has not seen patient mothers and nurses "bearing" from morning till night the humours of four or five discontented children, who are screaming and playing pranks with their metal plates and rag dolls? They seem to say: "Children are like this", and a benevolent compassion takes the place of the natural reaction of impatience. Of such persons we say: "How good they are! how patient they are!"

But the devil, too, is patient after this fashion: he too can contemplate the agonies and impotent rebellions of the souls which are in his power, which are prostrate among vanities, oppressed by a great quantity of means, the ends of which they have lost, souls in which the consciousness of sin is extinguished and which are gradually sinking into an abyss of moral error. He is patient in contemplating them, in supporting their cries – and he too offers them bears and rubber dolls and feeds them, stuffing them, that is to say, with new vanities, which mask their errors and nourish their bodies.

He who, seized with doubt, should ask concerning these mothers and nurses: "Are they really good?" might get an idea from the reply of Christ: "None is good save God", that is, the Creator. Goodness is the attribute of God. He who creates is good, only creation is good. Hence he only is good who helps creation to achieve its ends.

★ ★ ★

Now we come to the school. Conceptions of goodness and naughtiness must be very definite here, for when a teacher has to leave the classroom, she calls one of the children, who, during her absence, is charged to write the names of the "Good" and the "Naughty" in two columns on the blackboard under these headings. The child, however, who is called out is quite capable of judging, for nothing is easier than to distinguish between goodness and naughtiness in schools. The good are those who are quiet and motionless; the naughty are those who talk and move. The results of the classification are not very serious. The teacher gives good or bad "conduct marks". The consequences are not disastrous; they are, so to speak, akin to the social judgments passed upon men whose conduct is appraised as good or bad. This does not affect society and the judgment entails neither honours nor imprisonment. It is merely a pronouncement. But "esteem" and even "honour" depend upon it, things which have a high moral value. In school "good conduct" means inertia and "bad conduct" means activity. The "esteem" of the headmistress, of the teacher and of schoolfellows, the whole "moral" part, in fact, of the system of rewards and punishments, depends upon these appreciations. As in society, they require no "judicial qualifications", no "authority" in those who form them; they are based on something that "all" can see and judge; they are the true moral judgment of the environment; indeed, anyone of the children themselves, or even the classroom attendant, may write the list on the blackboard. There is, in fact, nothing mysterious or philosophical in conduct; it is the sum of acts committed, the facts of life itself, accessible to all, which determine it. And all can see it and pronounce upon it.

On the other hand, there are much more serious acts, the consequences of which affect the community and touch those principles of justice on which all are entitled to rely; they therefore require "authoritative judgments" against which there is no appeal; a kind of Supreme Court hastily convoked.

When in an examination the children, seated side by side, have there and then to give samples of what they have learnt, that is to hand in that veritable legal document an evidence visible and accessible to all judgments, the written task, be it dictation, composition or problem; if then one child helps another, he is not merely naughty, but wicked, for he has not only displayed activity, but activity for the benefit of another. The punishment may be very serious: the annulment of the examination, which may sometimes mean the loss of a whole year's schooling, the repetition of that year's course. A child who can help another is kind; well, he may be punished by having to sit the examination again several months later, or even by having to go back for a whole year of his life and begin over again. There are many cases of this kind: the family of this kind-hearted child may have been very poor, and the child may have been making a great effort to come out well, so as to be able soon to help his family by his own childish work; who knows how his comprehension of this family condition may touch the heart of a child? He may have seen in his bewildered schoolfellow another poor boy in like circumstances. How often some quarrel in his home, or insufficient food, may have caused him to lie in bed, sleepless and excited, for hours? In the morning his mind was confused. Perhaps his unfortunate schoolfellow had been in like case just on the eve of the examinations.

It is essential to understand certain situations: the mother at home counts the days of each school year that passes, because to her these are so many days sacrificed; she is certainly following her boy at the examination with a heart full of anxiety; her face at the window when the child comes in sight asks, when he is yet afar: "How did it go?" This picture was perhaps present in the heart of the good-natured child when he helped his comrade.

He might, of course, keep all this to himself, perfect his own work, or hand it in first. For justice decrees that the time spent on the work should be counted by the minute, almost as by the chronometers of psychological experiment. Justice is rigorous. On the paper handed in by the child the teacher writes the hour: handed in at 10.32, handed in at 11.5. If two papers are about equal in merit, so that it can hardly be said from the contents which is the better of the two, though both are superior to all the rest, a difficult case arises: it must be decided which is to be the first. It is a matter of great weight, because the prize is in question. When there is a doubt, the hour decides. One paper was handed in at 10.30, the other at 10.35. The one handed in at 10.30 is pronounced the first, because the writer was able to do work of equal merit in five minutes less than his rival. On what may not a prize sometimes depend! Hence a diligent child must be very careful in his preparations for an examination; the two in question were equally clever and equally quick; but one had taken care to have good pens and flowing ink, and the other had not. Thus his negligence cost him the prize. It is true that the parents and not the children provide the pens. In strict justice all should have the same pens, but here we enter into a sea of scruples which might obscure justice. No, justice must be rigorous, but without scruples. Now the kind child who helped his companion lost time, and so by this alone he lost part of his merit; he therefore "sacrificed" himself for a comrade.

No considerations, no extenuating circumstances will be allowed to mitigate the punishment. Family conditions, the mother . . . nothing can avail against the cancelling of an examination. Even in the case of great criminals extenuating circumstances are admitted in mitigation of punishment. But school is another matter; here we have to deal with definite facts: there has been an infiltration of one mind into another, and we are no longer able to judge the children individually by their work. Moreover, the examination is the individual test. If the cancelling occurs at the final examination, the culprit must go through the year again, and when a year is repeated it is the entire year. It is not so with convicts, where months and weeks are taken into account. Here the unit of measurement is the school year. And then there is another point to consider in the case of convicts: their crimes may have been induced by irresistible forces and conditions, driving them to do evil. . . . But who is there who cannot refrain from doing good? To do good is certainly not an irresistible impulse!

However, to obviate such inconvenient impulses, school educates children to refrain from mutual aid throughout the year. It goes even farther: it directly prevents the children from communicating one with another. What a chase it is! The clever, practical teacher adopts regular strategic tactics and is familiar with all the child's devices in this covert and deceitful contest. Children are "capable of anything" to support one another and communicate one with another. If "prompting" when one child is repeating a lesson might reach the teacher's ear, we find a companion sitting in front of him with the open book fastened to his shoulders, where the other is able to read it. Or if the wily teacher makes the patient come out from among the desks in order to prevent him from receiving any help, his companions may make signs to him, perhaps by means of the deaf-and-dumb alphabet. Then we find the teacher using the blackboard as a pretext for turning the pupil with his face to the wall, the while she keeps her burning eyes fixed on the class. Thus the patient is isolated. "Nothing escapes" a clever teacher; she is capable of surprising a rolled-up note slipped by one child under the desk of another; and of confiscating a piece of blotting-paper which two children interchange on the pretext of using it, when they have written upon it.

For this reason properly constructed desks should be open in front, because otherwise it is so easy to pass things under them; whereas with desks which are not only hygienic but "moral", such subterfuges would be difficult to carry out.

Indeed, these desks which are open in front also facilitate surveillance of the scholars from the moral point of view; because, always seated, placed side by side without any possibility of spiritual communion, their heads dazed by the continuous vociferation of the teacher, these children very often contract vicious habits, such as onanism, which originate in the school itself. These are less openly discussed than spinal curvature, myopia and exhaustion from overwork, but the evil has long been recognised, even before science entered upon the scene to make a study of the maladies engendered by school conditions. The sedentary habit impedes circulation in the pelvic basin and induces stagnation of the blood; moreover, what other outlet is provided for the nervous energies? And the evil spread in an alarming manner.

But open desks make subterfuges impossible. All moral devices for combating abuses flourish in the school. In the schools in Rome, for example, order and surveillance are so perfect that children are not even allowed to go to the lavatory. It is well known what disorder was caused by this "question of the lavatory". If a child became tired of sitting still or listening to the teacher, he asked for leave to go out: he was capable of remaining shut up in the lavatory for a considerable time in order to raise his spirits a little in a place he preferred to that he had just left, for pupils are not allowed to linger in the corridors; the attendants are always on the watch. But these visits to the lavatory had become such an abuse that it was decided to take remedial measures. Today the physiological time is reckoned more or less exactly, and at a stated hour the whole of the pupils accompanied by the teacher, marching two and two in line like soldiers drilling proceed to the lavatories. The children of the first file enter in succession and the others halt, but continue to mark time; as by degrees the children come out of the lavatory, they form in file again and begin once more to mark time together with their companions. The movement seems, indeed, appropriate to the occasion. We will say nothing of the state in which the last children in the file of forty or fifty (who did not go in as a pretence, since the "physiological time" had been reckoned) will find the lavatory; nor will we ask what has become of hygiene. Let us look at the exterior of the lavatories; they have little doors with a large space above and a large space below; thus modesty, and at the same time morality, are safeguarded; within, nothing but the proper duty can be performed. The more modern lavatories in schools, however, are made without seats; with an aperture in the ground to obviate contact and ensure hygiene: the uncomfortable position prevents a longer sojourn than is necessary. It appears that this is the best practical method for installations of this kind in common lodging-houses, casual wards, and schools.

★ ★ ★

School is the place where the "social sentiment" is developed; it is the child's society. As a fact, it is not the school in itself, nor the intercourse of the scholars, but the education given in the manner described above which is designed to develop this sentiment. Hence, when my method became known, although I had spoken therein of places where children live together agreeably and work, I was asked in a critical tone: "And how will the social sentiment be developed if each child works independently?" We must therefore conclude that this system of regimentation in which the children do everything at the same moment, even to visiting the lavatory, is supposed to develop the social sentiment. The society of the child is therefore the antithesis of adult society, where sociability implies a free and well-bred interchange of courtesies and mutual aid, although each individual attends to his own business; in the society of the child it implies identity of physical attitudes and uniformity of collective actions, together with a total disregard of all pleasant and courteous relations; mutual help, which is a virtue in adult society, is here considered the gravest fault, the worst offence against discipline.

Modern methods of instruction recommend the teacher to conclude every lesson with a moral, like the classic fables. Whether the lesson treats of birds, butter, or triangles, it must always end by pointing a moral. "The teacher must miss no opportunity," says the pedagogue; "moralisation is the true aim of the school."

"Mutual aid" is the burden of the pedagogistic refrain, for the Leitmotif of all moralities, not excepting that of the school, is "to love one another". To exhort children to help one another and show mutual affection the teacher perhaps adopts a psychological method in three periods, distinguishing perception, association and volition; or she may adopt the method of cause in its relation to effect; this is left to her discretion; but she must always keep her class in a state of "discipline" and "goodness", for these are its essential constituents.

But the factor which affords the most substantial support to the educative organism of the school is the system of prizes and punishments.

Pedagogues make this the main feature of their treatment. All admit, more or less, the need of some external stimulus to induce school-children to study and behave well, although some are of the opinion that it would be well to instill into the child the love of good for its own sake, and that a sense of duty rather than the fear of punishment should deter from evil. This opinion is generally recognised as lofty, but impracticable. To imagine that the child could be stimulated to work merely by a desire to do his duty is a "pedagogic absurdity"; nor is it credible that a child could persevere in the paths of industry and good conduct merely with a view to a distant end, such as the fine social position he might some day win for himself in the world by means of study. Some direct stimulus, some immediate token of approval, is necessary. True, it has been deemed advisable to make punishments less rigorous and the bestowal of prizes less ostentatious, and such modifications have now become general. Indeed, those fustigations and corporal punishments which not very long ago were usual in prisons, lunatic asylums and schools have been abandoned in schools; the penalties of today are slight: bad marks, reproofs, unfavourable reports to the family, suspension of attendance. The ceremonial prize-giving is also a thing of the past, the solemn function at which the scholars mounted the platform as in triumph to receive their prizes from the hands of the noblest and most distinguished persons of the neighbourhood, who accompanied the presentation with amiable words of encouragement, while the public, consisting mainly of proud and agitated parents, murmured their approval and admiration. All these superfluities have been abolished; the prize, the object, is simply handed to the winner in an ante-room of the school, in the presence of the beadles.

The important matter is that the child shall receive the object he has deserved. The medals, too, with which pupils were formerly able to adorn their breasts, are now abolished; the prize is a book, a useful object. A sense of the practical has found its way even into our schools. Perhaps the good children will presently be rewarded by the presentation of a piece of soap, or the material for an apron, in a *tête-à-tête* between giver and recipient.

But a prize there must needs be.

However, throughout all the discussions of the pedagogues and the evolutions of punishments and prizes, no one had dreamt of asking himself what is the good which is rewarded, and what the evil which is punished, or whether, before urging children on to an undertaking, it would not be well to cast a glance at the undertaking itself, and judge of its value.

At last positive studies on the school question have shed sufficient light to enable us to construct a new base for the old question. Is it well to allure children by a prize, to incite them to exhaust their nervous systems and injure their eyesight? And is it well to check them by means of punishments, when, urged by an over-powering instinct of self-preservation, they seek to avoid these perils? At last we all know that the prize-winners of the elementary schools are the mediocre pupils of the high school; that the prize-winners of the high school are the exhausted students of the academies; and that those who gain prizes throughout their school career are those who are most easily vanquished in the battle of life.

Knowing this, is it well to stimulate on the one hand and to repress on the other, to the end that children may remain in this ruinous condition? Are not the perils of school life already serious enough, without adding stimuli to induce them to throw themselves into these perils with all their energies? A number of deeply interesting comparative studies have been made of late on clever and stupid school-children, those who gain prizes and those who incur punishment. Certain anthropologists, some what ingenuous in matters of science, have studied the question in such good faith that they have even proposed to inquire whether the more brilliant prize-winners show evidences of morphological superiority, congenital marks of a natural privilege, a brain more highly developed than that of mediocrity. On the contrary, anthropological notes reveal their physical inferiority, i.e. their low stature and their remarkably narrow chest measurements. Their heads are in no way distinguished from those of less clever scholars; many of them wear spectacles.

Thus we get a clearer picture of the life of a child who diligently performs all his tasks with a dread of making mistakes which may become positive anguish; who learns all his lessons, thus of necessity depriving himself of a walk, a saunter, an hour of rest. Obsessed by anxiety to be the first, or even stimulated by illusions of a future more brilliant than that of his companions, exhilarated by the praises and prizes which make him believe himself to be "one of the hopes of his country", and the "solace of his parents", he rushes forward to future impotence, as if dazzled by a fairy vision. His careless companions, on the other hand, have well-developed chests and are the merriest boys in the class.

Other types of clever pupils are those who are helped at home by tutors, or educated mothers who devote themselves to their advancement; while other types of dull pupils, often punished, are poor children who are not made welcome in their homes, but are left to themselves, sometimes in the streets; or who are already working for their bread in the early hours of the morning before coming to school. In an inquiry I made, the children who were praised and passed without examination were in the category of those who brought a good luncheon with them; the children at the bottom of the class, who incurred punishments, were those who brought no provisions, or only a piece of bread.

It must not be supposed that the above is an exhaustive enumeration of the causes which contribute to the deceptive phenomenon connected with prizes and punishments; but it is obvious that a clearly defined road has been marked out which should lead us to comprehension of the facts.

Prizes and punishments are not merely final episodes, they are exponents of the moral organisation of the school. Just as the annulment of the examination of a pupil who has helped a companion is but the extreme instance of "an education" which tends to isolate the individual in his egotism; so the prize and the punishment are the extreme incidents of the constant principle on which the organism of the school is based: emulation. The principle is that children, seeing others cleverer than themselves, who get high marks, praises and prizes will be stimulated to imitate these, to do better, to overtake their companions. Thus what may he described as a kind of mechanism is evolved, which uplifts the whole school, not merely towards work, but towards effort. The moral purpose is to accustom children to "suffer".

Let us take an example of such emulation. When the observant doctor entered the school, his attention was directed to the organs of sense, and he found many slightly deaf children among the pupils. Hearing less than the others, they appeared less intelligent, and as a "punishment" they had been relegated to the desks at the very back of the schoolroom. They were often set to repeat because they had never learnt to write "from dictation", and made incredible and unpardonable mistakes. Emulation and punishment had alike proved powerless; not even when they were placed as far as possible from the teacher did these deaf children improve! They were also lively children, who were repeatedly punished to induce them to keep still, and who were vainly exhorted to imitate companions whose conduct was exemplary. A large number of children suffering from adenoids, who consequently breathed through their mouths, and were incapable of fixing their attention, got bad marks and punishments because they were never attentive; meanwhile this defect of the open mouth was vainly combated by the kind and careful teacher, who multiplied moral tales concerning the ugliness of children who keep their mouths open, and, terrible to relate, even sit with their fingers in their mouth!

Many of the lazy children, who would not do the gymnastic exercises like the rest, who made pretexts for stopping and thus set a bad example, were found to be suffering from heart affections, anaemia, or liver complaints. Yet one of the most brilliant examples of emulation is that of the gymnastic competitions, competitions in endurance and competitions in speed. The children are encouraged to continue the exercise as long as possible; or to cover the ground in the shortest possible time; here effort is the basis of the exercise. Now anthro-pological study has revealed the fact that there are two principal types of constitution; one in which the chest predominates, the other in which the legs predominate. When the chest is well developed and the lungs and heart strong, endurance is more natural than agility; the opposite holds good of the other type, in which, by reason of the length of the legs and the slightness of the chest, agility prevails. No emulation can change one type into the other. Morphological study of the child whose body is transformed in successive ages, should be the basis for the organisation of gymnastic exercises, and not emulation. That which has its origin in the body, as constitution or disease, should he considered in the body. No miracle can he performed by the sentiment of emulation.

This prejudice in favour of emulation is so deeply rooted that when in 1898 I began my campaign in Italy to procure the formation of separate classes for deficient children in connection with the elementary schools, the principle of emulation was urged against me: the deficient children would no langer be helped by the example of the clever, industrious children; and when these weaklings had been deprived of the stimulus of emulation, they would accomplish absolutely nothing.

But emulation can only avail among equals. When "competitions" take place, "champions" are chosen. To a deficient child, the example of a clever campanion is merely humiliating; his inferiority, his impotence are perpetually cast in his teeth by the victorious career of his comrade. He becomes more and more discouraged as the zealous teacher scolds and punishes him for his weakness and points out the radiant example offered by the strong. What would give him a ray of light, a glimpse of hope, would be for him to see the possibility of doing something within the limits of his own powers which might nevertheless have a value of its own; to penetrate into some sphere where he too might compete with someone and be encouraged. Then he would be like others, he would be exhilarated and comforted; and the feeble flower within him might expand. He has infinitely greater need of encouragement, solace and external stimuli to excite him to activity than the normal child.

And what happens to the normal child, the clever boy, who serves as an example to his inferiors? Whom does he emulate? Who carries him along that he may ascend? If all need to be drawn upwards in order to climb, who is to draw him who stands above all? This time the question is out of place. In his case the impulse will be retrograde. Here we have the thrice-happy type of him who competes with his inferiors! This makes me think of a description given by Voisin of a competition arranged by one of the idiots in his asylum. This boy, who was very tall, selected all the shortest and youngest of the idiots and challenged them to a race; he always came in first and was delighted. Such an example is not, however, peculiar to Voisin's asylum; it is the *moral attitude* of all who are ambitious, but idle, and are anxious to outshine others without too much fatigue, without perfecting themselves, counting much on the phenomena of contrast. Thus we find a fluent orator seeking to be preceded by an unskilful speaker; and pretty girls who have not the means to adorn themselves and thus set off their beauty, are fond of going about with their plainer friends.

I have read an amusing fable, which was evidently a parody of this phenomenon. There was once a king who had such a long nose that it was positively ridiculous. When a neighbouring king proposed to visit him, he was much perturbed, being ashamed to exhibit his defect to a neighbouring people. Then the prime minister thought of an expedient and propounded this practical plan to the king: "Your Majesty, on this occasion let your noble court retire; I will search throughout the kingdom for the men with the most prominent noses, and for the time they shall constitute your court." This was done; and such noses appeared on the scene that that of the king seemed quite normal in comparison. Thus the august colleague noticed that the court was remarkable for its noses, but did not perceive that the king had a nose of abnormal length.

These stories of the competition between idiots and the court of noses make us smile; but the normal competitions between our children are not matters for mirth. The healthy children who, when side by side with the deaf, the sickly and the deficient, are only conscious of their superiority; the fortunate children who have the help of educated mothers and are brought into contact with poor, unhappy, neglected children, merely feel that they are examples to these; well-fed children refreshed by a long sleep in comfortable beds, placed side by side with little busy workers who get up before sunrise to sell newspapers or deliver milk, and arrive at school already tired, imagining themselves to be superior to these, and to serve as a "stimulus" to them "to do better" all these normal children are on the wrong moral track. They are being misled into an unconscious acceptance of injustice. They are being deceived. They are not better, they are only more fortunate than their companions; their kindly hearts should be led to recognise the truth; to pity the sickly, to console the unfortunate, to admire the heroes. It is not their fault if, instead of all this, vanity, ambition and error spring up in their hearts.

It is true that the teacher makes an attempt to educate their hearts aright, reminding them of ailing, unfortunate and heroic children by means of moral stories which all learn without distinction in the same manner. She lays stress upon incidents illustrating the good feeling of mankind. Yet no one ever considers that the ailing, the unfortunate and the heroic are all there among them, since all children go to school; but they cannot communicate with each other and recognise each other; and thus these subjects who are actually present are distinguished only as the ones who receive all the scoldings, punishments and humiliations, while their more fortunate companions lord it over them arrogantly as their examples, gaining prizes and praise, but losing their own souls in the process.

In this moral confusion, where man "loses sight of God", as in hell, what strong spirit is stimulated to develop his entire precious activities and cultivate his own heart? All are lost, the strong as well as the weak; few indeed are those who possess an individual instinct capable of saving them, who do not succumb to the temptations of prizes, threats of punishment, to the continual suggestions of emulation and of fraudulent rivalry, and who come out with their powers still intact and their hearts pure, sensible of the great facts of humanity. Those who pass through the ordeal untouched by its empty glories and persecutions, and set forth on the path of a productive life which attains to beauty and goodness by internal energy and is susceptible to truth these are they whom we hail as men of genius, as benefactors of the human race.

★ ★ ★

When we come to analyse good and evil positively, we feel that in *reality* much of the "evil" we theoretically deplore in individuals may be resolved into external causes. The depravity of the masses revolves itself into the combined effects of pauperism and drunkenness; crime into degeneration; the faults of children and scholars arise from the darkness of prejudice. But as these causes are not absolute and immutable, but are related to transitory states which may be altered, the ancient philosophical conception of evil resolves itself partially into so many social questions and actions. To give work and combat the drink habit – this it is which contributes largely to morality by removing so many causes of evil. To undertake the regeneration and education of the degenerate, is to combat crime, and therefore to promote morality.

Thus, if in schools the dense darkness of prejudice is the cause of innumerable moral ills, to reform the school by the help of natural principles will be the first step towards its moralisation.

It is in this direction, then, that we must face the great question, not by analytical examination of the system of prizes and punishments, of the principle of emulation, of the most opportune and practical manner of inculcating moral principles, nor by the creation of new decalogues. That which we have hitherto regarded so slightly as a didactic problem is, on the contrary, a great and veritable social question.

When a moral problem is limited to the *effects* of preventible causes, it is merely apparent. Thus, for instance, let us imagine for a moment a populous quarter, where pauperism is rampant and the poor will fight for a piece of bread; where dirt, drinking-shops and civic neglect degrade the inhabitants; where all, men and women alike, give way readily to vice. Our sole impression of such people at the moment is: "What wicked people!" On the other hand, let us take the modern quarter of an industrial city, where the houses of the people are hygienic, where the workpeople receive a fair remuneration for their labour, where popular theatres, conducted with a true sense of art, have taken the place of public-houses; and let us enter one of the restaurants where workpeople are enjoying their food in a quiet, civilised fashion. We should be inclined to say: "What good people!" But have they really become good? Those who ameliorated their social conditions were the good people. But the individuals who have benefited by their exertions "live better"; they are not, strictly speaking, "more meritorious" in the moral sense.

If they were, we should only need to imagine a society in which the economic problem had been solved, to behold men who have become "moral" solely in virtue of having been born in a different age. It is obvious that the moral question is a very different one; it is a question of life, a question of "nature", and one which cannot be solved by external eventualities. Men may be more or less fortunate, they may be born in more or less civilised surroundings, but they will always be men confronted by a "moral question", which goes down deeper than fortune or civilisation.

It is very easy to be convinced that the so-called "naughtiness" of children is the expression of a "struggle for spiritual existence"; they want to make the man within them live and we try to hinder them; we offer them the poisons of darkness and error. They fight for their spiritual bread as the poor fight for material bread; and degrade themselves by falling victims to our seductions just as the poor degrade themselves by succumbing to the fascination of alcohol; and in this struggle and this degradation children have revealed themselves as the "poor" and "needy", neglected and destitute. None have ever demonstrated more clearly than they that "man does not live by bread alone", and that the "question of bread" is not the real "question of man". All the suffering, all the struggles, all the claims of society in the past with regard to bodily needs are repeated here with amazing clarity in connection with spiritual needs. Children want to grow, to perfect themselves, to nourish their intelligence, to develop their internal energies, to form their characters and to these ends they need to be liberated from slavery and to conquer "the means of life". It is not enough to nourish their bodies: they are hungry for intellectual food; the clothes, which protect their limbs from the cold are not enough for children: they demand the garments of strength and the ornaments of grace to protect and adorn the spirit. Why have we adults stifled these wants till we have almost come to believe that the economic question is the true solution of the problem of human life? And why have we never imagined that, even after such a solution, strife, anger, despair and degradation might reappear as a result of higher desires left unsatisfied? Such strife, anger, despair and degradation we encounter continually in the children of today, who are nevertheless well fed, well clothed and well warmed, in accordance with the standards of perfected physical hygiene.

To respond to the intellectual needs of man in such a manner as to satisfy them is to make an important contribution to morality. Indeed our children, when they have been able to busy themselves freely with intelligent work, and have also been free to respond to their internal wants, to occupy themselves for a long time with chosen stimuli, to perform abstract operations when they were sufficiently mature, to concentrate their minds in meditation, have shown that order and serenity have evolved within them; and after this, grace of movement, the capacity for enjoyment of the beautiful, sensibility to music, and finally, amenity in their relations to each other, have sprung up like a jet of water from an internal fount.

All this has been a work of "liberation". We have not made our children moral by any special means; we have not taught them to "overcome their caprices" and to sit quietly at work; we have not inculcated calm and order by exhorting them to follow the examples of others and explaining how necessary order is to man; we have not lectured them on mutual courtesy, to instil the respect due to the work of others and the patience with which they should wait in order not to infringe the rights of others. There has been none of all this; we have merely set the child free, and helped him to "live". It is he who has taught us "how" the child lives, and what other needs he has besides his material wants.

Thereupon an activity formerly unknown among little children, together with the virtues of industry, perseverance and patience, manifested themselves amidst cries of joy, in an atmosphere of habitual serenity. These children had entered upon the paths of peace. An obstacle hitherto opposed to nature had been removed.

And just as men, satisfied by nourishing food and removed from the dangers of poisons, have grown calmer and have shown themselves capable of preferring the higher pleasures to base and degrading indulgence, so the child, his internal needs satisfied, has entered the sphere of serenity and has shown his tendency to ascend.

All this, however, has not touched the roots of the moral question; but it has stripped and purged it of all the dross that encumbered it. The more fully a man's wants are satisfied, the happier he is; but he is not already "full of merit", as we divine that a man gifted with a lofty moral sense ought really to be. Rather have we deprived man of his merits; "goodness" has disappeared as well as "wickedness" at the advent of social reform. When we discovered that many forms of goodness were forms of good fortune, and many forms of evil-doing were forms of misfortune, we left man absolutely naked, stripped bare by truth. He must then take up his real life at its roots and "acquire merit". At this point he will begin to be born anew morally, emerging from the pure and essential chrysalis of the "hygienically" living man.

★ ★ ★

If the whole structure of our educative method starts from an act of concentrated attention to a sensory stimulus, and builds itself up on the education of the senses limiting itself to this, it would evidently not take the whole man into consideration. For if man does not live by material bread alone, neither does he live solely by intellectual bread.

The stimuli of the environment are not only the objects, but also the persons, with whom our relations are not merely sensory. In fact, we are not content to admire in them that beauty to which the Greeks were so sensitive, or to listen to their speech or their song. The true relations between man and man, though they are initiated by means of the senses, are established in sympathy.

The "moral sense" of which positive science speaks is to a great extent the sense of sympathy with our fellows, the comprehension of their sorrows, the sentiment of justice: the lack of these sentiments convulses normal life. We cannot become moral by committing codes and their applications to memory, for memory might fail us a thousand times and the slightest passion might overcome us; criminals, in fact, even when they are most astute and wary students of codes, often violate them; while normal persons, although entirely ignorant of the laws, never transgress them owing to "an internal sense which guides them".

Positive science includes in the term "moral sense" something complex which is, at the same time, sensibility to public opinion, to law and to religion; and multiplying it thus, it does not clearly define in what "moral sense" consists. We talk of it intuitively; each one has within himself something that "responds" to the appellation; and by this internal response he must understand and decide in what this "moral sense" consists. But religion is simple and precise: it calls this internal sense, which lies at the root of life, Love. Social laws do not enter into this any more than does the entire universe. Love is the contact between the soul and God; and when this exists, all the rest is vanity. Good springs therefrom naturally, as sunbeams radiate from the sun. Creation itself has been given in charge of this well-spring of love, and it is love which maintains it, as the contribution of the creature to the provident forces of nature.

Those biological studies, which seek to probe the secrets of Nature have also recognised love as the key of life. Scientists have at last perceived, after much research, this most evident fact: that it is love which preserves the animal species and not the "struggle for existence". In fact, the struggle for existence tends to destroy; and as regards survival, this is not the exclusive privilege of the "fittest" as was at first supposed. But existence is indeed bound up with love. Indeed, the individuals who struggle and conquer are adults; but who is it that protects the newborn creature and infantlife in process of formation? If a hard and horny covering is the natural protection of his species, he does not possess it; if it is strength of muscle, he is weak; if it is tusks, he is without them; if it is agility, he cannot yet move; if it is fecundity, he is not yet mature. Therefore, all species should have become extinct, for there is none so strong but that he once was weak; and there is no infancy, which is not more feeble than any adult life. It is love which protects all this weakness, and explains "survival". Our scientists, indeed, study maternal love, today with the deepest attention as a natural phenomenon. If the struggle for existence presented to us a uniform picture of destruction, the phenomena of maternal love are today revealed to us in the richest and most fascinating forms, which almost represent the occult and sentimental aspect of the marvellous varieties of forms in nature. It is seen at last to be one of the "fundamental characteristics of the species", which should be recognised by all students.

Even insects, which Fabre[48] has described with such a wealth of detail, small and remote as they are from ourselves, exhibit wonderful phenomena of maternal love. One of the first articles published by a naturalist on these phenomena, *La Psychologie d'une Araignee* (The Psychology of a Spider), might serve as the motive of a drama. The spider, as

---

48 Jean Henri Fabre (1823 – 1915) was a French writer and entomologist.

is well known, makes a bag of threads, which she generally attaches to the backs of leaves, and in it she deposits and preserves her eggs; she gets into it herself together with the eggs, to protect the treasure of the species. If the bag should be broken at any point, the spider promptly repairs it. By way of experiment, a spider was taken out of the bag and kept at a distance for twenty days. What is a spider? A few cubic millimetres of a dark, flabby substance without brain or heart, whose life is so short that twenty days constitute a very long interval for it; but this small creature never relaxed her efforts to escape and her agitation never abated; finally, when she was liberated at the end of the twenty days, she fled to the bag, hid herself in it, and repaired the walls. Where was all this love and memory concentrated? This mother-spider was then removed from the nest and another spider was introduced, which at once adopted the offspring, acted as the mother, defended the nest from attack, and repaired the walls if they were damaged. There must therefore be a maternal instinct in the species, independent of actual maternity. But when the real mother approached the adopted bag, not only did the fostermother make no attempt to defend it, but she fled and gave up her place. By what phenomenon of telepathy did the visitor concealed in the bag feel the maternal power approaching? The following was the end of the experiment: the little spiders were hatched and remained in the bag together with their mother; the experimenter tore the bag to see what would happen; the little spiders fled in every direction, but the mother remained crouching on the tattered fragments of the nest and died, almost violently, killed by the destruction of her offspring. Maternal love, therefore, does not require complicated organs; it needs neither brain, heart, nor senses, and seems almost to exist without matter; it is the force which life assumes to protect and preserve itself, a force which seems to exist before and to accompany creation, like that wisdom of which Solomon speaks. "The Lord possessed me in the beginning of his way, before his works of old. . . . When there were no depths, I was brought forth. . . . Then I was by him as a master workman, and I was daily his delight, rejoicing always before him. . . . Whoso findeth me findeth life."

But long before biologists perceived that love is the powerful force which protects the species and explains its survival, religion had pointed

to love as the force which preserves life. In order to live, it is not enough to
be created; the creature must also be loved. This is the law of Nature. "He
who loveth not . . . abideth in death." When Moses gave the Decalogue
which was to guide the Hebrews to salvation, he preceded it by the law:
"Thou shalt love the Lord thy God with all thine heart, and thy neighbour
as thyself." When the Pharisees came to Christ, asking Him to declare the
Law, He answered: "Do ye not know? Thou shalt love thy neighbour as
thyself;" as if to say: the law is evident and unique, it is the law of life, and
for this reason must always have existed, from the very beginning of the
world. But to St. Peter, who was to be the head of the new religion, love,
the transition from the old to the new order, was more fully explained:
"Love," said Christ, "even as I have loved you", that is to say, not as you
are capable of loving, but as I am capable of loving. There is a deep gulf
between the manner in which men are able to love themselves and that in
which Christ can love men. Men often rush headlong to their own perdition; they are capable of confounding good with evil, life with death, food
with poison. Little confidence can therefore be felt in the injunction: "Love
they neighbour as thyself". And it was in truth a new commandment that
Jesus gave, when He said: "Love even as I have loved you".

Moses, indeed, had been obliged to supplement the law of love by
a Decalogue of practical injunctions: "Honour thy father and mother,
Thou shalt do no murder, Thou shalt not steal, Thou shalt not bear false
witness, Thou shalt not covet." Christ, on the other hand, taught that it
will be enough if we do not demand measure for measure in love, and
that there will no longer be any need of the support of rules. We must let
the measure overflow; and behold! This in itself opens to man the door
of salvation. "If ye love them which love you, what thank have ye? for
sinners also love those that love them. And if ye do good to them, which
do good to you, what thank have ye? for sinners also do even the same.
And if ye lend to them of whom ye hope to receive, what thank have ye?
For sinners also lend to sinners to receive as much again. But love ye
your enemies, and do good, and lend, hoping for nothing again, and ye
shall be the children of the Highest."[49]

Set yourselves free from all bonds and all measurements and lay hold

---

49 St. Luke, 6. 32-5.

of the one thing needful: to be alive, to feel; this was the revelation made by Christ when, like Moses, He went up into the mountain, but without hiding Himself from the people, calling the crowd indeed to follow Him, and openly expounding all the secrets of truth: Blessed are those who feel, even if they suffer, for to suffer is to feel, to live. Blessed are those who weep, blessed are those who hunger for righteousness, blessed are the persecuted, blessed are those whose hearts are pure and free from darkness. For he who feels shall be satisfied; but he who cannot feel is lost; woe to those who lie down in comfort, woe to those who are full, woe to those who laugh – they have lost their "sensibility". And then all is vanity. What is the use of knowing all the moral laws and even practising them, if the heart be dead? It is as if we should whiten the tomb of a corpse. The moral, self-satisfied man, without a heart, is a tomb.

The education of the moral sense

Thus the conception of moral education, like that of intellectual education, must include a basis of feeling, and be built up thereupon, if we are not to lead the child towards illusion, falsity and darkness. The education of the senses and liberty to raise the intelligence according to its own laws on the one hand; the education of feeling and spiritual liberty to raise oneself, on the other – these are two analogous conceptions and two parallel roads.

Consider our position in relation to children. We are their "stimuli", by which their feeling, which is developing so delicately, should be exercised.

For the intellect, we have the various objects, colours, forms, etc.; but for the spirit, the objects are ourselves. The pure souls of children must derive nourishment from us; they should fix themselves on us with their hearts, as their attention is fixed upon some favourite stimulus; and by loving us they should exalt themselves in their intimate spiritual creation.

When interest leads the child to take the box of colours, and keeps him absorbed in them, the objects lend themselves passively to his manipulation, but the colours reflect the luminous rays of the sun, which then strike the virgin retinae of eyes not as yet completely matured and adapted. So, too, when the child's heart turns to us and fixes itself, asking nourishment from our souls, we ought to be always ready, like passive objects, inasmuch as we should never, through our egotism, fail to respond to the child's needs; we should respond with all our intimate energies, to reflect upon him the luminous rays required by his pure soul, as yet unadapted to life.

We ought not to call him by name and offer him our affection, inviting him to accept our help; but, like the material objects which attract him by their smoothness, their lustre and their varied and interesting forms, and by ocular demonstration of the means of lofty intellectual exercise, as in the coloured alphabets and the rods which contain the first secrets of numeration we, too, should wait; not coldly, but rather making the child feel that we contain a rich material which is at his disposal, ready to be taken as soon as he stretches out his hand to grasp it. Our "response" to the child should be as full, as prompt and as complete as that of the objects which he may manipulate, but which at every touch give an upward impetus to the intellectual life of the child. How many persons must have noted that on some occasion when they have caressed children, the little ones have retreated, as if repelled and offended; and many must also have remarked that when the affectionate impulse of a child has been checked, he shrinks into himself, humiliated, like the mimosa when touched. Now the respect we owe to the spiritual liberty of the child should manifest itself as follows: we must never force our caresses on him, greatly as we may be attracted by his fascinating graces; nor must we ever repel his outbursts of affection, even when we are not disposed to receive them, but must respond with sincere and delicate devotion. We are the "objects" of his love, the objects by means of which he is organizing his life. The most perfect teachers and mothers will be those who will take the didactic material for their model, and imitate this by filling themselves in every sense with moral riches and being full of response in every detail; passive in abnegation, yet active as well-springs of affection. And if all the sensorial objects combine all possible vibrations accessible to man the vibrations of light and colour, as also those of sound and heat, so too should they combine in themselves all the vibrations of internal sensibility, waiting for the thirsty soul to choose among them.

It may be asked: And how shall we make the child love us; how shall we make the child "feel"?

If a child could not see colours he would be blind; and no one could give him sight. And so if the child could not feel, no one could give him sensibility; but since Nature has united mother and child not only by the flesh, but even more closely by love, it is indubitable that at birth the child brings with him not only flesh but love. Now he who loves, even though it be only a single object, has in himself a *sense* which is capable of receiving impressions *ad infinitum*; he who sees an object possesses sight, therefore he who sees an object will see. He who loves a mother or a son, "loves"; that internal sense vibrates, and certainly not only to the object present to it at the moment.

Even that poor spider, artificially deposited in the bag of another mother, adopted and defended the alien eggs, because the spider is capable of maternal love.

Therefore, the child whom his mother has loved and who was helped by that love has that "internal sense" by means of which he is capable of love. The "human objects" which present themselves to that sense have reflections from it.

We should "wait to be seen" by him; the day will come when, among all the intellectual objects, the child will perceive our spirit and will come to us to take his ease within us. It will be to him a new birth, akin to that other awakening, when someone of the objects first attracted him and held him. It is impossible that that day, that moment, should not arrive. We have performed a delicate work of love towards the child, presenting to him the means which satisfy his intellectual needs, without making ourselves felt, keeping ourselves in the background, but always present and ready to help. We have given great satisfaction to the child by succouring him; when he needed to clarify the order of his mind still further by language, we offered him the names of things, but only these, retiring at once without asking anything from him, without putting forward anything from ourselves. We have revealed to him the sounds of the alphabet, the secret of numbers, we have put him into relation with things but restricting ourselves to what was useful to him, almost concealing our body, our breathing, our person.

When he felt a desire to choose, he never found an obstacle in us; when he occupied himself for a long time with an exercise, we were careful to protect the tranquility of his work, as a mother protects the refreshing sleep of her babe.

When he made his first plunge into abstraction, he felt nothing in us but the echo of his joy.

The child found us always indefatigable when he called upon us, almost as if our mission to him were to offer him what he requires, just as it is the mission of the flower to give perfume without limit or intermission.

He found with us a new life, no less sweet than the milk he drew from his mother's breast, with which his first love was born. Therefore he will one day become sensitive to this being who lives to make him live, from whose self-sacrifice his freedom to live and expand is derived.

And undoubtedly the day will come when his spirit will become sensitive to our spirit; and then he will begin to taste that supreme delight which lies in the intimate contact of soul with soul, and his ear alone will no longer hear our voice. The power to obey us, to communicate his conquests to us, to share his joys with us, will be the new element in his life. We shall see the child who suddenly becomes aware of his companions and is almost as deeply interested as we are in their progress and their work. It will be delightful to witness such a scene as that of four or five children sitting with spoons arrested over the smoking bowl, and no longer sensible to the stimulus of hunger because they are absorbed in contemplation of the efforts of a very little companion who is trying to tuck his napkin under his chin, and finally succeeds in doing so; and then we shall see these spectators assume an expression of relief and pride, almost like that of a father who is present at the triumph of his son. Children will recompense us in the most amazing manner by their progress, their spiritual effusions and their sweet obedience. The fruit they will cause us to gather will be abundant beyond anything we can imagine. Thus it comes to pass when the secrets of life are interpreted: "Give and it shall be given unto you: good measure, pressed down and shaken together, and running over shall men give into your bosom."

The essence of moral education

To keep alive and to perfect psychical sensibility is the essence of moral education. Around it, as in the intellectual education which proceeds from the exercise of the senses, *order* establishes itself: the distinction between right and wrong is perceived. No one can *teach* this distinction in all its details to one who cannot see it. But to see the difference and to know it are not the same thing.

But in order that "the child may be helped" it is essential that the environment should be rightly organised, and that good and evil should be duly differentiated. An environment where the two things are confused, where good is confounded with apathy and evil with activity, good with prosperity and evil with misfortune, is not one adapted to assist the establishment of order in the moral consciousness, much less is one where acts of flagrant injustice and persecutions occur. Under such conditions the childish consciousness will become like water, which has been made turbid, and more poisonous than is alcohol to the life of the foetus. Order may perhaps be banished forever, together with the clarity of the consciousness; and we cannot tell what may be the consequences to the "moral man". "Whoever shall offend one of these little ones, it were better for him . . . that he were drowned in the depth of the sea." "If thy hand or thy foot offend thee, cut it off and cast it from thee."

However, the properly organised environment is not everything. Even in intellectual education it was not the spontaneous exercise alone which refreshed the intelligence; but further, the lessons of the teacher which confirmed and illuminated the internal order in process of development. On these occasions she said: "This is red, this is green". Now she will say: "This is right, this is wrong". And it will not be unusual to find children like the one described above, who make good and evil the centre of consciousness, and, placing it above material bread and intellectual nourishment, will propound the question more vital to them than any other: "Where is good? and what is evil?" But we must not forget that moral lessons should be brief; and that Moses, the father of the sages, in order to inculcate morality, not in a child but in a race, gave ten simple commandments, which to Christ seemed superfluous. It is true, however, that at the head of these was the "law" of love; and that Christ substituted for the Decalogue an amplification of that law, which comprises within itself all legislations and moral codes.

★ ★ ★

It is possible that good and evil may be distinguished by means of an "internal sense", apart from cognitions of morality; and in such a case, of course, the good and evil in question would be absolute; that is to say, they would be bound up with life itself and not with acquired social habits. We always speak of a "voice of conscience" which teaches us from within to distinguish the two things: good confers serenity, which is order; enthusiasm, which is strength; evil is signalised as an anguish which is at times unbearable: remorse, which is not only darkness and disorder, but fever, a malady of the soul. It is certain that the laws of society, public opinion, material well-being and threats of peril would all be powerless to produce these various sensations. Often serenity is to be found among the unfortunate, whereas the remorse of Lady Macbeth, who saw the spot of blood upon her hand, gnawed at the heart of one who had acquired a kingdom.

It is not surprising that there should be an internal sensation which warns us of perils and causes us to recognise the circumstances favourable to life. If science in these days demonstrates that the means for preserving even material life correspond to the moral "virtues", we may conclude that we shall be able to divine what is necessary to life by means of the internal sensibility. Have not the biological sciences demonstrated an analogous fact? The biometer applied to man has made it possible to reconstruct the absolutely average man, that is to say, the man whose body gives average measurements in every part; and these average measurements have been found, by means of the statistical and morphological studies of medicine, to correspond to "normality". Thus the average man would be a man so perfectly constructed that he has no morphological predisposition to disease of the organs. When the figure of a man was reconstructed in accordance with average biometrical proportions, it was found to correspond in a remarkable manner to the proportions of Greek statues. This fact helped to give a new interpretation to "aesthetic sentiment". It was evidently by means of aesthetic feeling that the eye of the Greek artist was able to extract the average measurement of every organ and construct a marvellous and exact whole therewith. The "enjoyment" of the artist was his enjoyment of the "beautiful"; but he felt even more profoundly that which contained the triumph of life, and distinguished it from the errors of nature, which predispose to illness. The triumph of creation can give an intimate pleasure to him who can "feel it"; errors, even slight, will then be perceived as discords. Aesthetic education is, in short, akin to the mathematical approximation towards the absolute average; the more it is possible to approach to the true measure in its extreme limits, and the closer we can get to this, the more possible does it become to have an absolute means of comparison for the consideration of deviations. The great artist is thus able to recognise the beautiful in a detail even in the midst of other discordant details; and the more capable he is of possessing an absolute sense of the beautiful, the more readily will he perceive any disproportion of form.

Something of the same sort may happen in the conscience in relation to the distinction between good and evil; the more so as the good stands for real utility in life far more directly than the beautiful, and the evil may be roughly said to represent danger. Have not animals, perhaps, an acute instinct of self-preservation, which dictates infinite details of conduct to them, both for the maintenance of life and for its protection? Dogs, horses and cats, and generally speaking, all domestic animals do not await the imminent earthquake quietly and unconsciously as does man, but become agitated. When the ice is about to crack, the Eskimo dogs which draw the sleighs detach themselves one from the other, as if to avoid falling in – while man can only observe their amazing instinct with stupefaction. Man has not by nature these intense instincts; it is by means of intelligence and the sensibility of his conscience to good and evil that he constructs his defences and recognises his perils. And if this intelligence of his, which is actually capable of transforming the world, raises him to such a supreme height above animals, to what a lofty eminence might he raise himself by developing his moral consciousness!

But on the contrary, man today is reduced to the point of asking himself seriously whether animals are not better than he. When man wishes to exalt himself, he says: "I am faithful as a dog, pure as a dove, strong as a lion."

Indeed, animals have always that instinct which is admirable, for it confers on them a mysterious power; but if man lacks sensibility of conscience, he is inferior to the animals; nothing can then save him from excesses; he may rush upon his own ruin, upon havoc and destruction in a manner that might fill animals with stupefaction and terror; and if it were in their power, they might set themselves to teach man, that he might become equal to themselves. Men without conscience are like animals without instinct of self-preservation; madmen rushing on to destruction.

What shall it profit man to discover by means of science the laws of physical self-preservation in its most minute details, if he has no care for that which corresponds in man to the "instinct" of his own salvation? If an individual has a perfect knowledge of hygienic feeding, of the manner in which to weigh himself in order to follow the course of his own health, of bathing and of massage, but should lose the instinct of humanity and kill a fellowcreature, or take his own life, what would be the use of all his care? And if he feels nothing more in his heart? If the void draws him to it, plunging him into melancholy, what does his well-nourished and well-washed body avail him?

Good is life; evil is death; the real distinction is as clear as the words.

Our moral conscience is, like our intelligence, capable of perfection, of elevation; this is one of the most fundamental of its differences from the instincts of animals.

The sensibility of the conscience may be perfected like the aesthetic sense, till it can recognise and at last enjoy "good" up to the very limits of the absolute, and also until it become sensitive to the very slightest deviations towards evil. He who feels thus is "saved"; he who feels less must be more vigilant and do his utmost to preserve and develop that mysterious and precious sensibility which guides us in distinguishing good from evil. It is one of the most important acts of life to examine our own consciences methodically, having as our source of illumination not only knowledge of moral codes, but of love. It is only through love that this sensibility can be perfected. He whose sense has not been educated cannot judge himself. A doctor, for example, may be perfectly informed as to the symptoms of a disease, and may know exactly how cardiac sounds and the resistance of the pulse are affected in diseases of the heart; but if his ear cannot perceive the sounds, if his hand cannot appreciate the tactile sensations which give the pulse, of what use is his science to him? His power of understanding diseases is derived from his senses; and if this power is lacking, his knowledge in relation to the sick man is vanity. The same holds good of the diagnosis of our own conscience; if we are blind and deaf, innumerable symptoms will pass unobserved, and we shall not know on what to found our judgment. The tedium of futile undertakings will oppress us from the first moment.

On the other hand, it is "feeling" which spurs us on towards perfection.

There have been persons with an extraordinary power of recognizing good and evil, just as the Greek artists showed extraordinary powers of recognizing the normal forms of the body under the guidance of the aesthetic sense. Saint Teresa tells us that when some worldly person who was not good approached her, she suffered as if she were inhaling a bad smell. She explained that of course she did not smell anything at all, in the material sense; but that she actually suffered, not merely in imagination; her suffering was a real spiritual distress which she could not tolerate.

More interesting still is the following story, which refers to the early Fathers of the Church, who lived in the desert. "We were seated at the feet of our Bishop," says one of the monks, "listening to and admiring his holy and salutary teaching. Suddenly there appeared on the scene the leading 'mime', the most beautiful of the public dancers of Antioch, covered with jewels; her bare legs were almost concealed by pearls and gold; her head and shoulders were uncovered. A throng of persons accompanied her; the men of the period never wearied of devouring her with their eyes. An exquisite perfume, which exhaled from her person scented the air we breathed. When she had passed, our Father, who had looked steadfastly at her, said to us: 'Were you not fascinated by so much beauty?' We were all silent. 'I', continued the Bishop, 'experienced great pleasure in looking at her, for God has appointed that some day she shall judge us. I see her,' he added, 'as a soiled and blackened dove; but this dove shall be washed and shall fly heavenwards, white as snow.' As a fact, this woman returned and asked to be baptised. 'My name is Pelagia,' she said, 'or such is the name my parents gave me, but the people of Antioch call me The Pearl, because of the quantities of jewels with which my sins have adorned me.' Two days later she gave all her goods to the poor, put on a hair shirt, and took up her abode in a cell on Monte Oliveto, which she never left until her death."[50]

---

50 Charles Forbes René de Montalembert (1810 – 1870). *Les Moines d'Occident depuis saint Benoît jusqu'à saint Bernard* (The Monks of the West from St. Benedict to St. Bernard).

Our insensibility

How remote are we from that delicate sensibility which responds to evil by suffering and to the good perceived in others as it were miraculously, by a feeling of pleasure! In our society it is possible for us to live for a long time with a criminal, to esteem him, press his hand, etc. until he is at last exposed by the scandalous discovery of his misdeeds. Then we say: "Who would have thought it? He always seemed an excellent person."

And yet it is impossible that the criminal showed no signs, no perversities of feeling, no heartlessness which should have revealed him to us from the outset. No one will say that we ought all to become wonderful aesthetes like the Greek sculptors, or as sensitive as the saints; but if we admit that it is a barbarous thing to pass by the beauties of art without perceiving them; that it is the mark of defective civilisation to confound horrible coarseness and monstrosity with ideal beauty, to be unable to distinguish the strident noise of the tram-car wheels, or the deafening crash of ill-tuned instruments from the harmonies of Bellini or Wagner; that each of us would blush for such insensibility, and would conceal it – how is it we do not perceive that such obtuseness is habitual to us in moral matters? We see that we are capable of confusing virtuous persons and criminals without any foreboding. How is it that so often in the case of judicial errors, the voice of the innocent did not resound in our ears, although his trial was a public one and we allowed him to languish in prison for years? How is it that goodness should be so obscure a thing that we confound it with prosperity? How is it that those rich men of whom the Gospel says "Woe unto you, rich men, for ye have your reward", can think of "improving the morals" of the poor, without any examination of their own moral lives or the lives of those belonging to them, almost as if they believed that the rich are essentially good and the poor essentially bad?

If such darkness as this reigned in the intellectual field, we should be unable to conceive the form of madness which would present itself to our eyes. There are confusions in the moral field, which it is impossible to imagine in any other domain of life. If some day the youth of the nations, more clear-sighted than those of today, hear that the Christmas feast was kept on the battlefields of the European war, they will understand the origins of the war itself. In such a situation, David (to whom indeed it would have been inconceivable) would have accepted the taunt of his enemies as well deserved when they asked him: "Where is now thy God?" "We have lost God" would have been a fitting lamentation. But to celebrate His festival indifferently under such conditions is to be unconscious of having lost Him. How long ago did the soul die, and when did the building up on death begin? What a terrible episode of madness is this monstrous slaughter, upon which the tree of peace was planted in honour of the Saviour!

Far indeed are we from the delicate sensibility to evil of Saint Teresa, or the keenness of spiritual vision, which enabled the man of God to see the white dove beneath the soiled feathers of the sinful woman. The difference is not as that between the taste of a peasant and that of an artist, but as that between a corpse and a living man. It is evident that we have suffered death, albeit we are unconscious of having died.

Here then, and not in hygiene, must we find the secret of our life. We have something more corruptible than our bodies, a life more fragile than our physical life; and the peril of darkness hangs over us. This is the secret of man.

If man loses the light that leads him on towards a better world, he falls into an abyss far below all created animals.

He who loves, therefore, will bestow all his care on these wellsprings of life; how frail are the lungs of a newborn infant, how easily can an unnatural mother deprive him of air and so suffocate him! Yet what is this easily accomplished act, which nevertheless destroys a life, in comparison with the infinitely easier and more deadly act by which we may procure the death of the soul?

The death of the soul, like that of the body, may be readily distinguished from a state of insensibility; in vain do we apply a red-hot iron to a corpse; there is no response.

He, who is alive, however, is not only capable of reacting to a stimulus very much less intense than a red-hot iron; he who lives and feels may perfect himself – and this is life.

It is enough that souls should "feel". How, then, could they live quietly amidst evil? If under the windows of our house people were piling up refuse until we felt that the air was being vitiated, could we bear this without protesting and insisting on the removal of that which was causing us to suffer? If, moreover, we had a child, we should clamour still more loudly and should even set to work to clear away the nuisance with our own hands, in our solicitude for his health. But if the bodies of mother and child lay dead, they would no longer be conscious of the pestilential air.

It is characteristic of "life" to purge the environment and the soul of substances injurious to health. Christ was called "the Lamb that taketh away the sin of the world", not the Master who preaches, but He who purifies. And this is the morality that springs from sensibility: the *action* of purifying the world, of removing the obstacles that beset life, of liberating the spirit from the darkness of death.

The merits of which every man feels he owes an account to his conscience are not such things as having enjoyed music or made a discovery; he must be able to say what he has done to save and maintain life.

These purifying merits, like progress, have no limits.

"Leave all ties and follow *Me*", said Christ to those who asked him what they should do.

For man can reinforce his own strength by other powers, which will urge him on upwards towards the infinite; before him who sleeps is the invisible ladder of Jacob, trodden by angels who call him heavenwards, that is towards the supernatural life. Yes, to be *more* than man. This is a *dream* to him who lacks faith; but it is the realizable goal, the aim of life, to him who has faith.

To Friedrich Nietzsche the superman was an idea without practical consequence, strange and erroneous even when tested by the very theories of evolution, which inspired him. His conception offered no help in overcoming the ills of humanity; rather was it as a chain binding man to earth, there to seek means to create of himself the man superior to himself; and thus leading him astray into egotism, cruelty and folly.

But innumerable saints have felt and acted in accordance with their profession of faith: "I live; yet not I, but Christ liveth in me."

If, as our poet says, man is "the chrysalis destined to become the angelic butterfly", there is no doubt as to the road he must take: spiritually he must either *ascend* or *die*.

Hence it is not the whole of life to obey the laws of hygiene, physical and psychical; but it is only life which can draw from its environment the means of its own purification and salvation; that life, however, which is supernatural, asks of love and divine light the strength necessary for its transformation.

Of a truth, it is not *ecstasy*, which characterises the saints; it is the real and victorious struggle of the higher against the lower nature.

Morality and religion

It is well known that in strong religious impressions, such as the crises of what is called conversion, the phenomenon is characterised by "an inner light", an "order" which suddenly establishes itself, and by means of which that which was before unseen becomes manifest: the distinction between good and evil, and hence the revelation of oneself. Indeed, the converted, at the moment when the revelation takes place, seem little concerned with divinity, or dogmas, or rites; they are persons given over to a violent commotion, who seem forgetful of all their physical and intellectual life, and who are absorbed in contemplation of themselves in relation to a central point of their consciousness, which seems to be illuminated by some prodigious radiance. The cry of the convert in the majority of cases is: "I am a sinner!" It seems as if darkness had fallen away from him, together with all the evil which was corroding, weakening and suffocating him, and which at length he saw, when it was separated from him, terrible, obscure and full of hideous dangers. It is this which agitates him and makes him weep; it is this which urges him to seek someone who can understand, comfort and help him. The converted want help, as do the newly born; they weep and struggle like men who are born to a new life, and who are restrained by no human respect, by no restrictions. It is their own life they feel; and the value of their own life seems to them greater than the riches and convenience of the whole world. They feel an ecstasy of relief at having escaped from a great peril; their chief anxiety is that they may be liberated from the evil that oppresses them. Before they can take another step forward they are obliged to reconsider the terrible time when evil was rooted within them, and they felt nothing of it.

And as a man with difficult short breath
Forespent with toiling, 'scaped from seas to shore,
Turns to the perilous wide waste, and stands
At gaze; e'en so my spirit that yet fail'd
Struggling with terror, turn'd to view the straits
That none hath past and lived.
(Dante's, Inferno, Canto I in the translation of Francis Cary.)

This evil had held captive all the treasures of the spirit, which, set free at last, seem to refresh and reanimate the whole world before their eyes:

And what I saw seemed even as a mile
Irradiating all the universe. . . .
(Dante, Paradiso, Canto XXVII.)

One of the most singular cases of conversion I ever heard described was the following: A monk, famous for his oratorical gifts, was preaching in a crowded church to a congregation, which was listening to him with devout admiration. Suddenly he was interrupted by a loud sob, and a man in the crowd cried aloud, stretching out his hands towards the pulpit: "I am a great sinner." The monk, as is usual in such cases, came to the help of the convert and received all the outpourings of that soul, as it stripped itself of the evil which had been corroding it. Then, curious to know what argument had touched the heart of this man, he asked him what part of the sermon had specially borne upon the prodigy. "Ah!" answered the convert, "I never heard a single word of what you were saying; I entered the church without knowing why; at that moment you pointed your finger at me emphatically. Yes, it is true, I cried, I am a sinner, and I felt as if a heavy cloak of lead which had been oppressing me had fallen from my shoulders; then an uncontrollable flood of tears rose from my heart." Thus no intellectual element played any part in this conversion; it was not a "conviction", nor even new "knowledge", which had acted; what had happened was purely a spontaneous phenomenon of the conscience, which, perhaps after an unconscious preparation, divided the light from the darkness and initiated the creation of the new man.

The convert feels more clearly than any other that evil is an "obstacle" to a form of enjoyment higher than the loftiest enjoyments man can taste. He has not only been purified, but his purification has transformed him. He is like a diamond embedded in dross and mire which is suddenly separated from the overlying substances, and brought to the surface, clear and brilliant; it is not only a purified and magnificent stone; what really transforms it is the sun, which can now be reflected in it and make it sparkle. This is the unsuspected splendour, which is added to it naturally, and has nothing to do either with the dross that has been removed, or with the intrinsic qualities of the gem. The dross not only defiled it, but also prevented it from encountering the rays which should give it its characteristic beauty.

All devout persons know that evil is a "chain" for us, holding us down beneath the earth as in a tomb, and that sentiments hostile to love form as many obstacles which impede our expansion and our free contact with the divine essence which is within us. The slightest alloy, the most minute infiltration, suffices to impair our brilliance and to cause our ejection from the casket of the elect: a single glance which judges our brother instead of absolving him, a feeling which hardens our heart against him, or, finally, the envy which generates devouring hatred and fury.

"The works of the flesh are manifest, which are these: . . . hatred, variance, emulations, wrath, strife, seditions, heresies, envyings, witchcraft, murders." To approach the altar with a heart suffering, be it ever so slightly, from some seductive stimulus against, charity is vain; it is as if a wounded hare should rush to her form, bearing the arrow that has pierced her through and through; she goes, not to save herself, but to die in her form. "Likewise thou, if thou bring thy gift to the altar, and there rememberest that thy brother hath aught against thee . . . go thy way; first be reconciled to thy brother, and then come and offer thy gift."

He who forgives an offence does not perform a logical act of justice, nor does he benefit the person he forgives; hence it is waste of time to consider whether the offence deserves pardon or not, and whether the person who committed it needs absolution from us or not. We must pardon, not from a sense of justice nor for the benefit of the offender, but for our own sakes; he who forgives has divested himself of envy and resentment, of all that oppressed and fettered the spirit, making it powerless to rise. This is why we must forgive: that so we may burst the bonds which impede our free movement, our ascent. When we cut the cable of a balloon, we do not consider whether this is just towards the earth and whether the cable deserves it; we do it because it is necessary, to enable the balloon to rise. He who ascends, moreover, enjoys the marvels of a spectacle, which cannot be enjoyed on earth. Who would strike a balance between this gain and the sacrifice of the cable?

Forgive, and you will feel universal absolution rising to you from the whole world, in token of your ascent. *Haec est vera fraternitas, quae vicit mundi crimina.*

The religious sentiment in children

Only few researches have been made into the crises of conscience and the spontaneously religious sentiment of children. It is true that in recent years, during the remarkable religious movement which took place in England, most surprising instances of religiosity in children occurred; it was after the little Nelly, aged five, asked for the Eucharist on her deathbed that Pius X allowed it to be administered to children, irrespective of their age. But the subject forms a very inconsiderable part of the positive studies of today.

The solitary study of this kind which has been brought forward in public congresses on psychology was that which was considered during the First International Congress on Pedology[51], held in Brussels (August 1911): *Quelques observations sur le developpement de l'emotion morale et religieuse chez un enfant.*[52] The child who was the subject of observation had received no religious education whatever. One day he was seen to burst into a sudden fit of weeping for no apparent reason. When his mother asked why he was crying, the child replied: "Because I remember how I saw a puppy ill-treated two months ago, and at this moment I *feel* it." A year and a half later a similar crisis took place. He was looking at the

---

51 The term pedology ("pédologie") is used when talking about childhood and pedagogy. It is built from the ancient Greek word pais-Paidós (child) and means the scientific study of the development and behaviour of the child. Specifically, pedology claimed to study the child in all its aspects, in all its manifestations and in all of its activities.

52 Some observations on the development of moral and religious emotions in a child.

moon one evening from the window, when he suddenly burst into tears. "Do not scold me," said the child in great agitation, "while I was looking at the moon I felt how often I had grieved you, and I understood that I had offended God."

This interesting study reveals successive phases of a spontaneous phenomenon of moral consciousness: the first was the revelation of the lively feeling which provoked a fit of weeping two months after the event which distressed the child: he *felt* the sufferings of the cruelly treated puppy. And a long time after this activity of the conscience has been initiated comes the establishment of order: the child distinguishes between good and evil actions, and recognises the fact that he has incurred the displeasure of his parents; this displeasure was probably not very serious, indeed it was so slight that the child had been unconscious of it at the time; but at the moment when he is purging himself of these trivial impurities he feels God: "I understood that I had offended God", he said, and he knew well that he had not offended his parents. Now, no one had ever talked to him about God, or trained him to examine his conscience.

During my experience I have had no opportunity of witnessing a similar cycle of spiritual development. My experiences in religious education have necessarily been limited hitherto; indeed, in the Children's House kept by the Franciscan Sisters of the Via Giusti the religious education was given by the ordinary methods and it was not possible to make original studies or observations. On the other hand, the dominant political party in the municipalities has abolished religion from the public schools with a sectarian rigour, which causes the word "God" to be feared as bigots fear the word "devil".

My experience has, therefore, been limited to some of the children I have received privately in my own house, children belonging to non-religious families, who had consequently undergone no religious influence.

One of my little pupils was just over sever years old, when a friend of his family, noticing his intelligence and knowing that he had been educated in "freedom", thought he would test him by describing to him briefly animal evolution according to the principles of Lamarck and Darwin. The child followed his explanation very attentively and then asked: "Well, then, man comes from the monkey, and the monkey from some other animal, and so on; but from whom did the first creature come?" "The first," answered his friend, "was formed by chance." The child laughed aloud, and calling his mother, said excitedly: "Just listen; what nonsense! Life was formed by chance! That is impossible." "Then how was life formed?" "It is God", replied the child, with conviction.

This same child was prepared, with his mother's consent, for Holy Communion, together with his sister; a highly educated young priest of much aesthetic knowledge undertook the task. I was curious to hear what objections the child had raised; but I was not admitted to his lessons. I was present on only one occasion, when the course of instruction was almost at an end. The priest spoke of the reservation of the wine and of the practical situations in which the celebrant may find himself during the holy office. I thought such a dissertation entirely unsuitable for children and one, which was likely to distract their attention from the end in view; but I saw with amazement that their faces were turned intently to the altar; they were evidently unfamiliar with such minute explanations, but they were penetrated by a sentiment which attracted them; the chalice with the divine blood appealed to these souls ready to receive it, as it did to the innocent Parsifal. When they made their first Communion, I was convinced that their souls received the mysteries with the sweetest faith and with absolute simplicity, as if all that is of God were comprehensible to them, and only that which denies Him an absurdity. Their spiritual conquest accompanied them in life.

A little cousin of these children, who was prepared to receive the Communion a long time after them, and who had had no religious training in her own home, said one day when she was working enthusiastically in class: "How beautiful the anatomy of a flower is! I like arithmetic and geometry so much! But religion is the most beautiful thing of all."

There was an older child in the school, whose parents, both father and mother, were positively hostile to religion. This child, although she showed great interest in the school exercises, was always restless. Later, when some wonderful children's parties were given in the villa where she lived, parties, which were arranged with great skill and were veritable works of art, she became still more restless and cynical, almost as if she were suffering from some disillusionment. One day she called an orphan child from Messina, one of our children who had come from the school in the Via Giusti, and took her away into a quiet corner asking her to repeat the Lord's Prayer. The orphan recited it, while the rich child gazed at her eagerly. Then, as if in obedience to an inspiration, she went to the piano to play; but her hands trembled; she threw herself on one side, with her elbow on the keyboard and her head hanging, unable to conceal her agitation any longer. Her soul was seeking to satisfy its yearning; nothing could give her peace but the one thing those who loved her wished to withhold from her. Her heart was still alive and eager: "Like as the hart desireth the water brooks, so longeth my soul after thee, o God."

As yet the coarse scoria evolved from darkness, which makes it so difficult for the adult to embrace the mysteries of the spirit like a little child, had not formed around her. Later, such mysteries become incomprehensible; as to Nicodemus, who replied to Christ: "How can a man be born again? Can he enter a second time into his mother's womb?"

But this rapid survey will suffice to make us understand that the little child has other needs, in addition to his intellectual wants, and that long before his intelligence is developed and satisfied, his pure and open spirit reflects the divine light. He is perhaps the Parsifal for whom we are waiting, depressed and sick at heart, while because of the impurity of our hands the dove can no longer descend in the Holy Grail towards the chalice filled with the blood of Peace.[53]

---

53 The moral question is barely indicated and is not even comprehensively indicated. Such a work, indeed, represents an experimental contribution to the education of the intelligence. An experimental study of the moral and religious education of children has only just been initiated in the Montessori School of Barcelona, Spain. A book on this subject should form a sequel to this volume.

I cannot foresee whether my colleagues and I will be able to bring such a heavy task to a successful conclusion.

Books on religious education which later on were published are:

"The Child in the Church" (1922) [I Bambini nella Chiesa], "Life in Christ" (1931) [La Vita in Christo], "The Mass explained to Children" (1931) [La Santa Messa spiegata ai Bambini].

Index